Advance

"This is a groundbreaking book about one of the least understood groups of people: Filipinos. As a people, we're a lot American, we're definitely Asian, and we're undeniably Latino. *The Latinos of Asia* is essential reading not only for the Filipino diaspora but for anyone who cares about the mysteries of racial identity."
—Jose Antonio Vargas, Pulitzer Prize–winning journalist and founder of Define American and #EmergingUS

"Analyzing Filipino American experiences of 'looking Asian but having a Spanish last name' or 'looking Mexican but identifying as Asian,' Ocampo shows how the children of Filipino immigrants constantly challenge the prevailing racial-mapping rules in America. *The Latinos of Asia* is groundbreaking, offering an ingenious perspective on racial dynamics and formation."
—Min Zhou, Tan Lark Sye Chair Professor of Sociology, Nanyang Technological University, and co-author of *The Asian American Achievement Paradox*

"Are Filipino Americans Asian, Latino, or something else entirely? In this provocative book, Anthony Ocampo deftly combines survey analysis, in-depth interviews, and personal narrative to show that the answer is not a simple one. It depends critically on context and has important implications for matters such as life chances, life choices, and race relations in a rapidly diversifying nation."
—Karthick Ramakrishnan, Professor and Associate Dean of Public Policy, University of California, Riverside

"*The Latinos of Asia* is groundbreaking. Ocampo examines racial identities among Filipino Americans not just in relation to whites, but in relation to other minorities. Through candid and eloquent responses from Filipino American young adults, and engaging links to scholarly discussions, Ocampo tracks the fluidity of race and argues that place matters in how people come to think about themselves."
—Robyn Rodriguez, University of California, Davis

"Anthony Ocampo's fascinating study illustrates how Filipinos do not fit neatly into American racial categories. His highly accessible narrative carries the reader through different social and institutional contexts that draw Filipinos back and forth over panethnic lines, and challenge our notion of what panethnicity means in America."
—Wendy Roth, Associate Professor of Sociology, The University of British Columbia

"Engaging and timely, *The Latinos of Asia* shatters static, homogenizing, and binary categorizations of Asian Americans and Latinas/os. Presenting powerful testimonials by Filipinos from two Los Angeles communities and centering dynamics in schools and neighborhoods, this must-read book complicates understandings of race, identity, and Los Angeles."
—Gilda L. Ochoa, author of *Academic Profiling: Latinos, Asian Americans and the Achievement Gap*

"In this innovative book, Anthony Ocampo brings to light the ambiguities and ambivalences of a racial identity that is always Filipina/o but also contingently Asian, Latina/o, and even Pacific Islander. Brimming with unexpected findings and insightful explanations, *The Latinos of Asia* underscores the intrinsic instability and enduring power of race."
—Moon-Kie Jung, author of *Beneath the Surface of White Supremacy*

"*The Latinos of Asia* presents an innovative analysis of Filipinos as an 'in-between' people straddling the stigmatized immigrant groups from Latin America and model minority newcomer populations from Asia. This book convincingly demonstrates that race is not a fixed characteristic of individuals and groups. Anthony Ocampo's work will capture the imaginations of students of immigration, race, and ethnicity alike."
—Rubén Hernández-León, Associate Professor of Sociology and Director of the UCLA Center for Mexican Studies

"Anthony Ocampo shows that understanding race in today's America means understanding a group that toes different racial lines: Filipino Americans. Through rich interviews and accessible prose, Ocampo explains how Filipino Americans straddle Latino and Asian racial categories, and what that straddling says about race in the United States today. This is *the* definitive account of the contemporary Filipino American experience."
—Tomás R. Jiménez, Stanford University; author of *Replenished Ethnicity: Mexican Americans Immigration, and Identity*

The Latinos of Asia

The Latinos of Asia

How Filipino Americans Break the Rules of Race

Anthony Christian Ocampo

Stanford University Press
Stanford, California

Stanford University Press
Stanford, California

Printed in the United States of America

Library of Congress Cataloging-in-Publication Data

Ocampo, Anthony Christian, 1981– author.
    The Latinos of Asia : how Filipino Americans break the rules of race / Anthony Christian Ocampo.
        pages cm
    Includes bibliographical references and index.
    ISBN 978-0-8047-9394-0 (cloth : alk. paper) — ISBN 978-0-8047-9754-2 (pbk.   ) — ISBN 978-0-8047-9757-3 (electronic)
    1. Filipino Americans—Race identity—California—Los Angeles Region.
2. Filipino Americans—California—Los Angeles Region—Ethnic identity.
3. Filipino Americans—California—Los Angeles Region—Social conditions.
4. Los Angeles Region (Calif.)—Race relations.   5. Los Angeles Region (Calif.)—Ethnic relations.   I. Title.
    F869.L89F47 2016
    305.899′21079494—dc23
                                                                            2015021949

Typeset by Newgen in 10/14 Minion

For my Mom and Dad, the most important teachers in my life. I love you.

Contents

The Latinos of Asia

1 The Puzzling Case of Filipino Americans

IN THE SPRING OF 2011, I was in my last year of the sociology PhD program at UCLA. I'd been in the program for nearly seven years—long enough to have finished law school *twice* with time to spare. Like most graduate students, I wasn't making much money. Working as a college teaching assistant for the majority of my twenties hardly brought in the big bucks. So when I walked by this flyer in the UCLA sociology building, I thought I'd hit the jackpot:

ALCOHOL STUDY
Do you drink alcohol regularly?
Are you Asian American?
For completion of the study, participants would be
compensated up to $215.

This study was tailor made for me. Given the typical stresses of PhD life, my fellow grad students and I were no strangers to the local bars, and as a Filipino, my ethnic roots were from Asia. This would be the easiest two hundred bucks I'd ever make in my life, I thought.

Apparently, I was wrong.

I called the study coordinator to set up an appointment for the following Monday, but before I hung up the phone, I mentioned that I was Filipino. This was when everything went downhill.

"I'm sorry, but you're not eligible for the study," the coordinator said.

"Why not?" I asked.

"Because we can only have Chinese, Japanese, and Korean participants in the study."

"But I'm Filipino. Your flyer said it wanted *Asian American* participants."

"Yes, but we need a genetically similar sample."

"You've got to be kidding me."

"No, I'm sorry."

I knew the genetics argument was bogus. Anyone who's taken Introduction to Sociology knows that race is a social construction, not a genetic one. People, not biology, determine the meaning of racial categories. Besides, there is a consensus within the scientific community that with respect to genetics, "all human beings, regardless of race, are 99.9 percent the same."[1] Even though I had science on my side, the coordinator wouldn't budge. By her definition, I wasn't Asian American. I hung up the phone without bothering to say good-bye.

What was the big deal? Surely I could've shelled out a few bucks from my own wallet for a few drinks at happy hour. And so what if I wasn't going to make two hundred dollars? This was my last year of grad school, and within a few months, I'd be working as an actual college professor (finally). But this wasn't the main issue. What upset me most was that a researcher from a top university felt at liberty to exclude Filipinos from a study about *Asian Americans*. This researcher had no idea what she was talking about. Besides the plethora of scientific articles that have debunked the relationship between race and genetics, I also had the history books on my side. Any Asian American historian can tell you that Filipinos played a central role in the creation of the Asian American identity.[2] In fact, the term *Asian American* did not even exist until the late 1960s, when Chinese, Japanese, and Filipino activists coined the identity as an ideological strategy to advocate for their civil rights.

Although I was angry, I wasn't entirely surprised. For all intents and purposes, there are many out there who forget that Filipinos are, in fact, Asian American.[3] Most would also agree that when people hear the word *Asian*, Filipinos are rarely the first people that come to mind. This seems baffling considering the size of the Filipino population in America. There are more than 3.5 million Filipinos in the country, but it's as if nobody knows we're here.[4] Most Americans have no clue that Filipinos are the third-largest immigrant group behind Mexicans and Chinese. In California, the nation's leading destination state for immigrants, Filipinos outnumber every other Asian American group. Despite their size, people would be hard pressed to name anything distinctly Filipino: try naming a Filipino dish, a Filipino public figure, a Filipino musician. Most people would be stumped (interesting aside: many Filipino musicians have been marketed by record labels as Latino artists).[5] When it comes to their place in America—and in the Asian American community—how did Filipinos become an afterthought?

This is the puzzle I hope to unravel with this book. Over the course of three years, I interviewed more than eighty Filipino American young adults living in Los Angeles. Our conversations tackled a variety of questions: What was it like growing up in an immigrant family? What was it like growing up in the suburbs of Los Angeles? Who did you hang out with in your neighborhood? What were your interactions like with the people you went to school with? What was college like? Who do you feel Filipinos have most in common with?

Of course, these conversations took their fair share of twists and turns, but my aim was always central: I wanted to know how Filipinos carved out their racial place within American society. I was especially interested in studying Filipinos in Los Angeles, because the region, in many respects, foreshadows the America of tomorrow. Immigration from Latin America and Asia is reshaping the racial landscape of this country. While not discounting the continued legacy of the black-white divide, the United States is surely becoming a more multiethnic society. In Los Angeles, for instance, Latinos and Asian Americans now make up a collective majority. This book investigates how Filipinos understand their identity vis-à-vis these two fast-growing communities. In other words, I am interested in *panethnic moments*, or those times when Filipinos have felt a sense of collective identity with either Latinos or other Asians. That Filipinos share historical and cultural connections with both Latinos and Asians makes this an even more interesting puzzle to investigate.

Beyond the Filipino case, studying these panethnic moments reveals the constellation of institutional, social, and cultural factors needed for people from different ethnic backgrounds to develop a sense of common identity. Along the same lines, when panethnic moments don't happen, we gain a better understanding of the conditions when identities fail to resonate. My hope is that the puzzling case of Filipino Americans provides the proverbial "black box" that can reveal the unwritten rules of race in an increasingly diverse America.

Understanding how people fit into the American racial landscape matters tremendously. Race permeates nearly every aspect of our everyday lives, whether we realize it or not. It affects which neighborhood we live in, which schools we attend, our chances of finishing our education, our likelihood of getting a job, and whether we're paid well and get promoted at our job.[6] And these are just the socioeconomic outcomes. Race also affects who we become friends with and who we decide to marry.[7] It influences our physical and mental health, our musical interests, and what we do in our free time.[8] Race also affects how we judge other people—whether we think someone is a trustworthy person, a decent neighbor, an intelligent student, a hardworking employee, a capable leader, and even a great lover.[9] In other words, race is ubiquitous.

Immigration and the American Racial Landscape

Throughout its history, America has had an obsession with categorizing its inhabitants by race. From the early days of the republic, our nation's founders made it clear that the constitutional rights of life, liberty, and the pursuit of happiness applied only to whites, and not to African Americans and American Indians. By the nineteenth century, the US legal system had implemented the "one-drop" rule—the notion that someone with even one-sixteenth African blood was considered legally black, even if that individual appeared white to the outside world. For much of American history, race essentially determined one's life chances.[10] It determined whether one could own land, attend certain schools, live in certain areas, marry certain individuals, or vote in government elections. White Americans, in particular, have had a vested interest in maintaining these rules of race. Race has provided them with an ideological tool to systematically maintain economic, political, and cultural privileges at the expense of blacks and other nonwhites.[11]

Immigration has historically complicated American racial paradigms. How did immigrants fit themselves into America's racial classification system? At times, this choice was out of their hands. Many of the early European immigrants who made the trek across the Atlantic during the late eighteenth and early nineteenth centuries were poor and uneducated. They spoke different languages, practiced different religions, and had distinct ethnic traditions. Although they were European and legally categorized as white, they weren't always treated as white. The white Anglo-Saxon Protestant descendants of the early colonial settlers saw new European immigrants as "social and cultural threats to the American way of life."[12] In their eyes, these newcomers, who were mainly from southern, central, and eastern Europe, threatened American job security, public health, and patriotism.[13] European immigrants were even likened to African Americans, who occupied the bottom rung of the racial hierarchy. For example, there was once a time when Irish Americans were commonly referred to as "[negroes] turned inside out."[14]

Over time, however, Europeans eventually "became" white. The industrial economy allowed even the most poorly educated of European immigrants to achieve middle-class status within a generation.[15] When the United States closed its borders to immigrants in the 1920s, it became more difficult for European immigrants to maintain the languages and cultures that distinguished them from the white Anglo-Saxon Protestant groups that once discriminated against them.[16] Without a continuing influx of Europeans coming to the United States, the ethnic markers that once triggered their racial otherness were no longer being replenished.[17] European immigrants were also asserting their whiteness by actively distancing themselves from African Americans. By the middle of the twentieth century, the children, grandchildren, and great-grandchildren of early European immigrants blended seamlessly into the white middle-class mainstream.[18] Since then, they have continued to embrace their whiteness as a marker of privilege and status within their workplaces, neighborhoods, and everyday interactions.[19] Sociologists cited these experiences as proof that immigrants and their children would "acquire the memories, sentiments, and attitudes" of native-born white Americans.[20] They argued that assimilation was "inevitable."[21]

Unfortunately, claiming whiteness was never a viable strategy of social mobility for non-European immigrants who arrived during this period. In the same historical moment that Europeans' status as whites went from probationary to full-fledged, immigrants from Mexico, Japan, and India had also attempted to legally argue that they too were white.[22] Whether they were trying to gain American citizenship or attend desegregated schools, their attempts were usually denied. Judges cited everything from phenotype to commonsense understandings of whiteness to connections with the home country as reasons to deny their requests.[23] Immigrants from Mexico and Asia were never seen as white, and for most of the twentieth century, they were not granted the same basic privileges as their European-descent counterparts.[24]

By the 1960s, America had entered a new era of immigration. Part of the change had to do with the transformation of the American economy. With the postwar period came the end of American industrialism, which for decades had served as the economic stepping-stone for newcomers to this country. The industrial and factory jobs that had catapulted Europeans from poor to professional within a generation were rapidly disappearing. The US government decided to reopen its borders to immigration in 1965, but the collapse of American industry meant that the opportunities for upward mobility were severely compromised.[25] The American labor market became an hourglass economy—there were jobs in the professional ranks and low-wage service sector, but fewer and fewer in the middle. As a result, millions of immigrants who arrived after 1965 had to settle for jobs with essentially no chance for occupational mobility. The majority of occupations available to immigrants after 1965 had no built-in opportunity structures. Low-wage service jobs, hard physical labor, and domestic work provided little chance for millions of immigrants and their children to move up in society.[26]

The literal face of immigration today has changed. Immigrants who have arrived since 1965 are generally not coming from European societies. The overwhelming majority of them are from Latin America and Asia. Unlike their European counterparts of yesteryear, most of these immigrants do not have the privilege of white skin. For them and their children, assimilation into the mainstream is not a given. No matter how middle class they become, how well they speak English, and how familiar they are with American ways of life, race marks them as foreign.[27] Sociologists now believe that the continual arrival of immigrants from these regions means that even the grandchildren and great-grandchildren of today's newcomers could be subject to immigrant backlash, which is unlike the case of later-generation Europeans.[28] In short, immigrants today may become Americans, but they almost certainly will never become white.

But maybe that's OK. Given the dramatic changes in the demographic composition and political climate of the United States, immigrants and their children have had less of a need to become white to thrive in this society. Undoubtedly, whiteness brings privileges across nearly every political, cultural, and economic arena of American life.[29] All anyone needs to do is look at the racial composition of Congress, American television shows, and Fortune 500 CEOs (which are, by the way, 85, 84, and 97 percent white, respectively).[30] Even so,

communities of color in the United States have asserted their economic and political autonomy in unprecedented ways. Whiteness
is not always necessary for upward mobility in the same way it once
was. For example, when post-1965 immigrants could not find work
in the mainstream labor market, they developed thriving ethnic
economies.[31] They established businesses and community organizations that provided not only jobs but also the infrastructure of support to help them get on their feet in their adopted country. In these
spaces, ethnicity was an asset, not a liability. Immigrants came to rely
on their cultural sensibilities and ethnic networks to achieve middle-
class status.[32]

Undoubtedly, the 1960s civil rights movement also reshaped how
people came to value minority identities. The 1960s gave rise to race-
based social activism. Drawing inspiration from African American
civil rights leaders, such as Martin Luther King Jr. and Malcolm X,
other people of color in the United States began using their minority
identity as a strategy to galvanize their communities to fight for equal
rights. Ethnic groups that once considered themselves separate came
together under panethnic identities.[33] For the first time in American
history, Chinese, Japanese, and Filipinos began identifying as "Asian
Americans." Mexicans, Puerto Ricans, and Cubans began seeing
themselves as "Hispanic," and a few years later, as "Latino."[34] In the
decades since the civil rights movement, these new panethnic identities crystallized and became part of the American racial imaginary.
This was largely a result of the efforts of political activists, cultural
institutions, media organizations, and ethnic studies departments,
which collectively cultivated a sense of shared peoplehood among
groups that might otherwise have seen themselves as culturally distinct. Today, people take terms like *Asian American* and *Latino* for
granted, but the reality is that these identities only came into being
within the past half century. The additions of these new panethnic
categories are evidence of the increasing racial heterogeneity of the
United States. As such, sociologists today are less concerned about
whether immigrants and their children will become American and

more interested in understanding which "segment" of society they will assimilate into.[35]

Ever since *Asian American* and *Latino* have become part of our everyday vernacular, there have been debates about where Filipinos fit in. For the past fifty years, Filipinos have been part of the Asian American community. In the late 1960s, Filipino activists worked alongside Chinese and Japanese Americans to establish Asian American organizations, publications, and cultural groups.[36] However, the political implications of Asian American identity have given way to more cultural meanings. Most people do not think of the political movements of the 1960s and 1970s when they hear the term *Asian American*. They tend to associate Asian American identity with East Asian cultures, which have historically been portrayed as inherently foreign to Western culture.[37] Many Filipinos in turn have internalized this Orientalist understanding of Asian American identity. While this is obviously problematic, Filipinos nonetheless have juxtaposed their culture to those of other Asians.[38] Filipinos understand that nearly four centuries of Western colonization (by the Spanish and the Americans) have influenced their country in ways unparalleled in other Asian societies. And because race is often a matter of culture in most people's minds, some Filipinos feel that their categorization as Asian American is little more than a "geographical accident."[39] At the moment, though, the presence of Filipinos within Asian American organizations remains strong. Filipinos are active members of Asian American political organizations, academic associations, and cultural performance groups throughout the country.[40]

Because of the history of Spanish colonialism in the Philippines, there are some who believe that Filipinos should realign their pan-ethnic allegiances toward Latinos. As a result of their shared colonial past, Filipinos and Latinos have cultural commonalities that would enhance such a coalition.[41] Throughout the twentieth century, there have been hints that Filipinos could, under the right circumstances, function within Latino panethnic coalitions. When Latino activists and American bureaucrats became invested in promoting Hispanic panethnic identity, there were debates about who should be included. Some suggested that Spanish surnames or Spanish colonial history should determine panethnic membership,[42] a litmus test that Filipinos would handily pass. Historically, Filipinos have played key roles in some of the most notable Latino social movements in American history. During the same era that Filipino activists were building the foundations of an Asian American coalition, Filipino laborers were helping to establish the United Farmworkers with Chicano civil rights leader César Chávez and other Mexican American agricultural workers.[43] The League of United Latin American Citizens, a national organization dedicated to fighting anti-Hispanic discrimination, at one point had all-Filipino chapters in different parts of the country.[44]

Even before the rise of panethnic social movements, Filipinos were linked in with Mexican Americans and other Latinos. One of the first sociological studies to look at Latino immigration experiences from a comparative perspective, *Spanish-Speaking Groups in the United States*, included a chapter specifically on Filipinos. Filipinos also became part of Latino communities through intermarriage. Because the earliest waves of Filipino immigrants were overwhelmingly male, many ended up marrying Mexican women and forming "Mexipino" families and communities.[45] These historical and cultural overlaps have prompted many to develop a shared sense of commonality with Latinos in this country.[46] Despite their shared history, Filipinos generally do not identify as Hispanic or Latino. Nonetheless, history tells us that this possibility cannot necessarily be ruled out.

Breaking the Rules of Race

History has shown us that racial identities evolve.[47] The nineteenth-century Sicilian farmer became Italian upon arriving onto American shores; today, generations later, his grandchildren are white Americans. Identities can also shift in real time. Jamaicans and Haitians who migrate to the United States all of a sudden become black Americans.[48] There are select groups who can even vacillate between racial groups that people tend to view as separate. Dominicans are seen as African

American and Latino.[49] Indo-Caribbeans blend in with black, West Indian, and South Asian communities.[50] In part, this is based on how others perceive them. It also has to do with how people see themselves. In other words, identity is a two-way street.[51]

There were many Filipinos I interviewed who didn't feel that Filipinos were "fully Asian." During my conversations with them, they recounted moments when the people they interacted with didn't even know they were Asian. Joey Estrella, a recent college graduate, was one of these individuals:

> People think I'm half Hispanic. Even Filipinos do. But I'm full Filipino. That's the thing. You'll see dark skinned Filipinos and then you'll see some that look Asian. Then there are those who look mestizo [native Filipino mixed with Spanish]. It's hard to pinpoint who's Filipino because there's not a specific look. I have friends that look Chinese or Japanese, and their last name's Gonzalez. And they're full Filipino![52]

For Joey and many others, to be Filipino was to be racially ambiguous. Filipinos were racial chameleons—what color they were depended on the larger context surrounding them. Lia Manalo, an aspiring writer, grew up in Carson, California, and she went to elementary school mainly with Filipinos and Mexicans. She said many of her elementary school teachers thought she was Mexican because she was darker skinned. They even placed her into an English as a second language (ESL) class because they mistook her shyness for an inability to speak English. Toward the end of elementary school, there were teachers who thought Lia was Japanese because of the shape of her eyes. This consistent experience of being racially misclassified made it hard for Lia to identify as Asian.

"It's hard because we're the only Asian country that has been colonized by Spain for three hundred years," Lia said. "It really changed us because we're more Latin. We have more similarities with Latin culture than other Asians. Filipinos are the Mexicans of Asia."

In many ways, the phrase "Mexicans of Asia" perfectly captures the racial experiences of Filipinos in Los Angeles. They are neither black nor white; rather, they have vacillated between identifying with Asian American and Latino communities. Filipinos know they are considered Asian, but the cultural residuals of their Spanish colonial past—their surnames, their foods, their strict Catholicism—cannot be ignored either. "Filipinos and Latinos go hand-in-hand," said Jayson Carrera, a registered nurse: "I think it's the culture. A lot of the influences come from the Spanish. Because if you go to stores and markets, you'll find a Filipino store, and then not too far, you'll find a *carnicería* [Latino butcher] or a *panadería* [Latino bakery]."

And it isn't just Filipinos who feel this way.

Junot Díaz, a Pulitzer Prize–winning author and professor at the Massachusetts Institute of Technology, visited the Philippines for the first time in November 2011.[53] Díaz grew up in the Dominican Republic, but he later moved to New Jersey at the age of six. Having lived alongside Filipinos in New Jersey, he always felt an unspoken connection between his homeland and the Philippines.

"I've been waiting to come to Manila since I moved to New Jersey," he said to a Filipino reporter.

A month shy of his forty-third birthday, he finally made the trip.

As Díaz toured the Philippine capital, what he saw elicited vivid memories of life in the Dominican Republic. Both societies were colonized by the Spanish for more than three centuries, and you could see it in the architecture of the buildings. Though the era of Spanish rule was long over, the cultural residuals of this period remained in tact.

"I felt like we were talking about another chapter of Dominican history," he said of the tour he took in Intramuros, the preserved centerpiece of the Spanish colonial government in the Philippines. Though the colonial remnants were "fundamentally traumatic [and] fundamentally terrible," there was something to be said about the sense of familiarity this history created between himself and Filipinos.

"You should come to the Dominican Republic," Díaz told the reporter. "Because from what I've seen so far, Filipinos would have no problem over there. You wouldn't even noticed you'd left. . . . Our countries have been colonized by both the Spanish and the [Americans]. I feel the similarities very strongly."

Three thousand miles away from where Junot Díaz grew up lived Alicia Sanchez, a Mexican American office manager and mother of two. I met Alicia at a local gym a few months after I had finished my PhD at UCLA. Alicia had never heard of Junot Díaz, but she echoed his sentiments about Filipinos. When we first met, one of the first things she told me was that her best friend Camille Lopez was Filipina.

Alicia had met Camille more than ten years earlier at her previous job. Everything about Camille's family—the food, the customs, and the gossiping aunties—reminded her of her family. Camille's family was from the Philippines; hers, from Mexico. But for Alicia, geography was where the differences ended.

"I've always told her she's really Latina," Alicia said. In fact, for the first few months of their friendship, she hadn't even known Camille was Filipina. It wasn't until Camille had said she was "going home" to the Philippines for the holidays that Alicia finally found out her best friend wasn't actually Mexican. The revelation didn't seem to make too much of a difference.

As the years passed, Alicia joked she had enough evidence to "prove" that her friend Camille was "really Mexican." At Camille's family gatherings, she always noticed the food. "There was carne asada, there was pastor, there was flan. Some of them had different names, but they were pretty much the same," Alicia said.[54] The scale of Camille's typical family gathering was "pretty Mexican" too. "Filipino families are huge just like ours," she said. "Everyone and their mom was there. And it wasn't even a special occasion. The moms would shove food down your throat even if you're not hungry. That's just like what Mexican moms do."

These are just a few stories that show how Filipinos break the rules of race. There are many more in the chapters that follow. These chapters offer stories of Filipinos, in both history and the present day, trying to make sense of race. Sometimes these moments were painful, other times they were funny. In the end, there are lessons to be gained from the racial experiences of Filipinos in Los Angeles. We will learn how the legacies of colonialism collide with the demographic changes of today to shape different aspects of Filipinos' lives. We will see how Filipinos draw on the cultural residuals of their history to weave themselves into the racial tapestry of America. We will better understand how people conceptualize Asian American and Latino racial identity in everyday life by disentangling Filipinos' panethnic moments. Ultimately, we will learn that race is never as simple as checking a box on a form.

2 Colonial Legacies

THERE IS AN OLD FILIPINO SAYING that playfully attempts to capture the history of the Philippines: "The Filipinos have spent three hundred years in the convent, and fifty years in Hollywood." For more than three centuries (from the 1560s to the 1890s) the Philippines was under the control of the Spanish Empire, which throughout this period also held colonies throughout most of Latin America. After a brief period of revolution against the Spanish at the turn of the twentieth century, the Philippines—despite aggressive efforts for independence—soon found itself entrenched in a bloody war with the Americans. By the beginning of the twentieth century, the Philippines was under the rule of a new colonial regime under the United States, which lasted through the 1940s. Even when the Philippines became a sovereign nation in 1946, the US government maintained a neocolonial influence by way of its continued military, economic, and cultural presence in the country.[1] These four centuries of Western colonial influence left indelible imprints on the economic, political, and cultural landscape of modern-day Philippine society. How is it that the Philippines is the only society in Asia that is predominantly Roman Catholic? How is it that the Philippines has the fifth-largest English-speaking population in the world, when most societies in Asia have only a negligible proportion of English speakers? Although the era of Western colonialism is officially over, these anomalies are examples of how the aftermath of colonialism continues to shape the lives of Filipinos—even those who have left the homeland. With respect to Filipinos in the United States, both historically and in the present day, colonial legacies have influenced both their immigration and their adaptation to their adopted country in ways that are unlike those of many other Asian immigrant groups.

Spanish and American colonialism in the Philippines have influenced the economic, cultural, and social experiences of Filipinos in the United States—all of which in turn shape the way that Filipinos experience race in this country. From an economic perspective, the residuals of these colonial regimes helped determine which classes of Filipinos were able to migrate, which jobs they obtained upon their arrival, and which communities they could settle into. Colonialism has also affected different facets of Filipinos' cultural lives, from their language to their religion to their overall familiarity with American ways of life.

Within the past hundred years, there have been two major historical periods of Filipino immigration to the United States. Interestingly, the legacies of colonialism affected the experiences of these immigrants in almost opposite ways. During the 1920s and 1930s, tens of thousands of Filipinos were recruited for agricultural work in Hawai'i and the Pacific Coast of the US mainland when the Philippines was still an American colony. They were predominantly young, single males who conveniently filled the labor posts vacated when the US government restricted immigration from China and Japan. When US colonialism in the Philippines ended in 1946, immigration from the Philippines essentially halted.[2] The United States eventually reopened its borders to immigrants from Asia in 1965, and by the late 1970s, hundreds of thousands of Filipinos had migrated to the United States. This new generation of Filipino immigrants looked very different from their predecessors. There were both men and women who, for the most part, were college educated, middle class, and professional—

many were beneficiaries of the American educational system in the Philippines that had been established during the US colonial period.

Although the racial experiences of Filipinos who came in the early and late twentieth century could not be more distinct, both were direct by-products of the colonial regimes that dramatically transformed the society they called home. This colonial history provides an important backdrop for understanding the contemporary racial experiences of Filipino young adults growing up in an American society that is more multiethnic than ever.

Three Hundred Years in the Convent: Spanish Colonialism in the Philippines

Prior to Spanish colonization, the more than seven thousand islands that make up the modern-day Philippines were not a united society. The people who inhabited the islands had autonomous tribes and societies, each with its own distinct language, culture, and religion. In the early sixteenth century, the Spanish came to the Philippines in the hopes of gaining access to the trade markets of Asia and expanding their economic presence on a more global scale. Around the same time that Hernán Cortés led the Spanish takeover of the Aztec Empire in Mexico, Ferdinand Magellan attempted to claim Las Islas Filipinas in the name of King Philip II of Spain. Capitalizing on the cultural divisions among the island societies, the Spanish successfully quelled the indigenous resistance, and by the late 1500s, the Philippines had become an official colony of Spain. For the next two and a half centuries, the Philippines was governed by the Spanish via the viceroy of Mexico City. Throughout this period, the Spanish operated a trading system between Manila and Acapulco, which facilitated the exchange of foods, precious metals, agricultural goods, and cultural practices between the Philippines and Mexico for nearly three centuries.[3]

As was the case with most colonial regimes, the Spanish were not only concerned about the economic advantages of colonizing the Philippines; they were also interested in culturally transforming the islands. Just as they had done in Mexico and throughout Latin America, Spain used Catholicism to pacify the native population in the Philippines. Rather than teaching Filipinos Spanish, Catholic friars became fluent in local languages to Christianize the people (this strategy allowed them to more successfully convert the Filipino people, and at the same time, it prevented the possibility of Filipinos learning a common language and staging a rebellion).[4]

The religious influence of Spanish colonialism in the Philippines is alive even in the present day. More than 80 percent of Filipinos are Roman Catholic. In this respect, the religious landscape of the Philippines is more similar to Mexico and other Spanish colonies throughout Latin America than it is to other Asian societies. The Catholic population in other Asian countries—China, Japan, and Korea included—is negligible. The practice of Catholicism remains strong even among Filipinos who leave the homeland. Most Filipinos in the United States, whether they are immigrants or US-born, identify as Catholic.[5] In this respect, the religious orientation of Filipino American communities is more similar to Latinos than to other Asian American groups.[6]

Spanish colonialism has also influenced other aspects of Filipinos' cultural lives, especially when it comes to language and naming. Although Spanish never became the lingua franca of the Philippines, there are countless Spanish words and phrases embedded in Filipino languages. For example, in Spanish, it is common to greet another person with the phrase "¿Cómo estás?" or "How are you?" In Tagalog, the primary language of the Philippines, a similar phrase is used— "Kumusta?"—although it is spelled slightly differently. In addition to words, the majority of Filipinos have Spanish last names, such as Gonzalez, Santos, Rodriguez, and Torres.[7] As I discuss later in this book, these linguistic similarities at times become the building blocks for Filipinos' relationships with Latinos, even if it is subconsciously. As historian Rudy Guevarra argues, the Spanish colonization of the Philippines and Mexico "was the single most important factor that laid the foundation for [Filipinos' and Mexican Americans'] historical, social, and cultural interactions, although both groups did not (and still do not) always consciously acknowledge this connection."[8] Later in this book, I show how the cultural residuals of Spanish colonialism—religion, language, and surnames—affected the way people understood Filipino racial experiences in relation to other minorities.

Fifty Years in Hollywood: American Imperialism in the Philippines

The turn of the twentieth century witnessed a changing of the guard. For more than three hundred years, the Spanish Empire was a global superpower, having established colonies throughout Latin America, Africa, Asia, and the Pacific. Throughout the 1800s, however, many of Spain's colonies throughout Latin America began revolting against the imperial regime, and by the end of the nineteenth century, Spain had lost control over nearly all of its colonies in Mexico, Central America, South America, and the Caribbean. The Americans waged war against the Spanish in the late 1890s, in an effort to emerge as the new Western superpower, and in effect they were able to acquire the last of Spain's remaining colonies—Puerto Rico, Guam, and the Philippines. For the price of $20 million, the United States expanded its colonial empire across the Pacific. Not surprisingly, the Philippine natives did not automatically consent to American rule. Having already organized a successful rebellion against the Spanish, Filipino forces then had to wage war against the Americans to maintain their hard-won independence. This war went on for the first few years of American colonial rule, and the Filipinos lost their battle for independence.[9] It is estimated that anywhere between four hundred thousand to more than a million Filipinos died as a result of the conflict, prompting some historians to dub the bloody Philippine-American War as "the First Vietnam."[10]

Once the United States pacified the resistance, it initiated a project of "benevolent assimilation." Viewing the Filipino as uncivilized, unhygienic, and incapable of self-government, the US government aspired to transform the Filipinos into America's "little brown brothers."[11] In an interview with the *Christian Advocate* in 1903, President William McKinley famously told a reporter that he felt a tremendous, God-given responsibility to father the Filipino people. On more than one occasion, the oft-desperate McKinley asked God for guidance on what to do with the newly acquired colony:

> I walked the floor of the White House night after night until mid-night; and I am not ashamed to tell you, gentlemen, that I went down on my knees and prayed Almighty God for light and guidance more than one night. And one night late it came to me this way—I don't know how it was, but it came: (1) That we could not give them back to Spain—that would be cowardly and dishonorable; (2) that we could not turn them over to France and Germany—our commercial rivals in the Orient—that would be bad business and discreditable; (3) that we could not leave them to themselves—they were unfit for self-government—and they would soon have anarchy and misrule over there worse than Spain's was; and (4) that there was nothing left for us to do but to take them all, and to educate the Filipinos, and uplift and civilize and Christianize them, and by God's grace do the very best we could by them, as our fellow-men for whom Christ also died. And then I went to bed, and went to sleep, and slept soundly, and the next morning I sent for the chief engineer of the War Department (our map-maker), and I told him to put the Philippines on the map of the United States (pointing to a large map on the wall of his office), and there they are, and there they will stay while I am President![12]

As evidenced by McKinley's musings, what the US government called benevolent assimilation could more accurately be described as pater-nalistic racism. Without any regard for the wishes of the native pop-ulation, the Americans began their colonial mission by revamping the educational system in the Philippines—a project that historian Renato Constantino famously described as the "miseducation" of the Filipino people.

In an effort to "civilize" the Filipino people, the Americans estab-lished a public education system and made English the medium of instruction. Legions of American teachers, known as the Thomasites, were recruited by the US government to teach Filipino children American history, politics, and cultural traditions.[13] In doing so, the Americans wanted to inject a capitalist spirit into the Filipino people. Their hope was that "future generations would be inculcated with liberal American values, and with those, a desire to produce and consume within a society."[14] The colonial government also established scholarships for academically gifted Filipino men to pursue their college educations in the United States. These young scholars, who were better known as *pensionados*, studied everything from economics to politics to agriculture at American universities.[15] In exchange for their free education, the United States required that these men return to the Philippines and serve as teachers, engineers, and civil servants.[16] In fact, my own maternal grandfather, the late Sergio Crisostomo, was a part of the American *pensionado* program. Born in 1894, Sergio later migrated to attend DePaul University, a Catholic university in the heart of Chicago. Although he had already graduated from the University of the Philippines, he earned a second bachelor's degree at DePaul in 1926. Upon returning home to a small province in the Philippines, he spent several decades teaching American history to generations of high school students, until his death in 1961.

The Americanization of the Filipino people was hardly the US government's only objective with the Philippines. As is the case with most colonial relationships, economic exploitation was at the heart of the American regime. The United States capitalized on the agricultural riches of the Philippines, transforming the islands into a mass producer of sugar, a major cash crop at the time.[17] The Americans were also keen to establish a foothold within the Asian trade markets, viewing the Philippines as "the geographical centre of the oriental commercial field."[18] By colonizing the islands, American industries would have not only new opportunities to trade with China but also the chance to expand their consumer base by forcing the millions of Filipinos who lived on the islands to purchase goods manufactured in the United States.[19] This uneven economic relationship between the

United States and the Philippines would later contribute to the underdevelopment of the Philippine labor market in the decades following American rule.[20]

In addition to expanding trade relations to Asia, American colonial policies in the Philippines inadvertently fulfilled another important economic purpose—filling labor shortages in the US agricultural industry. Starting in the mid-nineteenth century, the United States had recruited tens of thousands of Chinese laborers each year to work on the railroads, in mining, and in agriculture.[21] Racist resentment from white workers eventually prompted the US government to pass the 1882 Chinese Exclusion Act, which led to the rapid decline of Chinese immigration. At this point, tens of thousands of Japanese migrant workers arrived to take the place of the Chinese agricultural workers. Ultimately, though, they met the same fate as the Chinese when the US Congress passed the Gentlemen's Agreement of 1907 and barred Japanese labor migration.[22] By the early twentieth century, two more restrictive immigration laws were signed into law—the Immigrant Act of 1917 and the National Origins Act of 1924—both of which essentially halted migration from Asia altogether.[23] There was, however, one major loophole to these anti-Asian laws. Because the Philippines was an American colony, and thus part of the United States, Filipino laborers were technically free to migrate at their will.[24]

Colonial Migrations

American colonialism in the Philippines quickly exacerbated class inequality within a society already plagued by poverty.[25] In both the urban and the rural areas of the Philippines, the vast majority of people struggled to make ends meet. Filipinos may have had access to education during the American colonial period, but the same could not be said about food and other basic necessities. For thousands of Filipino families around the islands, particularly those in the provincial regions, opportunities for work were extremely limited. Migration became the solution of choice for thousands of Filipino men struggling to support their families. Enamored of stories about life in America, many of these disheartened men looked to the United States to secure economic stability for their families. More than 150,000 Filipinos—mostly young men with minimal education and no money—would leave everyone and everything they knew behind, all in the hopes of finding work in the United States and building a better future for themselves and their loved ones back home.[26]

The government created the special legal category "US national," which enabled Filipinos to migrate en masse. Despite claims of wanting to "benevolently assimilate" the Filipino people, this legal status was hardly a gesture aimed at integrating Filipinos into the American mainstream. Instead, it was a legal loophole that the US government developed deliberately so that Filipinos would not be subject to the laws that barred immigration from Asia. As US nationals, Filipinos occupied a liminal legal space—they were free to migrate to the United States and remained under the jurisdiction of American law, yet they were not permitted to enjoy the basic rights of US citizenship.[27] Even before Filipinos began migrating to the United States, the American people had already internalized extremely racist views toward Filipinos. American soldiers referred to them as "niggers" throughout the Philippine-American War.[28] Popular newspapers and magazines such as the *Washington Post, Los Angeles Times, Life, and National Geographic* regularly depicted Filipinos as primitive, dirty savages who were unable to fend for themselves, let alone govern their own society.[29] In contrast, the US Congress willingly granted citizenship to Puerto Ricans, the colonial siblings of the Filipinos.[30] In the eyes of Congress, Puerto Ricans were more deserving of citizenship because they, unlike the Filipinos, were at least partly of European descent.[31]

The unique legal status of Filipinos as US nationals provided a ready solution for agricultural businesses that were struggling to find workers. Agricultural business interests, first in Hawai'i and then later in the US mainland, quickly turned to Filipinos to fill these labor shortages.[32] Tens of thousands of Filipinos were recruited to work in Hawai'i in the early twentieth century. By the mid-1920s, the harsh climate and exploitative working conditions on the islands prompted

Filipino workers in Hawai'i to migrate to the farms in California and along the Pacific West Coast.[33] Despite their dreams for adventure and a better existence, the majority of Filipino migrants did not find themselves in a "promised land" where the "streets are paved of gold."[34] Filipinos who opted for city life in places like San Francisco or Los Angeles ended up taking jobs as service workers, making their living as bellhops, elevator operators, and bussers.[35] Regardless of their occupational pathway, Filipinos remained at the bottom rung of the American social hierarchy.

Work conditions in the California fields were barely livable. Filipinos not only earned subpar wages relative to white workers but also worked long hours, had very few days off, and lived in quarters that were more appropriate for livestock than human beings.[36] To make matters worse, the colonial relationship between the Philippines and the United States meant that Filipinos could not receive much protection from their home government, unlike the Chinese and Japanese immigrants who came before them.[37] The tendency for Filipinos to be exploited for labor made them an easy target of racism. During the early twentieth century, native-born white workers were already resentful about competing with immigrant laborers for work. Growers often hired immigrant and other nonwhite workers as strikebreakers whenever white workers pushed for better conditions and higher wages.[38] Any efforts by Filipino workers to push for labor rights were met with tremendous animosity from white workers, who invoked their racial privilege as often as they could. Filipinos often saw signs on the streets that read, "Positively no Filipinos allowed," "This is white man's country. Get out of here if you don't like what we pay," or "Get rid of all Filipinos or we'll burn this town down."[39]

Despite these insurmountable challenges, Filipinos were resilient in building lives and community in America. They formed unions and organizations to protest the injustices they faced. They opened thriving businesses when whites excluded them from entering their establishments. And despite the lack of Filipina women in the United States, Filipino men developed romantic relationships with women across racial difference, especially with Mexican women.[40] Whites, however, were relentless about sending the message to Filipinos that they were not wanted. They constantly taunted Filipinos, especially those who fraternized with white women. In several instances, white men resorted to violence. In 1930, mobs of armed white men opened gunfire at a Filipino social gathering in Watsonville, California, and beat the Filipino men until the police arrived.[41] That same year, a different group of white men bombed a Filipino community center in nearby Stockton, which at the time housed one of the largest Filipino American communities in the United States.[42] Nonetheless, Filipinos did everything in their power to carve out a place within their adopted country.

By the 1930s, white antagonisms toward Filipinos prompted the US government to reconsider its colonial relationship with the Philippines. White nativists found themselves an ally with agribusiness owners in the Midwest, who at the time felt threatened by competition with Philippine agricultural products. Together, they successfully lobbied Congress to pass the Tydings-McDuffie Act in 1934, which would grant the Philippines its independence following a ten-year grace period. The passage of this law meant that Filipinos in the Philippines no longer had the freedom to freely migrate to the United States. The law also imposed a quota that restricted Filipino immigration to a mere fifty persons per year.[43]

Just as it had done with Mexican immigrants, the Immigration and Naturalization Service tried to incentivize Filipinos to leave by pushing the Filipino Repatriation Act, which offered free transportation back to the Philippines for immigrants.[44] Their efforts failed. Even in the face of tremendous racism and economic struggle, hardly any Filipinos took the US government up on the offer. There were some who did not want to be perceived as failures who could not hack it at life in the United States. There were some who could not leave because they had wives and children, whose travel was not covered by the US government's repatriation programs.[45] Most Filipinos felt that they had earned a rightful place in their new country, having kept their heads held high even through the worst of conditions.[46] Despite their efforts, however, to start families, build communities, or even pledge their allegiance by joining the US military, these Filipino pioneers would forever be seen by the vast majority of whites, not as full-fledged Americans, but as "strangers from a different shore."[47]

Setting the Stage

By 1946, the Philippines was an independent nation no longer under the jurisdiction of American rule. Nonetheless, the United States had left its cultural, political, and economic imprint on the islands. The public school system established by the United States continued to operate and kept English as the language of instruction. Within a few decades, the Philippines had one of the most highly educated populations throughout Asia, and its people became one of the largest English-speaking populations in the world.[48] From the provinces to the cities, Filipinos continued to be exposed to American popular culture through a variety of venues, from television to movies to stories from immigrants who had returned home. There were physical reminders of the American colonial presence that remained as well. For another half century following independence, the US Navy kept control over a military base in Subic Bay, located in the northwestern part of the Philippines.[49] The continued presence of the military played a major role in the recruitment of tens of thousands of Filipino soldiers for the US Navy during the post-independence period. In the face of harsh immigration laws, many of them saw enlistment as the only pathway to the elusive American dream (Filipinos happened to be the only foreign nationals allowed to enlist even before migrating).[50]

For the Filipinos who did not enlist, economic opportunities were scant. American colonialism had exploited the rich natural resources of the Philippines and had facilitated the underdevelopment of the national economy. The major irony of the public education system in the Philippines was that it created a large pool of highly educated workers who would then encounter a labor market with limited opportunities for high-skilled work. In the decades following American rule, unemployment in the Philippines was rampant. Government corruption further worsened the dire economic situation in the Philippines. The most notable case of governmental corruption was that of president-turned-dictator Ferdinand Marcos. Marcos was democratically elected president in 1962, but he eventually declared martial law a decade later, claiming that he was protecting the nation from the threats of communism.[51] Although Marcos ran on a platform of economic reform, he ended up stealing billions of dollars from the Philippine treasury and racking up the national foreign debt during his reign.[52] From his initial election in 1962 to the time he was removed from office by the Filipino people in 1986, the foreign debt of the Philippines grew from $360 million to a whopping $28.3 billion.[53]

The poor economic state of the Philippine economy coupled with the development of a highly skilled labor force prompted the Philippine government to take action.[54] By the early 1970s, the Philippine government needed a solution to its economic woes and turned to migration as an answer. President Marcos established an aggressive state-sponsored labor migration program intended to funnel unemployed Filipino workers to countries throughout the world experiencing labor shortages.[55] He created several government-sponsored departments, from which emerged the Philippine Overseas Employment Agency, an organization that to this day is dedicated to locating employment opportunities and encouraging the safety of the millions of Filipinos citizens who work abroad.[56] In addition, Marcos also implemented countless policies and programs that encouraged migrants to remit money and goods back to the home country.[57] Filipino immigrants became entrepreneurs, and over time they were crucial in the development of a Philippine "migration industry," a web of businesses and agencies whose profits were driven by the continued flow of international migration.[58] These organizations dealt with everything from money and in-kind remittances to job placement and legal services.[59] The Marcos regime was in large part the reason the Philippines emerged as an international model of state-sponsored labor migration. The Philippines became a well-oiled machine ready to send its surplus workers to any country willing to capitalize on their labor.[60]

When the Philippine government first conceived of the idea of sending their workers abroad, Filipinos did not immediately start migrating to the United States en masse. American immigration policies still restricted their entry at the time. Slowly but surely, though, Filipinos started to make their way to American shores. In addition to the Filipino men who would enlist in the US military, there was a select group of Filipino nurses who had received permission to migrate through the special Nursing Exchange Program in the 1960s, a time when the United States was experiencing severe shortages in health-care workers.[61] Ultimately, immigration reforms in the United States during the 1960s changed everything. In 1965, Congress passed the Hart-Celler Act, which effectively reopened its borders to Asian immigrants, including Filipinos, after nearly four decades of harsh restrictions. While Filipinos were hardly the intended beneficiaries of this immigration reform, they were primed and ready to migrate to the United States, having been groomed by American-style schools and institutions in the Philippines for the past several decades. As Filipino journalist Conrado de Quiros so eloquently put it: "Most of us [Filipinos] are expatriates here on our own land. America is our heartland whether we get to go to there or not."[62] De Quiros's remarks demonstrate how for Filipinos, assimilation was a process that began not upon their arrival in the United States, but long before they stepped foot off the islands.

From the time the United States first opened its borders in 1960s to today, the Filipino population has exploded. Figure 2.1 shows that the number of Filipino Americans increased from a mere 176,000 in 1960 to nearly 3.5 million in 2010. These figures include only Filipinos who migrated legally and those who were born stateside. By the best estimates, there are an additional 300,000 Filipinos who are undocumented.[63] Many of these are Filipino adults who deliberately overstayed their visas in order to make a better life in the States.[64] Others were young immigrant children with barely any memories of the

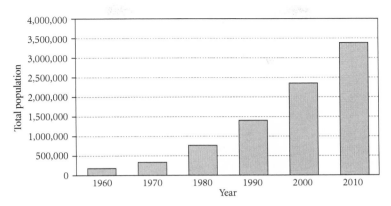

Figure 2.1 Population of Filipinos in the United States, 1960–2010
Source: US Census Bureau, 1960–2010.

Philippines who were brought here by their loved ones. The exponential growth of Filipinos in the United States after the 1960s was a direct by-product of new immigration policies that promoted both family reunification and professional recruitment.[65] These new immigration policies drastically reshaped the face of Filipino immigration. While earlier waves of Filipino immigrants were predominantly uneducated young men who went into agricultural work, the majority of Filipinos who arrived after 1965 came with their college degrees in hand and professional work experience to boot. Moreover, these Filipino immigrant waves included both women and men, as well as the old and the young, who in turn were entering a United States whose racial climate was being radically transformed by social activism.[66] All of these factors completely transformed the way that Filipinos in the United States were able to establish their livelihood, their families, and their communities in their adopted country.

Home Away from Home

After the 1960s, a new class of Filipino immigrants began migrating to the United States, which at the time was experiencing rapid economic and political change. America was no longer an industrial nation; it had begun the process of outsourcing industrial labor to countries around the globe.[67] The demise of American industry led to the bifurcation of the US labor market, which created two primary occupational pathways for post-1965 immigrants—the low-wage service sector and the professional ranks.[68] The educated classes of the Philippines, unable to find work in their own country, turned to professional opportunities in the United States. The United States was experiencing severe labor shortages, particularly in health care, and allocated a large segment of its immigration visas to foreign-born professionals who could fill those gaps. Instead of rural labor camps, these Filipinos were entering hospitals, classrooms, and engineering firms. In the latter half of the twentieth century, the Philippines became one of America's main sources of professional immigrant workers, especially in the health-care industry.[69]

When the United States reopened its borders in the 1960s, about half of Filipino immigrants came by way of an employment visa. These Filipino immigrants then capitalized on the family reunification laws and petitioned other relatives once they settled into their lives in the United States.[70] By the early 1980s, the proportion of Filipinos migrating via employment visa fell to about 20 percent, while those coming by way of familial petitions increased to 80 percent. It is important to remember that the newly arrived immigrants were the ones doing the petitioning—not the Filipino farmworkers who came in the previous era.[71] This was not surprising considering that these more recent immigrants generally had more resources and time to endure the onerous task of filing the paperwork to petition their loved ones.[72] Considering that most professional immigrants were petitioning relatives who were in their same social class as they were in the Philippines, these new immigration policies rapidly transformed the face of Filipino American communities—from extremely poor to solidly middle class.[73]

What remained consistent between early and contemporary waves of Filipino immigration was the sense of community that developed among the newcomers.[74] Sociologists used to believe that assimilation into the American middle class depended on whether immigrants weakened their ties to their ethnic community.[75] Nowadays, most studies show that maintaining ties with the ethnic community can actually facilitate immigrants' pathway into the American middle class.[76] The case of Filipino immigrants supports this argument. Filipino households have the highest median annual income among any other immigrant group in the country (about $70,000 annually).[77] However, their socioeconomic status has not prompted them or their children to fully assimilate with white Americans. Rhacel Salazar Parreñas, a sociologist at the University of Southern California, has extensively researched Filipino immigrant families in the United States and throughout the world. Parreñas writes:

> Much like other immigrant groups in the United States, Filipino migrants turn to family for support against the social and economic pressures that they encounter upon settlement. . . . Filipino migrants are known to have preserved various cultural practices to secure the use of the family as a source of support in settlement. They create fictive kinship, enforce a keen sense of obligation among kin, and use an extended as opposed to a nuclear base for the family. In general, Filipino migrants preserve various cultural practices so as to secure from the community mutual support for the economic mobility of the family and assistance in difficult periods of adjustment in settlement.[78]

In other words, Filipino immigrants rely on other Filipinos in America to maintain their middle-class standing in their new homeland. In the process, they and their children maintain a strong sense of Filipino identity.[79] It is rarely the case that Filipinos of either generation will identify as a "just" American, a label they almost always equate with being white.[80]

Nonetheless, Filipinos have the unique ability to culturally straddle the line between their immigrant communities and mainstream America. Language plays a major role in this. The vast majority of Filipino immigrants have a high school degree (more than 80 percent), and nearly half have at least a bachelor's degree.[81] Although other Asian immigrants, such as the Chinese, Koreans, and Japanese, are on par with Filipinos in terms of education, Filipinos are the only ones whose educational institutions use English as the main language of instruction. Not surprisingly, then, Filipinos report the highest level of English proficiency of any Asian immigrant group. Figure 2.2 shows the language patterns of Asian immigrants and their children in Los Angeles, one of the largest settlement cities for immigrants from Asia and Latin America.

Nine out of every ten Filipino immigrants speak English proficiently. By comparison, the level of English proficiency among other Asian immigrants is much lower. Only about 60 percent of Chinese and Korean immigrant men and 50 percent of Vietnamese immigrant men are fluent in English. There is also a gender disparity in the English proficiency of Chinese, Korean, and Vietnamese immigrants — the rates among immigrant women are comparatively lower. The English-language abilities of Filipinos have clear effects on the second

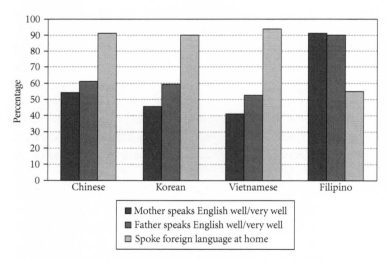

Figure 2.2 Language background of immigrant and second-generation Asians in Los Angeles, 2004 ($n = 1,617$)

Source: Immigrant and Intergenerational Mobility in Metropolitan Los Angeles Survey, 2004.
Note: Sample size for each group: Chinese (413), Korean (401), Vietnamese (401), and Filipino (402).

generation. Only half of Filipino children of immigrants grew up bilingual, in comparison to 90 percent of their Asian counterparts. Moreover, second-generation Filipinos are the most likely to prefer speaking English only.[82] The English-language proficiency explains why Filipinos are more likely than other Asians to live in more ethnically diverse neighborhoods as opposed to traditional immigrant enclaves and to obtain jobs in the mainstream US labor market as opposed to an ethnic-based economy.[83] Despite their linguistic advantages, some Filipino immigrants still feel that they are discriminated against because of their accents, which peg them as "forever foreigners" to the people they encounter in their everyday lives.[84] Although Filipinos possess certain cultural and linguistic advantages inherited from the US colonial period, their status as racial minorities still hinders some whites from seeing them as full-fledged Americans.[85]

In the end, the decision to migrate is not an easy one. Immigrants uproot themselves from the places they have called home to build a better life in a new land. They endure financial difficulties, broken families, and even physical dangers all in the hopes of creating better opportunities for themselves and their children. Every single day, immigrants from all over the world—from Latin America to Asia to Africa—make their way to the United States to pursue the American dream. Among the hundreds of nations that send immigrants to the United States, the Philippines is the third largest among them. How is it that an archipelago society located seven thousand miles away from American shores has managed to send millions of its people to the United States over such a short time?

Colonial legacies, an Americanized school system, economic underdevelopment, government corruption, US immigration reform, and a bourgeoning Philippine migration industry have created the perfect storm for this phenomenon to occur.[86] The economic, cultural, and institutional impact of the United States set the stage for Filipino migration to happen, and the Philippine government and business interests have further perpetuated the movement of Filipinos to the United States en masse.[87] Yet America's third-largest immigrant population has managed to fly under the radar. The historical legacies of American colonialism, coupled with US immigration policies that have left the front door open for professional migrants, have transformed Filipino America.[88] A community that only a century ago was relatively uneducated and predominantly male has evolved into one that is English speaking, well educated, and middle class.[89] Even so, Filipinos' status as racial minorities means that their ability to become fully incorporated into mainstream spaces of American society remains limited.

3 Suburban Ethnicity

NEIGHBORHOODS HAVE ALWAYS played a pivotal role in how immigrants and their children adapt to life in the United States. Historically, immigrants settled into ethnic neighborhoods out of necessity, as xenophobic attitudes were commonplace among most Americans. Unable to integrate into the mainstream middle sectors of American society, many found refuge in residential spaces that resembled their homelands, at least in terms of the cultural landscape. Within these ethnic enclaves, immigrants could form intimate connections, attend places of worship, and practice their cultural traditions with others from their home country, all the while slowly sharpening their English skills and learning American ways of life.[1] For early American immigrants, who mostly arrived from European societies like Ireland, Italy, and Germany, these neighborhoods were important sites of cultural incubation that provided some solace from the poor working conditions and discrimination they faced in the larger society.[2] For these early newcomers, immigrant neighborhoods helped explain why the land of milk of honey would take only a generation to yield its promises. For example, the Irish—once seen as racially on par with African Americans—went from illiterate railroad workers, maids, and factory laborers to college graduates, police officers, and respected members of the American middle class within a generation.[3]

Immigrant neighborhoods today have strong similarities to the ethnic enclaves of yesteryear. They still provide a social space of cultural familiarity that breeds intimate connections with other coethnics.[4] Immigrant institutions — ethnic grocery stores, English-language-learning schools, and employment placement agencies — continue to play a prominent role in facilitating the adaptation of newcomers and their children.[5] There are ethnic enclaves in Southern California such as Chinatown, Koreatown, and Little Saigon that resemble the Little Italys and Germantowns of the past in that they provide much-needed job opportunities for immigrants who cannot find work because of their limited English proficiency and education.[6] In many respects, they also provide important sites of incubation that help position the second generation for a decent shot at making it into the American middle class.

However, the landscape of immigrant neighborhoods has changed dramatically over the past half century since the demographics of immigration shifted from primarily European to predominantly Asian and Latino. Part of the reason for this is that waves of immigrants who came after 1965 are much more diverse in terms of their educational and class backgrounds. In 1965, Congress passed the Hart-Celler Act, which reopened the immigrants after a forty-year hiatus and initiated a set of laws that incentivized highly skilled immigrants to come to the United States.[7] Although there are still immigrants who come to America with little more than the money in their pockets, consistent with the immigrant narrative of yesteryear, there are also those who arrive with a significant amount of human capital — college degrees, large savings, strong professional networks, and extensive familial ties.[8] Some of these more well-to-do immigrants even have a decent familiarity with the English language and American cultural values.[9] The socioeconomic diversity of immigrants has yielded tremendous heterogeneity in the institutional, social, and cultural resources available in contemporary ethnic neighborhoods.[10]

This post-1965 wave of immigration gave birth to the modern-day "ethnoburb," a clever scholarly integration of the terms *ethnic* and *suburb.* Just east of Los Angeles lies Monterey Park, the quintessential example of the American ethnoburb. Hailed as America's "first suburban Chinatown," Monterey Park houses the largest concentration of Chinese Americans in the United States.[11] Half of the residents are of Chinese descent—mainly Chinese (and Taiwanese) professionals and entrepreneurs who migrated after 1970 and upwardly mobile Chinese Americans eager to move out of a rapidly declining Chinatown. The Chinese influence in Monterey Park is unmistakable. Although the city mandates the use of English on business signs, most establishments more prominently display the Chinese-language names of their buildings. Driving down Valley Boulevard or Garvey Avenue, the main streets of Monterey Park, one sees signs in English, but the configuration of the letters is at times confusing to outsiders (such as "H&H" restaurant).[12] The plethora of Chinese supermarkets, restaurants, businesses, community centers, and billboards at times makes local residents feel as if they are not even in the United States, particularly those who are not Chinese.[13] The immigrant population has even made an impact on local, state, and national politics by electing Chinese officials at each of these levels. Four out of the five local council members of Monterey Park are of Chinese descent. The Monterey Park city council has proved an important training ground for Chinese American politicians.[14] One former council member, Judy Chu, became the first Chinese American elected to Congress in 2009.

Filipinos do not have a Monterey Park. Filipino immigrants have the economic means to move into the suburbs, given that many come with college degrees and valuable professional experience. However, their ability to speak English and their relative familiarity with American ways of life as a result of US colonialism has allowed them to settle in more racially integrated neighborhoods.[15] There are no cities or neighborhoods throughout the entire United States where Filipinos constitute a majority. In fact, there is only one major city in the United States—Daly City—where Filipinos constitute even a third of the population.[16] Filipinos' English proficiency and educational background have preempted the establishment of a thriving Filipino ethnic economy in the United States that is comparable to New York City's Chinatown or Miami's Little Havana.[17] In Los Angeles, the area officially designated as Historic Filipinotown is in actuality a predominantly Mexican and Central American neighborhood. Only 3 percent of Filipinos in the county live in Historic Filipinotown (although the area is home to several Filipino community outreach organizations).[18]

Two places that quintessentially capture the ethnic neighborhood experiences of Filipinos are Eagle Rock and Carson. In both Eagle Rock and Carson, there is no racial group that holds the majority. Nonetheless, many people casually refer to Eagle Rock and Carson as "Filipinotowns," even though neither neighborhood embodies the same institutional ethnocentrism as an immigrant ethnic enclave or ethnoburb. Eagle Rock and Carson are indeed suburbs, but the level of immigrant ethnic influence is not nearly as visible as that of Monterey Park or other nearby Asian enclaves, such as Koreatown or Little Saigon. Benji Bautista, one of the Filipinos I interviewed, migrated from the Philippines to Los Angeles, where he and his family settled with more established relatives in Eagle Rock when he was just ten years old. His memories of his first weeks in America captured both the suburban ambiance and the subtlety of the Filipino ethnic influence in his adopted neighborhood:

> My first impression was how quiet it was and how clean it was. There's that isolation from interacting with other people. Because in the Philippines, where I was growing up, right when you come out of the house, there's already interactions between people, even if it's someone selling food on the street. You already have interactions.
>
> When we moved into our first home [in Eagle Rock], I knew my boundaries. But the first place we moved, it felt like it was the Philippines. We were living with relatives. That was an easy transition at that point. But later we moved into our own house, and I was like, this is America. You have borders. You have fences. I didn't make friends in the neighborhood. It didn't seem like there were people my age living in the neighborhood, or maybe I just never saw them. I think there

were kids a few doors down from us, but I never got to meet them, and there was no chance to meet them anyway.

I think silence was the best word for it. That silence is really deafening. The streets are pretty empty, and you have perfectly maintained lawns. Once you've transplanted yourself from a crowded street like in Manila, that's how it's deafening. . . . My image of America was prosperity and money. That image of America was what I saw on television and the movies—like *ET*. It's going to be nice and clean and comfortable, but it seemed surreal once you are transplanted into it. . . .

To my surprise, Eagle Rock was not so *puti* [white]. My image of America was like in the movies, surrounded by white people. That's what I was expecting when I came. At first, I thought I could feel comfortable being surrounded by other Filipinos in Eagle Rock [and] being around familiar faces. But surprisingly, it wasn't the same comfort. Part of it was, unlike the Philippines, everyone seemed to lead their own private life. People were indoors most of the time. I see faces of Filipinos to my left and right, but I still felt like they were inaccessible. In that way, I know there are people like me out here in this very same neighborhood, but it's still very isolating.

Benji's eloquent description of Eagle Rock depicted the quintessential aspects of American suburban life, such as privacy, boundaries, and manicured homes. At the same time, Filipinoness remained embedded throughout, albeit in subtle ways among Benji's family and neighbors. However, for him, they also embodied an Americanness that he was not accustomed to back in Manila. This was suburban ethnicity in action.

As Benji's narrative suggested, the Filipino presence in suburban communities like Eagle Rock and Carson was not overwhelming. Nonetheless, both neighborhoods were home to a plethora of Filipino businesses, most of which catered to the immigrant contingent. Both neighborhoods housed Filipino grocery stores, restaurants, video and music stores, employment placement agencies, and money remittance companies. Most of the Filipinos I interviewed did not frequent these

Filipino establishments regularly, but the sites still provided them with a symbolic sense of ownership over the neighborhoods. Marie, a college student from Carson, said she felt a tremendous sense of comfort in the presence of establishments like Jollibee, a fast-food chain that is the Filipino equivalent of McDonald's. "I think one thing I liked about Carson is that there's such a large Filipino community here," she said. "If you're craving something, you can always go to Jollibee or some other Filipino restaurant." However, when I asked her how often she ate there in the past year, she responded, "Almost never." In suburban neighborhoods like Eagle Rock and Carson, ethnic businesses were never the primary hangout spots for the Filipinos whom I interviewed. As a point of contrast, it is rather commonplace to find large groups of second-generation East Asians congregating within their respective ethnic establishments in other Asian enclaves and ethnoburbs like Monterey Park, Koreatown, and Rowland Heights.

Even though everyone appreciated the presence of Filipinos in their neighborhood, it was the racial diversity of their communities that they valued most—the idea that Eagle Rock and Carson "were Filipino, but not too Filipino." The existence of cities like Monterey Park and other Asian enclaves led some Filipinos to stereotype other Asians as being overly ethnocentric. "I feel like Asians are more to themselves. Asians hang out with other Asians. I feel like we have more exposure," said Ines, a graphic design artist who grew up in Eagle Rock. "My friend Alice grew up in Alhambra where everybody is Chinese, but I feel like Filipinos are more open." She added: "Filipinos are bound to have Hispanic friends and black friends. Asians are not." Lucy, a nursing student from Carson, echoed Ines's sentiments. "I don't see Asians interact with blacks and Latinos," she said. It was commonplace for Filipinos to unconsciously demarcate Filipinos from Asians, just as Ines and Lucy did. Both felt that the diversity of their communities made all the difference. "If I didn't have that diversity, I probably wouldn't know how to deal with other cultures," Ines said. "It made me more open minded." A *Los Angeles Times* survey of Asian Americans lent some credence to their remarks. Their findings revealed that more than 40 percent of Asians expressed angst about interacting with people outside their ethnic group, while the vast majority of Filipinos, both immigrant and US born, reported feeling comfortable making friends with whites, African Americans, Latinos, and other Asians.[19] This tendency helped shed light on why "there is no Filipino equivalent of Chinatown or Koreatown in Los Angeles, even though Filipinos are the largest Asian group in the city."[20] As one Filipino American community leader put it, "We won't ever get ourselves a Monterey Park."[21]

As Ines and Lucy's remarks suggest, Filipinos tend to believe that their residential choices are because they are somehow more open-minded than other Asians groups, as was also suggested by the *Los Angeles Times* survey. However, what most of them do not seem to realize, is that the tapered presence of Filipinos in both Eagle Rock and Carson is also a by-product of the immigrant backlash that earlier generations of Filipino residents faced in the early 1980s and 1990s.

Eagle Rock: Anytown, USA

In the 1970s, Eagle Rock was the stereotypical all-American small town — picturesque, residential, and predominantly white. Most of the residents were police officers and firefighters who had settled there to be close enough to respond to emergencies in any part of the city but still ensure that their families were far removed from the chaos of inner-city Los Angeles.[22] Eagle Rock residents also had a reputation for being conservative, typecast in a similar way to modern-day Orange County.

A decade later, immigration rapidly changed the face of the neighborhood. According to the 1980 US Census, two out of every three residents were white, and Latino and Asian immigrant families accounted for the remaining third. However, as the white residents became older, their children were no longer replenishing the neighborhood population. By the middle of the decade, two-thirds of the students in the local junior and senior high schools were either Latino or Asian American, a stark contrast to the demographic patterns of the neighborhood's residents. Eagle Rock's shift from a predominantly white to a majority-minority community was evident in neighborhood institutions beyond the local public school system. "When I first came here in 1972, I couldn't get over how white [and] Anglo-Saxon this area was," said Father Vincent Serpa, the associate pastor of the local Catholic Church, to a *Los Angeles Times* reporter in 1985. Longterm residents of Eagle Rock were not entirely pleased with the influx of new immigrants to their tight-knit community. "Sure, you hear certain squawks about new people moving in," said a local historian. One local city official added: "I think some of the people are threatened by other lifestyles. The mental attitude is generally conservative and, if you're not white, you're going to have a harder time."[23]

During the 1980s, the population of Filipinos grew from fewer than one thousand to an estimated five thousand. The *Los Angeles Times* commended Filipinos in Eagle Rock for bringing "a new, exotic touch" to a neighborhood once described as a "bastion of working-class whites and conservative values."[24] Throughout the decade, neighborhoods all over Los Angeles experienced similar demographic shifts due to ongoing Latino and Asian immigration, which frequently elicited backlash from longtime white residents.[25] However, Filipinos in Eagle Rock felt that their English proficiency and relative familiarity with American ways of life helped buffer their entrée into the neighborhood. "Ethnic enclaves exist because of necessity," said Eagle Rock resident and Filipino community leader Gilroy Gorre to the *Los Angeles Times*. "That does not happen with the Filipino, who is an American creature, the product of an American educational program. He watches Clint Eastwood and reads *Playboy* magazine." Gorre, the longtime editor of the local *Philippine American News*, would publicly laud the positive reception of Filipinos in the United States, often juxtaposing their experiences to those of other Asian immigrants in an almost boastful fashion. "For the first five or even ten years, the Koreans who come to America are most likely to go to a Korean bookstore, grocer, and insurance agent," Gorre argued. "That creates a geographically defined center for them. But the Filipinos don't feel subject to those same forces. . . . Filipinos are comfortable in the U.S. language and the culture."[26] For Gorre, these factors explained why Filipinos would even consider settling in predominantly white neighborhood like Eagle Rock. "Eagle Rock . . . that is where Filipinos move after they have climbed up the economic ladder to where they can buy their own homes," he said.

By opening ethnic establishments, Filipinos have reshaped the institutional landscape of Eagle Rock, but not to the same extent as in other Asian ethnic enclaves. "With its ethnic grocery stores, small restaurants, and musical dialects, the Filipino community is changing the landscape of Eagle Rock, splashing daubs of exotic color on the staid main streets and homes with white picket fences that characterize the area," reported the *Los Angeles Times*.[27] Unlike the ethnic shopping plazas of Monterey Park or Koreatown, Filipino businesses "sit tucked among purveyors of more traditional Americana—the sixty-year old hardware stores [and] the neighborhood barber shops."[28] In the early 2000s, Filipino business owners began leasing space in the Eagle Rock Plaza, the neighborhood's only major shopping mall. For a decade prior, Eagle Rock Plaza was practically a ghost town. The mall had a reputation for high turnover in its businesses, and many residents wondered why the mall even remained open at all. However, when Filipino eateries and stores began popping up in the first floor of the plaza, it attracted a new ethnic niche of patrons who started frequenting the mall en masse. "That is ground zero," said one Filipino local resident. "The mall has really come to symbolize the centerpiece of the Filipino community in Eagle Rock." By the late 2000s, the Eagle Rock Plaza had become a social gathering spot for Filipino immigrants, who felt going to the mall was like "walking into Manila" and "[being] back in the Philippines."[29] The *Los Angeles Times* even dubbed Eagle Rock Plaza the "anchor" of a "thriving Filipino community."

While not discounting the impact of this new ethnic presence in Eagle Rock Plaza, the reality was that only seven of the more than sixty retailers in the mall were Filipino businesses. Ultimately, the dramatic response of both the local residents and the *Los Angeles Times* spoke to the newsworthiness of seeing Filipinos institutionally and socially concentrated in a public space. The idea that a "Filipino mall" could not only exist but also thrive—even if just a few stores on a single floor of a once-defunct shopping center—was almost unbelievable for some Filipinos.

Alvin Contreras was one of those Filipinos. Alvin was the cousin of someone I had interviewed from Carson. He had been visiting from San Diego and had come to the coffee shop as his cousin and I were wrapping up our interview. After being introduced, Alvin and I got into a conversation about the respective neighborhoods where we had grown up, and we were joking casually about whose hometown was "more Filipino." To leverage our friendly debate in my direction, I told him that Eagle Rock had its own Filipino mall. "You're so full of shit," Alvin said. "You're lying." I offered to prove it by driving him there, and he happily agreed since he was in the mood for Filipino food anyway. Throughout the half-hour drive to Eagle Rock, Alvin remained skeptical and continued to assume that I was messing around with him. "There's even a Seafood City [a Filipino American grocery store chain] *in* the mall," I told him, to which he quickly responded, "Yeah, uh-huh. Sure."

We parked the car and started walking toward the plaza entrance on the first floor. A few steps into the mall, Alvin spotted the Seafood City, as well as a parade of Filipinos pushing Seafood City supermarket carts toward the exit, and he immediately burst into laughter for what seemed like a solid minute. "Oh my God!" Alvin said repeatedly, vacillating between this and uncontrollable laugher: "You *weren't* lying." Once his laugher subsided a bit, Alvin pulled out his iPhone and asked me to snap a picture. "I want to send it to my mom." Alvin stood in front of the indoor Seafood City and pointed at it as if were some type of major tourist attraction. After we ate lunch, Alvin bought some Filipino DVDs and CDs for his mother and aunt, and I drove him back to Carson. Alvin's surprise perfectly captured how unusual it was for Filipinos to see something that even remotely re-sembled the landscape of a typical Asian immigrant enclave.

Since their initial arrival in the 1980s, Filipinos in Eagle Rock have not been entirely exempt from immigrant backlash from white long-time residents. Filipinos have encountered major pushback whenever they have attempted to publicly codify their presence in the neighbor-hood. For example, in 2002, Filipino residents petitioned to have the city post a street sign that read "Philippine Village." From the view-point of the Filipinos who spearheaded the project, the sign was meant to celebrate the Filipino presence in the neighborhood and recognize an area that housed a number of ethnic establishments—a church, newspaper, radio station, remittance agencies, and restaurants—that catered to their community. Many opponents, most of whom were white residents, felt that the move was an act of ethnic favorit-ism and separatism that would ruin the neighborhood diversity. Betty Tyndall, an elderly white woman who had lived in Eagle Rock since World War II, was a fervent opponent to the decision. "The people in Eagle Rock are up in arms about this," she complained. "Eagle Rock is a diverse community where no particular ethnic group should separate itself from the community. I've never seen any group come and ask for this." Another longtime resident, Roe Muzingo, echoed Mrs. Tyndall's thoughts, despite her own immigrant roots. "We're in a melting pot, and we don't want to change it," she said. "I'm Ital-ian, OK? Italian is my heritage, but I'm an American. We shouldn't be separated." Ultimately, the Los Angeles City Council unanimously approved the sign, largely due to the public support and politicking of Latino council member Nick Pacheco, himself the son of Mexican immigrants and a resident of Eagle Rock.[30]

Given the potential for such immigrant backlash, Filipino busi-ness owners have remained keenly aware that being too visible could pose problems for their establishments. When trying to secure space in Eagle Rock Plaza, the Filipino grocery chain Seafood City took extra precautions "to ensure that the market's fish was packaged well enough to mask any unpleasant odors."[31] Of course, this company's standard for what constituted an "unpleasant" odor was based not on the perspective of Filipinos but on that of white residents more unaccustomed to the commonplace smells of an ethnic market. Ultimately, most of these neighborhood incidents related to "ethnicizing" public space have mainly involved Filipino *immigrants*. In most cases, the *children* of these immigrants—the primary segment of neighborhood residents I interviewed—remained relatively uninvolved in such debates about Eagle Rock's public space.

Carson: America's Most Racially Balanced Neighborhood

Unlike Eagle Rock, which became a minority middle-class neighborhood only in the past two decades, Carson has been a bastion for upwardly mobile people of color throughout the twentieth century. Carson has long appealed to minority families who were looking for a middle-class neighborhood existence that was unavailable in the city center. From the early twentieth century to the post–World War II period, the opportunities to purchase a home and land were generally unavailable for the majority of racial minorities, Filipinos included. Most people of color at the time lived in overcrowded housing units clustered in the center of Los Angeles. Given these constraints throughout most of Los Angeles, Carson was unique in that it provided people of color the chance not only to own homes but also to be part of community organizations and local politics. Since 1968, people of color of diverse backgrounds—African Americans, Asian Americans, and Latinos—have served as local public officials at every level, from city council members to mayor. The potential of Carson as a space of minority upward mobility even prompted the state to establish a college, California State University–Dominguez Hills, to serve the needs of students of color who were historically being shut out of other institutions for higher learning.

Filipino immigrants first moved to Carson in the early twentieth century. This pioneering group of Filipinos in Carson was part of the first major wave of Filipino labor migrants who arrived while the Philippines was still an American colony. Unlike today's Filipino immigrants, who are mostly college-educated professionals, many of these early settlers worked in agriculture, canneries, and fishing. Some of them were members of the US Navy, which permitted and actively recruited Filipinos to enlist because of the existing colonial relationship between the Philippines and the United States. The Filipino community that formed in Carson was unique from other pockets of Filipino settlements in the state. Unlike their counterparts who endured poor living and working conditions in the labor camps of northern and central California, Filipinos in Carson had more opportunities to at least sample the American dream.[32]

"They had families and their children attended local schools in the South Bay and played on sports teams in their communities and beyond," said Eloisa Gomez Borah, of the Filipino American National Historical Society. As noted earlier, because most Filipino migrants were male and not permitted to marry across racial lines, they generally found it difficult to form families.[33] However, Carson's proximity to Mexico allowed Filipino men to circumvent these constraints. In Mexico, they were not subject to antimiscegenation laws, and thus were able to marry the women they loved.[34] Most Filipinos married Mexican women, who at the time were considered white and were technically off limits. Ultimately, though, their common history of Spanish colonialism in their home societies meant that they shared many cultural sensibilities, which in turn allowed their marital unions to flourish.[35] In this respect, these marriages demonstrated how Filipinos in Carson had long been engaged in developing close relations across racial lines for most of the twentieth century.

The size of the Filipino community in Carson ushered in unique opportunities for them to become involved in local politics, unlike in Eagle Rock. In contrast to the residents of Eagle Rock, the Carson electorate had long been used to seeing people of color as local political leaders, which made the idea of a Filipino elected official a more acceptable idea. Filipinos had served as leaders in Carson's city council since the 1980s. In 1997, residents of Carson elected its first Filipino mayor, former council member Peter Fajardo, who at that time became one of the few publicly elected Filipino officials in the country. Despite his ability to garner voter support from a diverse array of constituents, many believed that Fajardo was guilty of ethnic nepotism. During his tenure, he appointed unprecedented numbers of Filipinos into local leadership positions, which other minority leaders argued would ruin Carson's reputation for being America's "most racially balanced community."[36]

The Fajardo administration stirred up worries among other racial groups that the Filipino presence was becoming too powerful. Many African American and Latino leaders accused Fajardo of earmarking certain positions specifically for Filipinos, a charge that Fajardo vehemently denied. Fajardo had long been a respected local leader even before serving as mayor both among Filipinos and other racial groups, but the perceived disruption in Carson's balance of power caused his political reputation to rapidly erode.[37] "It's certainly not a level playing field if a portion of the elected officials are working toward one ethnic group and not looking to help the remainder of the city," said Steven Caudillo, a Latino resident and local city organizer. The strong backlash against Fajardo's perceived attempts to increase Filipinos' political cachet was ultimately indicative of local residents' unwillingness to upset the balance of power among its different ethnic populations. Regardless of whether Fajardo was exhibiting ethnic nepotism, the responses of other minority leaders demonstrated their uneasiness at the idea that Filipinos would somehow come to dominate the local public sphere.

More recently, Filipino leaders attempted to rename a local street as a way to institutionalize their community's presence in Carson. In 2010, a Filipino council member proposed that Moneta Avenue in Carson be renamed Jose Rizal Avenue both to commemorate the longtime presence of Filipino residents and to pay homage to the national hero of the Philippines.[38] Almost immediately, local residents protested the attempted proposal. "The proposal threatens to open ugly racial rifts in Carson . . . where no racial or ethnic group has a majority," stated the *Daily Breeze*, a local South Bay newspaper. Even some Filipinos expressed their discontent with the council member's proposal. "It's not fair for everyone," argued Manny Flores, a local Filipino resident. "It doesn't make sense. Everyone knows we live on Moneta." Flores's remarks echoed the sentiments of other Filipinos who preferred that their community fly under the radar rather than provoke racially charged confrontations with other ethnic groups in Carson.

Second-Generation Perspectives

In both Eagle Rock and Carson, Filipinos constitute about 20 percent of the population. The majority of the Filipino children of immigrants who grew up in Eagle Rock and Carson did not speak a Filipino language (although most acknowledged that they understood Tagalog when immigrant family members spoke it to them). These second-generation Filipinos said they seldom frequented Filipino businesses and establishments unless it was to accompany their immigrant parents or relatives. Only two of the people I interviewed participated in Filipino-specific cultural activities. These two individuals, both Filipina young women, were part of a cultural folk dance troupe, and both had been coerced by their mothers to join initially. When they were at home, hardly any of them watched Filipino television except passively when their immigrant relatives were watching a *teleserye* (soap opera) or newscasts about the Philippines. When they were out in the neighborhood, they were more likely to patronize the local Starbucks than a Filipino establishment. Overall, their neighborhood experiences diverged tremendously from the experiences of other second-generation Asians, who were more actively engaged with their respective ethnic institutions. To a much greater degree, second-generation East Asians and Southeast Asians were bilingual. They translated on behalf of their non-English-speaking parents, they worked for their parents' restaurants and businesses, and they attended language and supplementary tutoring schools operated by their coethnics.[39] In other words, on an everyday level, Filipinos were not as engaged in the cultural activities that, some would argue, define ethnic authenticity.[40]

Were Filipinos who grew up in Eagle Rock and Carson totally assimilated into American culture? Did most of them consider themselves "just" American? These patterns of their cultural engagement might suggest that the answer is yes to both. However, the majority of Filipinos that I interviewed, even those who admitted not being able to speak a lick of Tagalog or who rarely patronized the local Jollibee or Goldilocks (another famous Filipino food chain), still maintained a strong sense of Filipino ethnic identity. Jen, a retail manager who grew up in Eagle Rock, felt it was a given for Filipinos there to have pride in their heritage and to want to "learn new things about the Philippines," even if those opportunities were not readily available. She contrasted her own sense of identity with that of her cousins who grew up closer to Downtown Los Angeles, in a more predominantly white area: "My cousins that live near Downtown, all of their friends are white. Every time they went to a Filipino event that I was part of, they always complained and said it was a waste of time." Renee, a nursing student from Carson, echoed Jen's thoughts when talking about her own cousins who lived in nearby Orange County: "My cousins who live in the OC [Orange County], they're more whitewashed. They don't even like it if their parents speak to them in Tagalog. They never eat Filipino food either. You're not real Filipino if you don't eat Filipino food." As Jen and Renee's comments suggested, neighborhoods seemed to matter a great deal when it came to maintaining ethnicity, even if the institutional landscape of the neighborhood was "not that Filipino."

Even so, most still considered Eagle Rock and Carson "very Filipino" because of the community of coethnics who live there. Although Filipinos did not make up more than a quarter of the residents in either neighborhood, the vast majority overestimated the percentage of Filipinos who lived in their neighborhood. These were some of the demographic approximations made by Filipinos from Eagle Rock:

RAYMOND: Maybe 60 percent to 70 percent Filipino? God, I don't
know. Generally the rest is Latino and white.

JOEY: 30 percent Filipino, 40 percent to 60 percent Latino, and the
maybe 5 percent black, and then the rest, the other 3 percent to
4 percent, would be white. I don't really know about the other
[races] other than Filipinos and Latinos.

VINCE: I would say 40 percent Filipino, 40 percent Hispanic, and
20 percent Caucasian maybe.

ANGIE: Maybe 60 percent Filipino, 30 percent Latino, and 10 percent
other and white.

GRACE: I would say 80 percent Filipino. The remainder would probably be Latino, maybe 15 percent or 20 percent. There's probably
some whites too.

INES: I'd say, like, 80 percent Filipino. And then 15 percent Latino.

MONICA: I'd say 95 percent are Filipino.

These were the racial breakdown estimations of Filipinos from Carson:

JACOB: Probably like 40 percent Filipino, 40 percent African American, and then I guess, like, 10 percent Samoan and the other
10 percent white and Mexican.

JEFF: One side would be populated by Mexicans and blacks. Over
where I live, I'd say it's 60 percent Filipino, 20 percent Mexican,
20 percent Samoan.

BRYAN: I'd say blacks and Mexicans are tied, maybe 30 percent each.
And then 25 percent Filipino and the rest of the 15 percent
Samoan.

ALMA: I'd say there's 30 percent Filipino, 30 percent African American, 30 percent Hispanic, and 10 percent of other. Oh, wait!
There's also the Samoan population.

RENEE: Filipinos would be maybe, like, 70 percent and the rest would
be divided between blacks and Hispanics.

Given that most Filipinos were not in the habit of regularly consulting
demographic statistics, how did they come up with such exaggerated

estimates? Filipinos' overestimations of their ethnic presence in Eagle Rock and Carson were an indication of their regular engagement with other Filipinos in their respective communities.

Eagle Rock and Carson solidified second-generation Filipinos' sense of ethnic belonging. "I think Filipinos in Eagle Rock are aware of their culture," said Franky, who worked at a local bank in the neighborhood. When Franky left Eagle Rock to attend UC Santa Cruz, he constantly "got into it" with other Filipinos on campus who "talked shit" about him for being whitewashed, mainly because he opted out of joining the Filipino student organization. In Franky's mind, there was no need to prove himself precisely because of where he was from. "My Filipinoness is rooted in Eagle Rock," he argued. "I don't feel like I have to be super Filipino everywhere I am *because* I'm from Eagle Rock. Eagle Rock is what makes me Filipino. That's how I feel." Most from Carson felt that their neighborhood gave them the same type of ethnic authenticity. "When you say Carson, you think Filipinos," said Renee. "When I look back, in hindsight, I thought everyone was Filipino."

It was within their neighborhoods that these children of immigrants learned what it meant to be Filipino. And for the majority of Filipinos, most of these lessons about Filipino ethnic identity started in the household.

Ethnicity Happens at Home

Cesar had never been to the Philippines, but he still felt that he knew everything he needed to about Filipino culture. "Why go to the Philippines when the Philippines comes to you?" he asked rhetorically, alluding to the countless relatives who had lived with him and his parents throughout his entire life in Carson. Cesar said he was always proud about his ethnic identity. He was so proud of being Filipino that he always felt the need to display his discontent when people would call him "Asian," a label he felt "erased" his identity. Every time people described him as such, he was quick to correct them and always left them knowing that he was Filipino. Being Filipino was so important to him that he even had the Filipino flag tattooed on his left arm, along with his two family names—Perez and Torres—written in cursive right under. I asked Cesar where he had learned so much about Filipino culture and history.

"Mainly from my grandparents," he said. "They'd have all these stories about the Philippines and what they did back there. I remember my mom and dad would have parties and events with people from their hometown. Every time we'd go to these events, there were always these little parties with Filipino dancing. I'd ask my grandparents what that was, and they would name all the dances. So my access to learning about Filipino culture was mainly through social events."

In the absence of ethnic institutions, the family became the primary "classroom" where Filipinos learned about Filipino culture. The family was where Filipinos accumulated their knowledge about Filipino traditions, foods, and even history. For Cesar, there was never any shortage of opportunities to learn about the homeland, especially when a new relative came to live with his family. Living in multigenerational, multifamily households provided Filipinos raised in the United States a symbolic connection with the homeland. Moreover, interacting with Filipino immigrant relatives also helped those born and raised in the United States develop a deeper appreciation of the struggles associated with migration.

Middle Class Dreams, Immigrant Realities

Joey, a medical student from Eagle Rock, had vivid memories of his parents' immigrant struggles. When they first contemplated migrating to the United States from the Philippines, Joey's parents anticipated that their American dreams would come into fruition rather quickly. After all, they both held degrees from the University of the Philippines, their home country's most prestigious college institution. Before moving to the United States, they both worked as accountants, which allowed them to maintain a comfortable life in a suburban neighborhood not too far outside of Metro Manila. When Joey was five years old, they decided to uproot themselves from their comfortable life in the Philippines and move to Eagle Rock. Joey's grandmother and her sister had been living there since the early 1980s and had recently opened a nursing home in the neighborhood. Although neither of the women was trained as a nurse, both had found work as caretakers for the elderly through other Filipino immigrants who were nurses working in the home health-care industry. Joey's grandmother and sister decided to open up their own nursing facility, and they needed help with the business operations. His parents were happy to oblige their need, assuming that their accounting skills would go to some good use. Their petition to migrate was approved shortly after Joey's sixth birthday, and they packed up their belongings and moved to America. However, their first home in the States was the nursing home that Joey's grandmother owned—not exactly the American dream home his parents were expecting.

After a few months of living in the nursing home, Joey and his family moved into a bungalow adjacent to the facility. Their living situation did not seem to improve all that much, mainly because they shared their home with several other relatives. "It was me, my brother, my parents, my great-grandpa, my aunt, and my grandpa, all under one roof," Joey remembered. Even as professional accountants, living in an overcrowded bungalow was all they could financially manage. It would be almost a year before his family could finally afford their own home, a modest apartment about a mile away from the nursing home. The apartment was located in the "shadier" part of Eagle Rock, closer to the more working-class community of Glassell Park, but even then, his parents still had to scrape together extra cash by doing odd jobs in the neighborhood. "They were working as accountants the whole time, but they also worked as gardeners on the side," Joey said. "Some of the local families needed gardening services, and so they would do that on the weekends." Joey remembered that his parents could not afford new furniture for their new apartment. In fact, it was even a struggle for them to buy toys for him and his brother. "I remember on weekends, we would drive around looking for yard sales, trying to get furniture and toys because stores were too expensive," he recalled.

Despite their own financial struggles, Joey's family maintained a sense of obligation to other relatives, especially those who had just arrived from the Philippines. "At one point, we had, like, ten people living in my apartment. It was totally illegal," he said. "There were people on my couch, four in my bedroom, another four in another bedroom, and two people on the couch." Their apartment became the initial stopover for relatives who needed a few weeks, or even months, to get their feet on the ground in America. "Our aunts and uncles would come from the Philippines, one by one. And they'd live with us first before they got established," Joey remembered.

As Joey's story demonstrates, middle-class living was not all it was cracked up to be. This was true even for Filipinos who lived in the "bourgeois" side of the neighborhood. Monica, a registered nurse, re-membered growing up in a quaint two-bedroom house just north of Colorado Boulevard, an area of Eagle Rock where the families, and their homes, were thought to be more affluent. Although the house where she grew up was much larger than Joey's family's—it had a large yard and a garage with an extra room on top of it—it did not seem any more spacious from the way she described it. "My house was the house where all the relatives would go when they first got to the States," she said. Monica, her parents, and her three siblings moved to Eagle Rock when she was just three years old. "When we first got there, we lived with my mom's parents, my aunt, and all my cousins," she said. "Random cousins would come in and out for months at a time. We were all living there in that house."

Although their home was spacious from the outside, Monica's family had to get creative to fit upward of twelve people "comfort-ably," given the limited space that they had:

> We had a pullout bed in the dining room. There was one master bed-room that we converted into a two bedroom. And then my grandpa had a den that was converted into his own room. For my family, there was the garage that they had converted into a regular room—no bath-room or nothing. And it was the six of us. I remember there were

three of us on the bed, and my older brother on the floor. I remember my brother would sleep on a laundry bag. That'd be the pillow he would use.

Even though she was very young when they migrated, she was old enough to know that life back in Manila seemed much more prosperous than this. "In the Philippines, we were pretty well off there. I remember my mom gave us everything. My older brothers and sister were in private schools," Monica recalled. Even today, she vividly remembered these early days as tough times. "We were there a couple of months. It seemed like forever," she said. "It was so cold. The heater was in the house. It was a big change for us." Although her mother worked as a nurse, it would be a few years before her parents were stable enough to rent their own home and financially provide for her and her three siblings.

These multigenerational households were the norm for many Filipinos. Even when their immediate family had the means to live on their own, most said their parents felt a sense of obligation to help new relatives get on their feet, especially if they themselves had been beneficiaries of such familial generosity. Erik, an outreach coordinator at a local community health organization, said this was his family's story. When Erik and his family moved out of his grandmother's apartment located close to the more working class neighborhood of Highland Park and into their own house in Eagle Rock, there were only a few months when he could remember it being only his immediate family in their home. "After we moved, it was just my parents and my newborn baby brother," said Erik. "But then two of my cousins moved into the back house. It was my dad's brother's daughter and my mom's sister's daughter." Erik said he never minded the extra company growing up. "They were all like siblings growing up," he said. If anything, Erik and others saw such household setups as the norm for Filipino families. "Whenever I meet Filipinos who don't have large families and it's just their family, that's kind of weird," said Rachel, a college academic adviser who grew up with several cousins in her own home in Carson. "That's definitely not the typical Filipino family," she said.

Even if they were not accommodating relatives in their home, many Filipinos remembered that their parents still provided financial assistance to loved ones back home. With so many relatives coming back and forth from the Philippines, it was rather common for Filipinos to see their parents send envelopes of cash or care packages to their family members in the homeland. Some even said that there were entire rooms or sections of the garage that were partitioned specifically for the preparation of *balikbayan* (homecoming) boxes, large cardboard boxes that Filipino immigrants would regularly ship back to the Philippines or take with them when traveling there. Filipinos sent back everything from clothing to shoes, towels, canned goods, electronics, medicines, vitamins, and other goods that were more affordable stateside. And typically, the senders would squeeze as many items as they could into the box. By the time a box was ready to send, its contents were as tightly packed as a can of sardines.

For the Filipinos I interviewed in their homes, I observed just how visible these *balikbayan* boxes became. When I would enter, some would excuse themselves for the mess in one of the bedrooms or the living room. More often than not, there was not really any significant mess. Rather, they were just excusing themselves for the large cardboard box that was awkwardly positioned next to their living room couch or dining room table, seemingly out of place amid the other furniture. "We're sending stuff back home," one young woman said. The choice of words—*we're* and *home*—became all the more interesting as I came to find that the young woman was not actively assisting with the preparation of the *balikbayan* box, nor was she making frequent trips to the Philippines. Nonetheless, the regular practice of sending *balikbayan* boxes back home gave her some sense of connection with her relatives abroad.[41] In one case, *balikbayan* boxes, as well as the goods about to be sent, took over the family home. When I met with Arianna, a community college student from Carson, her living room looked like a wartime bomb shelter. The furniture in the living room was beautiful, and there was even a seventy-inch flat-screen television. However, all of the furniture was buried under piles of clothing, canned goods, cereal boxes, shoes, and even jugs of wine. Arianna and I carved out a nook in her kitchen dining table to do the interview. After our interview, Arianna took inventory of her family's living room, caught me doing the same, and then said, "See? We're not *really* middle class because my mom uses all her extra money to buy stuff for people in the Philippines." Behind the beautifully kept lawn of their Carson home was a storage room of goods piled up over a period of months and waiting to be sent back to the Philippines. From the outside, Arianna's family was a middle-class household of four people; however, in reality, the income of that household supported many other families beyond their actual home, thousands of miles away in the Philippines.

For many of the Filipinos I interviewed from both Eagle Rock and Carson, being middle class often came with a caveat of family obligation. In their lives in the United States, most agreed they were never deprived, even if their early days of childhood involved some form of economic struggle, just as Joey and Monica's stories show. In general, Filipinos felt they grew up with everything they ever needed and wanted, Joey and Monica included, whether it be school supplies, computers, even cars. Yet despite their privileges, several Filipinos felt compelled to point out that middle-class life was not entirely what that label suggested. Most Filipinos said that their families were embedded in a larger system of reciprocity with relatives in the United States or back home, which dispelled any notions that they were affluent.

Never Miss a Family Party

One of the first questions I asked every Filipino during an interview was "What was your favorite part about growing up in your neighbor-hood?" By and large, the two most common responses were "the diversity" and "family." Rachel was among the Filipinos who responded with the latter. "Carson for me has *always* been about family," she said. "It's always been a large extended family, a bunch of aunts and uncles who aren't really related to you *obviously*." When she said the word *obviously*, she made eye contact and chuckled, a tacit gesture meant to signal a mutual understanding between two Filipinos. "It was a very Filipino, very immigrant experience," she said, despite not having been born in the Philippines herself. "That's what I loved about Carson. It always felt like home because there were always a lot of people. That's what Carson was—family." As she shared her story, it became clearer why Carson, family, and Filipino came to be synonymous concepts in her mind.

Rachel's parents moved to Carson in the late 1970s. Both her parents had occupations that made it relatively easy to migrate to the United States—her mother was a nurse and her father was in the US Navy. Their choice of professions also made it relatively easy to connect with other Filipinos, given that a large number of their coethnics entered nursing and military professions. By the time Rachel was born in the early 1980s, her parents had a close-knit group of friends in Carson. "It's actually funny. The way that they made them my 'real' family was that they made them my godparents [at Baptism]. So I had sixteen godparents," Rachel said. As was custom among many Filipinos, kinship titles were liberally applied to anyone and everyone. "Everyone is your *tita* or *tito* [aunt or uncle], even if you've just met them. For me, everyone was either *ninong* or *ninang* [godfather or godmother], or *lolo* or *lola* [grandfather or grandmother]," she joked. It was not until the fifth grade, when she had to create a family tree, that Rachel learned that her relatives were not "really" relatives. "We started to learn about kin in school, and I got confused because my teacher kept asking, 'Whose sister is she?'" Rachel recalled. "I'd be like, 'They're not sisters, but she *is* my aunt.'" Even twenty years later, Rachel continued to see her parents' closest friends as close as blood and their children as her cousins.

Beyond her circle of fictive kin, many of Rachel's blood relatives also settled in Carson upon migrating to the United States. Like many other Filipinos, Rachel's family took full advantage of the immigration policies that encouraged family reunification during the 1980s. In the early 1970s, Rachel's great aunt moved to Carson and shortly thereafter petitioned her husband and sisters, one of which was Rachel's grandmother. While her mother became a permanent resident on her own, her maternal grandmother was able to catalyze the migration of her mother's entire family. "My grandma petitioned all of her kids who were under twenty-one, and so now all of my mom's brothers and sisters live in Carson," she said. Rachel's entire social circle growing up consisted of family, both blood related and fictive, who were born both in the Philippines and the United States. "Christmas at my house is always about sixty people, minimum," she shared proudly. At the time of our interview, Rachel had just started to have a family of her own—she was the mother of two small children. She herself was now taking part in reifying the kinship ties among her relatives and close family friends. "When my older cousins and 'cousins' had kids, I became their godparent," she said, gesturing air quotes to denote her fictive kin. "And some of their kids are now *my* kids' godparents. It all perpetuates."

Edward's experience growing up in Eagle Rock involved much of the same. Edward, a recent college graduate and part-time tutor for a private company, reasserted the strong association of neighborhood, ethnicity, and family. When I asked him what he thought what it meant to be Filipino, he said:

Family is number one. Living with more than just the nuclear family. You live with your grandparents and other extended family nearby. And then having family gatherings pretty frequently. Respect for your *titos* and *titas* [uncles and aunts], and they are pretty invested in your life. They babysit you and things like that. It's big and close.

Edward also reiterated the mutual sense of reciprocity and kinship felt by members of a Filipino clan:

There's definitely a need to help each other a lot. There's a lot of money exchanged, time spent taking care of each other's kids. I really do think I do it out of love. Now that I am getting older, I take care of [my cousin's] kids. . . . When I meet with other Filipinos, especially if they are older, they'll introduce me to their other [older] coworkers and say, "This is *tita* or *tito* whoever," and they immediately welcome me. We would eat Filipino food and have potlucks all the time. It's like a connector. It's a conversation starter. If you have cultural proficiency and can prove your authenticity, then it's cooler.

Embedded in Edward's remarks were notions of what it meant to be an "authentic" Filipino. This included everything from being knowledgeable about Filipino ethnic cuisines to applying fictive kinship titles immediately after meeting someone to adhering to family obligations at the drop of a hat. These became the criteria for how Filipinos, even those born in the United States, gauged how Filipino someone "really" was.

"My Filipino friends completely understand the following two words—*family party*," said Ronald, a graphic designer from Eagle Rock. "When you have a family party, you *have* to be there. It's considered really disrespectful if you don't attend. My white friends were like, 'So you don't have to be there. It's probably boring.' They don't understand the idea that the family *has* to be together." Ronald said that it was even considered faux pas in his family to miss social gatherings, even if he had academic obligations. This specific willingness to drop everything for family was something that distinguished Filipinos from his white peers in Eagle Rock (in contrast, family was something that he argued was very similar between Filipinos and Latinos in the neighborhood). In high school and college, he said that he would prioritize family gatherings over studying for midterms, a trend common among other Filipinos. Along these lines, Joey spoke extensively about how atypical his parents were from other Filipino parents precisely because they allowed him to miss family obligations to study:

My parents were nice in that way if I wanted to study. Like at family gatherings, when we'd have birthday parties, everyone would be there. I'm pretty close to my aunts and uncles so I always had to be there. But then they would defend me if I wanted to study. They'd be like, "Joey is upstairs studying." This helped because pretty much every weekend there was a social gathering.

As Joey's remarks suggested, his choice to prioritize his academic obligations was something that might go against custom within Filipino families. His parents were able to serve as brokers between him and his extensive family so that he would not be perceived as snubbing the family, and by extension, rejecting Filipino tradition. Overall, the degree to which Joey felt he needed to strategize to save face within his family is quite telling about how the family defined the symbolic boundaries of Filipino ethnic identity.

The Neighborhood Parish

"The church thing is pretty common in Carson," said Jacob, an elementary school teacher from the neighborhood. "I think it's pretty common. I'm dead serious, about 90 percent of my Filipino friends went to St. Felipe." All of Jacob's friends were closely connected to St. Felipe, the main Catholic church in Carson. Many had been baptized there as infants. As they became older, they also participated in other Catholic sacraments, including First Communion and Confirmation, the ritual where young adults publicly reaffirm their religious faith in front of their local congregation. As he saw it, church was more of a meeting place than anything else. "My friends would all sin every week, but they would go to church. They said that was just what they had to do." Jacob himself had not grown up in the same parish. Part of it had to do with his multiracial background. His mother was a Filipino immigrant, and his father was African American. While they were both Christian, they had different religious affiliations. Not growing up too close to the Catholic faith was one arena in which he said some Filipinos might feel like an "outcast."

As Jacob's story suggests, being Filipino is often synonymous with being Catholic. Catholicism was one of the major influences of the Spanish colonial period—the vast majority of Filipinos in the homeland and in the United States are Roman Catholic, a trend quite similar to the case of Mexican Americans and other Latinos. In both Eagle Rock and Carson, there is one primary Catholic parish that houses most of the Filipinos in the area. In Eagle Rock, there is St. Daniel's; in Carson, as Jacob mentioned, there is St. Felipe, often jokingly referred to as "St. Filipino" by the people I interviewed. For many, Catholic religion, as well as attendance at these respective parishes, functioned as a litmus test of Filipino ethnic identity.

Church was much more than attending mass every Sunday. The local parish was the place where Filipinos formed connections with other Filipinos beyond their immediate families. Ronald said many of his memories of childhood and adolescence involved St. Daniel's parish. When he was five years old, Ronald started kindergarten at the parish elementary school and remained there through the eighth grade. As a youth, he remembered waiting after school with his other Filipino classmates as their parents socialized in the parish parking lot. The same thing would happen on weekends after Sunday mass, but he and his friends would wait even longer. "Sometimes as kids, we'd just be waiting there in the parking lot after church waiting for our parents to finish talking to the other Filipino parents," Ronald remembered. "They'd take forever! Everyone would already be long gone by the time my mom was finished talking to her friends." In this moment, the parking lot served the same function as most ethnic institutions. Impromptu interactions in the church parking lot became the building blocks for more intimate connections with other Filipino families in the neighborhood. Casual conversations eventually evolved into birthday invitations, babysitting favors, and car-pool groups. When Ronald participated in Confirmation classes during his first two years of high school, some of the other parents at his local parish became his "sponsors" for the sacrament. As was custom with Catholic tradition, these other Filipino parents at St. Daniel's were considered godparents, which made their kinship connection "official" in his eyes. As Ronald's story demonstrated, the church became the de facto ethnic institution for many Filipinos who grew up in the United States, particularly in the way it helped crystallized strong connections among Filipinos families in the neighborhood.

The Catholic parish strengthened Filipinos' connections to their neighborhoods, particularly those who temporarily moved away for school. Lynette, a recent graduate of UCLA, said that many of her relatives, including her parents, had been attending St. Felipe's parish since they arrived in Carson in the 1970s. St. Felipe's was especially important for them as newly arrived immigrants from the Philippines since it gave them opportunities to connect with other Filipinos. She and her siblings all attended St. Felipe's from kindergarten to eighth grade. "It was mostly Filipino, like 97 percent. The others were Mexican," Lynette described. Once Lynette reached high school, however, her parents sent her Marymount High School: "And then there were no Filipinos. I could count the Filipinos on two hands. It was mostly Mexican people and black people," she said.

St. Felipe's youth ministry programs were Lynette's only connection to her old friends in the neighborhood. "I kept in touch with my Carson friends because we all had Confirmation classes," she said. After her "weird transition" to Marymount, St. Felipe's Confirmation program became just as much about staying in touch with Filipinos from Carson as it was about the religious signification. "It was weird because I never thought of us as Filipino until I moved for high school," she said. "It was more like we all grew up together. I mean it was nice that many of us [in the parish] were Filipino and we could relate to each other's family experiences. And we felt very much at home at other people's homes as if they were our own homes." Like many others, Lynette's conversations about Filipino ethnic identity, neighborhood, family, and Catholicism all happened within the same breath.

Outside the Box

Even with the financial struggles and family obligations that their families faced, most Filipinos said their families had achieved some sense of economic stability. The vast majority never worried about not having a place to live, even if their living quarters were cramped. Unlike many working-class children of immigrants, many of the Filipinos I met did not work in high school or even college. Those who did work did so primarily to have some extra spending money, not necessarily to make significant contributions to their family's household income.

Andrea was the exception to this trend. Andrea's parents, like many other Filipino immigrants in Eagle Rock, were college-educated professionals. Her mother was a nurse, and her father was a computer technician. For most of her childhood, Andrea remembered living in a small but charming home in Eagle Rock with her parents and her sister. Unfortunately, everything changed around the time Andrea was ten years old. Her parents filed for bankruptcy and her family lost practically everything:

> My parents filed for bankruptcy when I was in the fifth grade. So we didn't have the house. We didn't have anything. For a while we had to live in Fontana [approximately fifty miles east of Los Angeles], but we still went to Eagle Rock for my parents' work and our school. We only had one car at that time. We couldn't afford a second, so we would wake up at 3 a.m., take a shower, drop off my mom at work in Downtown LA, eat breakfast in the car, and get milk from Jack in the Box just to eat our cereal. My dad would go to work in Burbank while my sister and I went to Glenrock Junior High. Since he was working, after school me and my sister would have to stay at the library for hours by ourselves. That was also the hangout where everyone would go.

By "everyone," Andrea was referring to other Filipino kids in the neighborhood. At the library, Andrea and her sister often kept to themselves and to a few of their other classmates from Glenrock. Because the library was across the street from St. Daniel's, many of the other students hanging out in the library were from the parish elementary school. I asked Andrea whether she made friends with the Filipino students from St. Daniel's. Andrea said her self-consciousness about her family's financial situation often got in the way of this:

We always thought the St. Daniel's kids were too good for us. They were snobby. Because we're public school kids and they're private school kids. In our minds, we're harder [tougher] than you, you guys are spoiled, you're too religious, you don't know what it's like out there [outside the neighborhood], you're stuck in your little fence in St. Daniel's. We would never talk to each other, especially to those St. Daniel's kids in their uniform, doing their homework, doing their own thing. Us public school kids, we were running around making noise everywhere.

At the library, Andrea could literally see the class differences between her and her Filipino peers, particularly those from the local Catholic school. In many ways, her class background alienated her from other Filipinos, whom she disparaged for being overly sheltered and naive about the "real world."

After three months of commuting from Fontana, Andrea's family was finally able to move back to Eagle Rock. However, bankruptcy made it difficult to secure an apartment lease in the area, and their only option was to live in a local extended-stay motel. Their new home had a small bedroom, a tiny kitchen, and a small living room. Living in a motel made it even more difficult to make friends with other Filipinos, who were generally accustomed to visiting one another's homes and forging kinship ties with their friends' parents:

Of the Filipino friends we made, they were well off. They got everything they wanted. They got all the school supplies they wanted while me and my sister had to share everything. And then we were ashamed to say we were living in a motel. When they would ask to go to our house, we would say our mom was busy. It was embarrassing, especially because it wasn't even a nice motel. It was really hard, but it made me and my sister more thankful for things.

Eventually, Andrea's family became stable enough to rent a one-bedroom home in a working-class Latino neighborhood adjacent to Eagle Rock. Although many of the other Filipinos I interviewed spoke about their experiences growing up with Latinos, most of them were referring to the middle-class segment in Eagle Rock. In contrast, the Latinos who Andrea grew up with were mostly poor or working class. Gangsters, drug dealers, and street crime were just part of the scenery on their block. Despite this, Andrea characterized her surroundings as friendly. "We understood that just because you're a gangster doesn't mean you're a bad person," she said. "We were able to be on level ground with them, talking about people who were passing away or talking about not having a place to live. We knew we all had it hard."

Over time, Andrea befriended more Filipinos whose financial situation converged with her own, especially as she entered high school where many of the Filipinos were lower middle class. Although her economic struggles did not compel her to completely distance herself from her Filipino identity, her narrative nonetheless demonstrated how class differences hindered the ability of low-income Filipino youth to become part of the neighborhood ethnic community.

Beyond class, religious differences also made it challenging for some Filipino youth to relate to other coethnics in the neighborhood. Five of the young Filipinos grew up Protestant. Although most people presumed that Filipinos were Catholic (a presumption made about many Latino groups as well), there were some who were part of the Lutheran, Baptist, or the increasingly popular Church of Christ (Iglesia ni Cristo) denomination. Of course, there were some similarities between Filipino Catholics and Protestants. They both belonged to the Christian faith, attended weekly church services, and celebrated sacraments such as Baptism. Filipino Protestants also developed tight-knit ethnic connections in their churches. Even though they had ethnic niches within churches, those who were Protestant sometimes felt out of place with other Filipinos. As a child, Rachel said that she could not relate to some of the religious rites of passage that her Filipino classmates in Carson were participating in:

A.O.: Did you ever feel weird around Filipino Catholics?
RACHEL: Absolutely. Because the Catholic religion is so tied in to Filipino culture, it's so difficult to separate.
A.O.: Can you give me an example?

RACHEL: I think when my classmates at school started to have their
First Communion. I also couldn't understand why they didn't
have Baptism as an adult, or even as adolescents. It took me a
while to figure out what was going on.

Rachel said she even felt a bit disconnected from her relatives who
were Catholic, even those who lived with her family after migrating
from the Philippines:

People who came from the Philippines and lived with us, they'd have
a Santo Niño (a statue of Jesus as a child). There's always a point of
contention because we don't put a Santo Niño in our house, and it's
contrary to our belief system. That's always an issue. . . . My cousin,
my dad's brother's daughter, she brought her Santo Niño and brought
all her different saints and such. It became an issue. I'd ask my parents, and they'd be like, "That's what they believe in. That's not what
we believe in."

As Rachel's story of her cousin demonstrated, there was a difference in
the way that Catholics displayed their faith. Many Filipino Catholics
openly displayed religious paraphernalia in their homes—large photos and statues of Jesus, as well as the Virgin Mary and other religious
saints. In contrast, Protestants tended not to display the same type of
reverence toward the Virgin Mary, nor were they as inclined to display
religious iconography in their homes in the same way as Catholics.

Vince, a nursing student from Eagle Rock, grew up attending a
Filipino Protestant church in the neighborhood, but it did not seem
to bother him as much as it did Rachel: "I don't really think about it
much. The only time it comes up is when my girlfriend brings it up.
She's a big-time Catholic." Vince said that his girlfriend used to constantly badger him about converting to Catholicism, especially when
they first started dating. Over the two years of their courtship, she
eventually became less persistent about pushing for Vince to convert.
Part of Vince's relative indifference about the issue might have been
due to the nature of the relationship. Although he said that they were

serious, he and his girlfriend were still technically dating. Getting married was a whole other issue altogether. Edward grew up in a "super Catholic" family in Eagle Rock and said marrying someone of a different faith, even if they were Christian, was a big deal for his relatives:

> I know very few Filipinos that aren't Catholic. Interacting with Filipinos who aren't Catholic is kind of weird. You're surrounded by other Filipino kids who are like you. Some of my cousins married Protestants and one even married a Muslim, and they both converted. You can feel that there was a rift between her and the family afterward. It's hard to communicate because of the difference in religion. I think a big thing for a lot of Filipinos is the bonding you do during church. Sometimes you do Confirmation, community service, and because of that, you have that common knowledge. And when you grow up this way, you're pretty oblivious to other religions.

Edward often overheard his immigrant relatives disparage his cousins among one another: "They would say, 'It's too bad she married someone who's not Catholic. What are they going to do with their kids? *Sayang naman* [what a waste].'" Edward said that his cousins, who were mostly second generation, rarely became fixated on the issue. For them, religious differences were not a big deal. Nonetheless, because they were so closely connected with their immigrant relatives, who were much more concerned and judgmental about religion, it sometimes became an issue for them. This was particularly the case at large family gatherings, when Edward and his cousins would sometimes have to deal with older relatives gossiping about their other cousins behind their backs.

Ethnicity Matters

Neither Eagle Rock nor Carson would be considered immigrant ethnoburbs in the same way as a Monterey Park or a Koreatown, but this was what Filipinos seemed to like the most about these neighborhoods. In many respects, Filipinos felt that their multiethnic neighborhoods complemented their ethnic identity—both neighborhoods were significantly influenced by a diversity of cultures. Traditionally, sociologists interested in the children of immigrants have argued that the maintenance of ethnic identity is predicated on their living in neighborhoods with large concentrations of other coethnics.[42] However, what the Filipinos of Eagle Rock and Carson have demonstrated is that the diversity of their neighborhood environment reinforces what it means to be Filipino, not necessarily with respect to traditional measures of identity such as speaking the native language but in terms of the hybridity of their ethnic culture. In other words, Filipinos feel that their culture is inherently diverse because of the historical influences from Spain and the United States, and the diversity of their neighborhoods reinforced this belief. "We got along with everybody. We can make fun of everybody," said Franky. "When you're around a bunch of your people and a group of culturally diverse people, you joke about that. You talk about race. I can joke about Mexicans to my Mexican friend because it doesn't matter. I think it's because I grew up with Latino friends." Cesar from Carson echoed Franky's sentiments: "I think Filipinos have more diverse friends because we're diverse to begin with," he said in reference to his identity. "We get along well with a lot of different cultures. From my experience, you could stick us in a group of black people and we'd get along with them. We can hang out with any group of people. Filipinos could go up to any group of black guys or Hispanic guys and it's fine. They don't sweat us."

The existence of places like Monterey Park and Koreatown led Filipinos to believe that they were different from other Asians. In other words, their neighborhood identity shaped their panethnic identity— their sense of "we-ness" beyond their ethnic group. Although there are countless examples of Asians displaying the same bonds with Latinos and other minority groups in their neighborhoods, schools, and political coalitions, Filipinos still perceived other Asians as ethnically cliquey.[43] In this sense, the Filipinos from Eagle Rock and Carson I interviewed felt that they had the best of both worlds. They were able to regularly engage with their ethnic identity and culture with Filipinos in their households and churches, but at the same, their everyday encounters with people of other racial groups prompted them to think of themselves as racial chameleons. As the following chapters illustrate, these particular beliefs about their ethnicity and race that Filipinos developed in their neighborhoods deeply influenced how they racially positioned themselves vis-à-vis Latinos and Asian Americans. The process by which Filipinos negotiated their relative position is particularly important given that Latinos and Asian Americans are the two fastest-growing racial groups in the United States today.

4 The Latinos of Asia

ONE OF MY MOST MEMORABLE conversations was with Nelson, a twenty-nine-year-old mortgage broker from Carson.[1] Before we were about to part ways, Nelson asked me at the last minute to join him for a beer at a bar next to the coffee shop where we had just finished our interview. After ordering our drinks from the bartender, we sat down in the bar's front patio because Nelson wanted to smoke a cigarette with his beer. He took a few swigs of his beer, lit his cigarette, and then asked if he could solicit some friendly dating advice. He was visibly anxious, which was surprising, considering how confident he came off during our earlier conversation.

Up until that point, I had thought Nelson to be a social butterfly, the last person anyone would think would be nervous about dating. He saw himself as a work-hard, play-hard kind of guy. By day, he was clocking long hours processing loans at a mortgage company in Carson. By night, he and his work buddies were making their way to local happy hour events at least a few times a week. On the weekends, his work crew would be either at a Hollywood club ordering bottle service or, if they felt more low key, at someone's house drinking until three or four in the morning. Given how outgoing he seemed to be, I wondered what about the young woman he was dating was making him so anxious.

Six months ago, Nelson met Sara, a Vietnamese American woman working for a real estate agency that his company was doing business with. Although Sara was dating someone else when they first met, Nelson had heard through the grapevine a month later that the relationship had ended. Nelson did not wait too long to seize the opportunity. Two months after their initial encounter, Nelson asked Sara out on their first date. Everything seemed to be going well, but he could not shake his anxieties.

"I'm kind of nervous about the girl I'm dating," Nelson confessed. "This is the first time I'm dating someone of a different race."

"A different race?" I thought, intrigued at his categorization of "Vietnamese" as a "different race" from Filipinos. Sara was not the first woman whom Nelson had dated from the real estate and mortgage company circuit. When he first started working for his company, he dated a Filipino coworker named Hazel for a few weeks, but nothing came of it. After Hazel, Nelson dated two other women he met through work, Jennifer and Gabriela, both Mexican Americans who had grown up in Carson. I wondered why Nelson had not said anything about Jennifer and Gabriela being of a "different race." I felt compelled to inquire.

"Wait a second," I interjected, "Didn't you say earlier that the last two girlfriends you had were Mexican? What about them?" Nelson grinned at me as if I had said something nonsensical.

"That doesn't count," he said. "Mexicans are the same as Filipinos."

Nelson explained that with Jennifer and Gabriela, he never remembered feeling out of place whenever he hung out with their family and friends. Whether it was at a large family barbecue or an intimate dinner at home, he was able to blend in seamlessly. Even though Gabriela's mother wasn't the best at speaking English, Nelson could get by with her by using the everyday words that were the same in both Spanish and Tagalog. "It felt just like my family," he said. "I never had a problem when I hung out with their folks."

In contrast, Sara's family just felt different. "I didn't have the same feeling with Sara's parents as I did with [Jennifer and Gabriela's] families. I was intimidated," he admitted. "It's such a different culture." Nelson said he kept an open mind whenever he spent time with her family but said that "it would take more work" to get comfortable with her parents. Almost all of their communication had to go through Sara, as her parents spoke little English. Nelson certainly did not know how to speak Vietnamese. He said he was trying to learn a few words here and there, but the lack of overlap between Vietnamese and Tagalog made this task rather difficult. In the end, Nelson said Sara was "the one," and so he was not going to let these cultural differences get in the way of courting her.

Racial Ambivalence

Why did Nelson's relationship with Sara feel more *interracial* than his previous ones with both Jennifer and Gabriela, both of whom were Mexican American? A major reason was that Nelson experienced a number of cultural collisions with Sara's family and community that rarely occurred during his two previous relationships. Another explanation is that Filipinos generally do see themselves as a racial group that is distinct from other Asian Americans. When I asked people to specify their *racial* background, nearly every person that I interviewed identified as "Filipino." Not a single Filipino volunteered "Asian" as their racial background.

Filipinos in Los Angeles did not necessarily identify as Asian unless they were confronted with a survey that prompted them to select their race from a discrete set of racial categories. Cesar, a store manager from Carson, spoke about the hesitation he felt whenever he had to fill out such forms:

A.O.: Do you ever identify as Asian?

CESAR: [Sighs]. Yeah, I have before. Not orally or verbally when I'm speaking. Maybe when I take a test, and it asks if I want to fill out ethnicity, and there's no choice for "Filipino," and there's only a choice for "Asian." That's the *only* time I ever "say" I'm Asian.

A.O.: Does it feel weird to pick that?

CESAR: At first, no. But then when I think about what Filipinos are, I start questioning it. Why can't we pick Filipino? If they have "Other" as an option, I'll pick it and then write in "Filipino."

Cesar was not the only person who felt torn when encountering the racial identification question on a form. Many spoke about opting to identifying as "other," rather than Asian, on a number of platforms, from social media websites to employment demographic forms. As part of the study, I asked participants to fill out a brief survey at the end of our interviews. I included an open-ended question about self-identification. All but one participant wrote "Filipino" as their response. However, the survey also asked them to select one of five choices for their racial background: White, African American, Hispanic or Latino, Asian, or Pacific Islander. Although I did not think to record their response times to this question as part of my research, it quickly became clear that many Filipinos were reluctant to choose among these options. A few objected to the question outright. "Do I *have* to pick one of *these* choices?" one young woman asked begrudgingly. Another young man refused to answer the question entirely, instead choosing to cross off one of the options and instead write in "Filipino." In the end, only about half of the Filipinos in the study chose "Asian" as their racial identity.

Following my conversation with Cesar, a white patron at the same coffee shop politely approached me to ask a question about Filipinos' "true" racial background after Cesar had left. After apologizing for unintentionally eavesdropping on my earlier conversation, she introduced herself and said she was a marriage and family therapist at a nearby hospital. Having overheard Cesar and I discussing racial identity, she felt compelled to inquire about a lingering question that had bothered her since working as a therapist. "Can I ask you something? Why is it that whenever I ask Filipinos about race, they're the most likely to say 'other'?" The woman's question illustrated two important things. First, Filipinos opted against identifying as Asian even when their responses would be kept strictly confidential and had essentially no consequences for the social situation they were in. And second, many become uneasy, at times even bothered, when the people they encounter break the rules of race and refuse to check a box.[2]

Beyond the experiences of the Filipinos in this study (and those that the white therapist encountered), Filipinos in the greater Los Angeles displayed a similar level of ambivalence about Asian American identity. Researchers from UCLA and UC Irvine conducted a survey of about 1,600 Asian American adults in the greater Los Angeles area, the vast majority of which were second generation. Similar to this study, the survey asked participants to select their racial background among a discrete list of racial categories. Figure 4.1 shows their patterns of racial identification based on my analysis of the surveys.

As Figure 4.1 shows, more than 90 percent of Chinese, Korean, and Vietnamese chose "Asian" as their racial background. In contrast, less than half of Filipinos did the same. Filipinos' unwillingness to identify panethnically speaks volumes about their ambivalent relationship with Asian American identity. During the 1990s, two of the

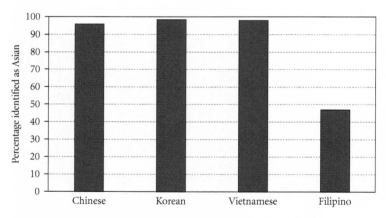

Figure 4.1 Panethnic identification of second-generation Asian Americans in Los Angeles by ethnicity, 2004 ($n = 1,617$)

Source: Immigrant and Intergenerational Mobility in Metropolitan Los Angeles Survey, 2004.
Note: Sample size for each group: Chinese (413), Korean (401), Vietnamese (401), and Filipino (402).

researchers from the Los Angeles study conducted a similar survey of teenage children of Asian immigrants from San Diego, a region where Filipinos also tend to live among Mexican Americans and other Latinos. The racial identification patterns of Filipino youth in San Diego paralleled these findings. Filipinos in San Diego were also the least likely to identify as Asian. About 90 percent of other groups identified as Asian, but only three out of every five Filipinos did the same. The Los Angeles and San Diego studies demonstrate how Filipinos across age groups and regional contexts displayed comparable patterns of racial ambivalence.

What explains the racial ambivalence of Filipinos in both Southern California regions? While neither of the studies included qualitative responses that might highlight an explanation, my conversations with Filipinos from Eagle Rock and Carson yielded important insights into why their racial identification patterns differed so starkly from those of other Asian Americans.

"Are Filipinos *Really* Asian?": Panethnic Divergences from Asian Americans

Growing up in Eagle Rock and Carson, Filipinos were just Filipinos. There were rarely moments when Filipinos felt compelled to identify as Asian. They never had to, given the strong presence of Filipino communities in both neighborhoods. Throughout our conversations, Filipinos tended to separate themselves from Asians in the same manner that they did from whites, blacks, and Latinos, as if Asians were a separate racial group altogether. This became clear when Filipinos would describe the racial makeup of their neighborhoods and schools:

> JACOB: There aren't really a lot of Asians in Carson. But if you go to Torrance, it's mostly white and Asian, but not a lot of Filipinos there.
>
> JOEY: The valedictorians at my high school were always Asian or white. You'd never really see a Filipino be valedictorian.
>
> VINCE: Growing up in Eagle Rock, I didn't get to know too many Asians.

GRACE: There was so much diversity at my high school. It wasn't just
Filipinos. There were also Hispanics, Asians, and a couple of
Armenians and blacks.

These descriptions revealed the implicit disassociation that Filipinos
held between themselves and other Asians. In other words, in their
understanding of "us versus them," Filipinos generally did not consider Asians part of the "us." Whenever Filipinos demarcated themselves from Asians in this way, I would probe them as to why they
did so. "If someone were to ask me if I were Asian, I guess I'd be
like, 'Yeah,'" Ronald said hesitantly, as if he were conceding to such
a response. I asked him whether there were any times when he can
remember identifying as Asian outright. "Not really," he said. "It's like
denying what I am. It's like denying that I'm Filipino. Like not really
acknowledging my own culture."

Because of the racial makeup of their neighborhoods, Filipinos had
minimal contact with other Asian ethnicities. As such, they tended to
lump all other Asian ethnicities together. "In Carson, I always just
knew Filipinos," said Dustin, a graduate student and school counselor. "If I had never left Carson, I would have thought Filipinos were
as huge a race as other ones. Chinese, Japanese, Korean—those seem
like all the same to me." A few Filipinos remembered having neighbors who were of other Asian ethnicities, but for the most part, the
only other Asians they came into contact with in the neighborhood
were those who had set up businesses in the neighborhood. Walking through the primary commercial areas in Eagle Rock and Carson,
the primary Asians I came into contact with were immigrant business owners. For example, whenever I walked along the commercial
areas of Colorado Boulevard in Eagle Rock, the only Asians I would
pass by were the Korean family who owned a dry-cleaning service, the
Chinese couple who ran a Chinese takeout restaurant, and the Vietnamese immigrants who worked at a local nail salon. The majority of
Filipinos described their interactions with these other Asian immigrants as little more than polite small talk.

Not surprisingly, then, the meanings that Filipinos associated with Asian American identity tended to be problematically stereotypical. Because Filipinos in Eagle Rock and Carson lacked significant opportunities to interact with other Asians on a more intimate basis, they often relied on caricatured notions of Asian American identity, ones that were often Orientalist in nature. These oversimplified understandings, in turn, prompted many Filipinos to distance themselves from the "panethnic" label, as illustrated by my conversation with Michael, an army reserve from Carson:

> MICHAEL: I don't think we're *Asian* Asian.
>
> A.O.: What do you mean by "*Asian* Asian"?
>
> MICHAEL: What comes to mind in my head? A host of different images—chopsticks, Japanese mountains, pho noodles. I think of those objects. Chopsticks mainly. When you think of Asians, you think of chopsticks. When I think about Filipinos or when I go to the Philippines, I always use regular utensils. I guess that's why I'm really hesitant about the whole Asian thing.

Michael admitted that he did not have many friends of other Asian ethnicities besides Filipinos. In Carson, most of his friends growing up were either Filipino or Mexican American. The first time Michael interacted with other Asian ethnicities was when he transferred to a magnet school in nearby Torrance, which had a significant number of East Asian students, but no other Filipino students.

"There were Asians there who didn't know what Filipinos were," said Michael. "It was interesting because I knew where China was, but they didn't know where the Philippines was. I had to explain what a Filipino is. I told them we're basically a mix of Spanish and Chinese. And we used to be an American colony." Michael said he ended up keeping his old set of friends from his high school in Carson because of these cultural differences with his new classmates.

As Michael's remarks suggested, Filipinos often juxtaposed the Westernization of their culture to the foreignness of other Asian cultures. "I don't pick Asian because I know that they're a separate culture from the Philippines," said Franky. "Aside from the whole immigrant parent thing that everyone can relate to, we just have a different history. I can't think of a time when I picked Asian or identified as Asian." When I asked Franky to elaborate, he referred to the American colonization of the Philippines as a reason for his racial ambivalence. "I don't think Filipinos fall into the Asian category. I want to say that Filipinos tend to want to assimilate or exude American culture a lot more because of the fact that America came to the Philippines," Franky argued, "When whites see other Asian groups, they see them as being 'fobbier' [more 'fresh of the boat']. But then they see Filipinos and we're more assimilated to American culture." These differences were most salient for those who were most knowledgeable about Filipino history and culture. As a teenager, Jen had been involved in a Filipino cultural dance troupe in Eagle Rock. Through dance, she learned about the multiple colonial influences of other cultures on Filipino dance—Spanish, Muslim, and Chinese—which made her feel like she was "less Asian. I guess having delved into the Filipino culture, I feel we're not Asian. We're just so different in terms of culture," she said, again illustrating how Filipinos' conceptions of race were often culturally determined.

Many felt that other Asians looked down on them because of their colonial history, which further deterred them from identifying with other Asians. "I feel like other Asians looked down on Filipinos because of our history," said Mary, a college student from Carson. Raymond, a registered nurse from Eagle Rock, echoed Mary's sentiments:

> It seems like in terms of Asian culture in the history books, there's a lot of stuff written on it. Whereas with Filipino history, the story is all about us being invaded. That's the only thing people really know about it. When it comes to the Chinese and the Japanese, there's a lot more history, a lot more culture about it. The only history I know is that we got invaded.

Both Mary and Raymond also expressed their disappointment about the way American society seemed to valorize and exoticize other Asian cultures while Filipinos remained relatively invisible. They felt that Chinese, Japanese, and Koreans had a history that was more "pure" and "real," which for them meant that Filipinos had significantly less cultural cachet in the eyes of other Asian Americans and the larger American society.

Some of the more politically conscious Filipinos I interviewed cited the position of Filipinos in the global labor market as yet another reason to distance themselves from other Asians. As it stands, there are nearly ten million Filipino workers, about 10 percent of the Philippine citizenry, currently working outside of their home country as a result of the long-standing instability of the Philippine labor market. Filipinos have found work in a variety of occupations, from nursing and teaching on the higher end to domestic work and factory labor on the lower end.[3] Filipinos work in more than two hundred countries throughout the world, many of which are in East Asia. In countries like Japan, Hong Kong, and Singapore, Filipino immigrants work primarily as domestic workers, even if they hold a college degree. "I think we're just different," Raymond said. "We're like the Mexicans of the Asians because we do all the labor work over there [in Asia]." Kevin, a graduate student in ethnic studies from Eagle Rock, gave the most politicized response when I asked him whether he felt Filipinos were Asian American:

> There's a disconnect when people say "Asian." It refers to East Asians. China, Korea, Japan—the three countries that have power. I think the connotation of Asian is based on power. When people think of Asians, they only think of the more successful developed nations. When you say Asian, you're referring to the most influential in global politics. So if I were to choose that, I'm excluded from the term *Asian*. I'm consenting to a term that means "East Asian."

Of course, Kevin was one of the few Filipinos who I spoke with who articulated his ambivalence in such terms. Nonetheless, Kevin's primary references for negotiating Asian American identity had to do not only with his upbringing in Eagle Rock but also with his interest in reading about world issues in *Time*, the *New York Times*, and the *Economist*. Although he was among the few Filipinos I met who engaged with these issues, even a cursory examination of these media outlets would support his theory. Whenever news stories referred to Asia, they were rarely ever talking about the Philippines. The noninclusion of Filipinos in public discussions of Asia and Asian America, coupled with the cultural differences that Filipinos observed in everyday life, further fueled their racial ambivalence. Kevin summed the issue up when he said: "The face of Asian Americans is an East Asian face, literally. Not a Filipino one."

Pacific Islanders by Default

The circumstances in which people select a racial identity on a form are most often private ones. People have to specify their racial identity when they apply for college, obtain a driver's license, fill out a random survey, complete paperwork for a new job, or register to vote. However, with the emerging popularity of social media in the past two decades, racial identity choices have become more of a public matter. People explicitly specify their racial identity on a number of social media websites, such as those used for friendship connections and dating. It was through my casual observations of racial identity choices on social media that I observed a unique trend among Filipinos—a sizable proportion of them racially identified as "Pacific Islander." This phenomenon was particularly intriguing because there was never an instance when I heard a Filipino, either in this study or beyond, say the words, "I am Pacific Islander."

According to the survey conducted by researchers from UCLA and UC Irvine, "Pacific Islander" was the most common racial identity option selected by Filipinos who did not identify as Asian American.[4] Did this mean that Filipinos developed a sense of panethnic consciousness with other ethnic groups within the Pacific Islander umbrella, such as native Hawaiians, Samoans, Chamorros (natives of Guam), and Tongans? Not really. The Filipinos whom I interviewed were fairly open about their lack of knowledge about Pacific Islander politics, culture, and identity, as illustrated by my conversation with Ines, an art director from Eagle Rock. Ines said that she preferred to select Pacific Islander as her race when Filipino was not one of the options provided:

> A.O.: Do you consider Filipinos to be Pacific Islander?
>
> INES: No.
>
> A.O.: So what made you pick that on the survey?
>
> INES: Because that was the only option. I don't think that Filipinos are Asian. I don't know. I think we have more of an island culture, I guess you could say. We're just down-to-earth people.

Franky had similarly vague reasons for preferring Pacific Islander identity over Asian American identity. "I just choose it. Maybe it's because of region," he reasoned. "The Philippines are islands in the Pacific. But Pacific Islander doesn't mean anything to me. I just pick it." The majority of Filipinos from Eagle Rock followed suit with Ines and Franky—they "identified" as Pacific Islander merely as a means to opt out of choosing Asian American.

Filipinos in Carson expressed a similar sense of racial ambivalence during our conversations as those from Eagle Rock. They tended to identify as Asian American because they felt they lacked the "right" to say they were Pacific Islander. In Carson, there was a sizable presence of Samoans, most of whom were lower middle class or working class. "Pacific Islander is for the Samoans," said Bryan, an account manager from Carson, "A lot of Samoans live in Scottsdale, which is pretty ghetto. It's probably the scariest place in Carson. There aren't any Asians in Carson besides Filipino, so I guess we can fill that in." These patterns revealed how racial ambivalence manifested differently in the identity choices of Filipinos from Eagle Rock and Carson. Ultimately, Filipinos' identity options depended largely on the availability and meaning of categories within their local neighborhood context.

When it comes to understanding identity, some sociologists focus on racial identity *choices*. In the end, Filipinos generally expressed ambivalence about the "Asian versus Pacific Islander" question altogether, regardless of which identity they eventually selected. As Joey put it: "Filipinos stand out. They're not Asian. They're not Pacific Islander."

In the summer after he graduated high school, Joey spent three months working for an Asian American news magazine. The magazine covered a variety of topics related to the Asian American community, everything from local political issues to relationship and dating advice. This was the first time Joey remembered having everyday face-to-face interactions with other Asians, since everyone he interacted with in Eagle Rock was either Filipino or Mexican. "I started to really struggle with the whole Asian question, but then again I never really identified myself as being Pacific Islander either," said Joey. "I don't feel right picking Asian, but I don't check Pacific Islander either. I don't know what they go through, so I don't want to haphazardly pick it." In the end, he said he tended to go with Pacific Islander because of his working-class roots growing up. In his mind, Asian American identity denoted privilege, and he felt that identifying as Pacific Islander signaled some of his family's struggles with class.

"Filipinos Are Basically Mexican": Panethnic Experiences with Latinos

"So which group of the two do you think Filipinos are closest to *culturally*?" I asked Joey. With respect to culture, neither Asian nor Pacific Islander was a viable option for Joey. "Latinos," he said without hesitation. "Is that even a question? In my part of Eagle Rock, Filipinos and Mexicans are part of the same class." Living alongside Latinos, it was relatively easy for Filipinos to become mindful of similarities between the two groups. Vince, a former classmate and neighbor of Joey's, expressed the same sentiments. "I would say Filipinos are closer to Hispanics," he said, "just because the way we do things. It's kind of like us, like Filipinos. They have big families. They are very welcoming as well. Whenever I go to a Hispanic friend's house, their parents are always nice." Other times, Filipinos could not articulate the specific similarities between themselves and Latinos. Similar to the way Dominican American author Junot Díaz expressed an implicit connection between Latinos and Filipinos, the people I interviewed "just felt the similarities very strongly."

In many ways, the sense of panethnic consciousness that Filipinos felt with Latinos was contingent on the racial makeup of their neighborhoods. I asked Vince whether he felt Filipinos were closer with Latinos or other Asians. "That's a tough one," Vince said. "I'd say in Eagle Rock, we're definitely closely related to Latinos because we live side by side here. We live together. We go to school together. You just bond because of proximity." At the same time, Vince felt that this might not necessarily be the case for Filipinos beyond his immediate neighborhood. "I think more general[ly] maybe, we're more closely related to Asian." Even then, Vince's rationale for aligning Filipinos with other Asians had to do with surface-level cultural similarities. "Filipinos' diet is very Asian, like rice, fish, and stuff a normal American wouldn't eat," he said.

While Filipinos were not identifying as Latino or Hispanic, per se, they frequently highlighted their cultural proximity with them. As my conversations with Joey and Vince revealed, many Filipinos felt more culturally aligned with Latinos than other Asian Americans. "When it comes to Filipino families being strict, that seems more Asian, but when it comes to culture and the whole 'family comes first' thing, that seems more Hispanic to me," said Amy, an architecture student from Eagle Rock. "For Filipinos and Hispanics, it's family before anything. I'm pretty sure other cultures have that too, but it's not as big."

Intuitively, people make assumptions about the cultural similarities among ethnic groups within the same panethnic category, a practice that is fundamental to the process of racialization.[5] However, in observing closer cultural ties to ethnic groups outside their presumed panethnic community, Filipinos needed an explanation. Spanish colonialism served as their explanation for these moments when these cultural commonalities came to light. They continually cited the cultural residuals of Spanish colonialism to explain their shared experiences with racialization, language, religion, and family. The cultural and historical link that Spanish colonialism established between Filipinos and Latinos became a major reason they racially demarcated themselves from other Asian Americans. As their narratives demonstrated, Filipinos developed what I term *colonial panethnicity*, the sense of shared peoplehood that they implicitly felt or openly invoked, on the basis of the historical, cultural, and social similarities rooted in Spanish colonialism that remain alive in their everyday lives.

Racialization Experiences

After Teddy graduated from high school, he left Eagle Rock to attend Claremont McKenna College, a small private college twenty miles east of Los Angeles. Teddy described the diversity of the student body as "decent, but still pretty white"—nothing compared to the racial mix of his neighborhood. Although the college reported that Asians and Latinos collectively accounted for about a quarter of the undergraduate population, there were not many Filipinos on campus despite their large numbers in the greater Los Angeles area. Despite the lack of Filipinos, Teddy said he made it work by befriending other students of color and making his way back to Eagle Rock whenever he needed his fix of Filipino food and culture.

At the end of his freshman year, Teddy remembered a conversation he had with Akilah, an African American with whom he had shared a dorm hallway in the previous year. "I started talking about where I grew up and that my parents were from the Philippines. As I was saying this, Akilah stopped me and was like, 'Wait, you're Filipino? I thought you were Hispanic.'" Teddy remembered how dumbfounded Akilah was upon finding out that the dorm mate she had just spent nine months living with was not, in fact, Latino. Teddy and Akilah had eaten meals together in the dining hall, had shared many late-night conversations in their hallway, and had even taken a class together their first semester at Claremont. "She was seriously shocked," Teddy said, "'No way. Are you serious?' she kept saying." Even more interesting was the fact that Akilah was someone who thought of race on a regular basis, especially as an African American woman.

Teddy, in turn, was not as surprised that Akilah had made that mistake. "She was from Queens. There weren't a lot of Filipinos where she grew up," Teddy explained, noting that she might not have developed a set of rules for recognizing who was Filipino. If anything, Teddy fit her rules for what a typical Latino was. His last name was Ramirez, he was of a darker complexion, and all his friends at Claremont were Mexican American. Teddy also noted that his haircut and voice probably gave Akilah further probable cause about his supposed Latino identity. "At that time, I had a shaved head, so that makes me seem more Latino to people," he said. "Even my girlfriend, she's Filipino, and she says I talk like a Mexican, especially when I'm with my friends from Eagle Rock." Teddy does not have the accent of a Mexican immigrant, but he unconsciously used a lot of Chicano vernacular and inflected his words in a way that resembled Mexican Americans born and raised in East Los Angeles. "It didn't bother me," Teddy admitted. "I'm pretty used to being called Mexican."

How was it that Akilah went nine months without realizing that her own neighbor was Filipino and not Latino? Teddy had never tried to fool Akilah or any of his dorm mates into thinking he was Mexican. He said that he had always had a strong sense of Filipino identity. "I'm from Eagle Rock. I'm as Filipino as it gets," he proclaimed, without an ounce of hesitation. Teddy's experience demonstrated an essential feature of the way race works in everyday life—race fundamentally entails a dialectical relationship between how individuals see themselves and how others, in turn, perceive them. Teddy may have seen himself as Filipino all the time, but what Akilah's "mistake" showed him was that there were likely other moments when the people he encountered assumed that he was Latino. For all intents and purposes, Teddy *was* Latino in Akilah's eyes. For the first nine months that she knew him, there was nothing about his phenotype, presentation of self, or choice of friends that signaled otherwise.

Of course, other Filipinos spoke about being perceived as Asian. Whether or not Filipinos were perceived as Asian depended on two main factors: phenotype and social context. With respect to phenotype,

Filipinos had very rigid understandings of how Asian American were "supposed" to look. When I asked Filipinos about the distinguishing characteristics of Asian Americans, light skin and slanted eyes were the most commonly cited physical traits. These physical markers, in turn, affected the degree to which others saw themselves as Asian, as well as whether they saw themselves as Asian. "The lighter I am, the more Asian people think I am," said Alexis, a college student from Carson. "A lot of my friends in college thought I was Chinese or Korean because I'm light." Alexis noted that these experiences happened mainly when she traveled to Orange County, an area with sizable pockets of Vietnamese and East Asian residents but very few Filipinos. In contrast, Angie said she felt "less Asian" because she did not fit these criteria:

> You know there are some Filipinos who have Chinese blood, and they have more of that Asian look. I guess it's more convenient for them to say they're Asian 'cause others can't tell. But me, I don't look Japanese or Chinese, so I can't do that. I really don't consider us Asian. Asians have really chinky eyes. We just all look different. We don't look like the stereotype of Asians.

Angie's remarks demonstrated the relevance of phenotype in how Filipinos conceptualized Asian American identity. Angie acknowledged that some Filipinos were able to "pass" as Asian, but she also wanted to point out that there were many who did not, which in turn made her ambivalent about their status as Asian Americans.

Some Filipinos said that it was more common for others to perceive them as Latino, more so than Asian American, particularly if they were darker skinned and had eyes that were "not slanted." "I confuse people a lot," said Angie. "Sometimes people think I'm Asian, but most of the time people think I'm Latina. Even other Filipinos think that I'm Latina!" Again, racialization experiences were context dependent. Whenever Filipinos went to places with a large presence of Latinos, there was always the possibility of being perceived as Mexican American. At the time of our interview, Franky worked at a bank in the south side of Eagle Rock, the area of the neighborhood with a larger population of Latinos. Like Teddy, he had a darker complexion and kept his head shaved, which he believed affected how people racially categorized him. "Working at the bank, I have a lot of Spanish-speaking customers who start speaking to me in Spanish the moment they sit down," said Franky. "And then when I tell them I don't speak Spanish, they seem confused." Other Filipinos noted that some Latinos even expect them to speak Spanish, even if they disclosed that they were Filipino. Jon, a hotel manager in Carson, said he was constantly mistaken for Mexican by the Latino immigrants with whom he worked:

> When they see me in the hall, they speak to me in Spanish. Then I tell them, "No hablo español," and they're like, "Why don't you speak Spanish?" And then I tell them I'm Filipino. And then they insist, "Well, some Filipinos speak Spanish. You have Spanish last names, right?"

The racial narratives of Angie, Franky, and Jon demonstrated the frequency with which Filipinos fit the "rules" of Latino identity more so than Asian American identity, which in turn affected the way people interacted with them. "People don't really see me as Asian," said Jon. "I'm dark, dude. You don't find many Asians that are dark skinned." In the end, it seemed that what "color" Filipinos were—whether Asian or Latino—depended largely on the social context surrounding them.

These complicated racialization experiences prompted many Filipinos to question where they racially "fit" in relation to Asian Americans and Latinos. While most generally conceded that Filipinos were part of the Asian American collective, some were persistent in pointing out the "Spanish roots" of Filipinos. Cesar attributed his experiences of racial miscategorization to his "Spanish blood":

> If we're in a Hispanic place, people assume I'm Mexican. It happens to Filipinos a lot, especially to my cousin. He just looks Mexican, but he's Filipino. We both have that Spanish influence. We both have that Spanish blood. Sometimes we [Filipinos] look Hispanic or Latino.

Cesar was one of many Filipinos who used genealogy as a rationale for their racialization experiences. Many Filipinos believed that, as a people, they had Spanish blood running through their veins, which helped them comprehend why others might perceive them to be Mexican or some other Latino ethnicity. The irony of this claim was that racial mixing did not occur in the Philippines to the extent that it did in other Latin American societies. Nonetheless, this belief of being part of a mixed people provided another rationale for Filipinos to develop a sense of panethnic consciousness with Latinos. Benji, a media outreach coordinator at a nonprofit agency, exemplified this sentiment: "I would say Filipinos are racially more like Latinos because of the Spanish influence. The glaring thing between us is the history of Spain, the hybrid identity of two cultures—that's why I feel Filipinos lean more toward Latinos than Asians." Benji's comment was all the more telling, given that he worked for an Asian American nonprofit agency.

Language Experiences

After one of my interviews in Carson, I stopped by a local market to grab some groceries before my drive back to West Los Angeles. As I was parking, I caught two elderly men in my periphery, one Filipino and one Latino, sitting at a table by the front of the entrance. From their body language, I could tell that the two men were fairly familiar with each other. They were exchanging stories, patting each other on the shoulder, and sharing laughs throughout their conversation. After about twenty minutes in the market, I walked out with my groceries, and the two men were still immersed in conversation, not seeming like they had anywhere else to be that weekday afternoon. My curiosity caught the best of me, and I walked by more slowly to catch a little bit of what seemed like a fascinating conversation. It was only then that I realized that the two men were not speaking the same language. The elderly Filipino had been speaking Tagalog to his Latino friend, who in turn was responding back in Spanish. At times, I heard them repeating lines and speaking more slowly than a typical conversation.

But at certain moments, I observed the two men vacillate between intent listening and "aha" moments whenever certain words were used—words like *merienda* (afternoon snack), *misa* (Sunday mass), *sábado* (Saturday), *compadre* (close friend), and *familia* (family). There were everyday words in Tagalog and Spanish that needed no overt translation. From the looks of it, it seemed that these linguistic overlaps helped these two men develop a friendship that transcended ethnic differences.

Language happened to influence the way Filipinos view themselves in relation to other Asians in the opposite way. Filipinos have very different language patterns from other immigrant and second-generation Asians. Most US-born Filipinos are not fluent in both English and their parents' native language.[6] Given the high levels of English proficiency of their immigrant parents, there is little need to be bilingual. As compared to other Asian immigrants, Filipino immigrant parents are more likely to speak English in the home and generally do not need their children to serve as language brokers to communicate with others outside the home. Ronald observed this among most other Asians he knew. "Sometimes their parents don't speak English at all, unlike Filipino parents," he observed. "I have never met Filipino parents that didn't know English." Relative to their second-generation counterparts, Filipinos are by far the most likely to be monolingual English speakers.[7] This was certainly the trend among the Filipinos I interviewed from Eagle Rock and Carson. Nearly all of them understood Tagalog "decently well," so they were not entirely divorced from their parents' native language. Nevertheless, only a tiny fraction of them felt confident enough to have a full on conversation in Tagalog. "All the Chinese and Vietnamese friends I know, they're more in tune with language. A lot of my Filipino friends only understand Tagalog or don't know it very well," he pointed out.

Filipinos cited their subpar Tagalog skills as a reason for their ambivalence about Asian American identity. Many felt that bilingualism was a litmus test for Asian American identity. Lynette felt that the different language experience of Filipinos was the main distinction from

Asians. "Not that many Filipinos who grew up here can speak the native language of their parents," she said. "Whereas I see other second-generation Asians that can speak their languages fluently. Plus, there's like Chinese school, Korean school, and I'm like, 'Wow, I would have liked to know how to speak Tagalog when I was younger.'" Bryan, an army lieutenant and neighbor of Lynette, implicitly attributed this trend to the influence of American colonialism. "They all speak their own languages, but we don't," he said. "We try to be something else. We try to be American."

The prevalence of bilingualism among other Asians also created challenges for Filipinos' social relationships with other Asians, particularly when it came to interacting with their immigrant parents. Ronald said part of the reason he preferred to have Filipino friends was that it was easier to befriend their families as well:

> What made it difficult for me to get close to other Asians was that it was hard to get close to their parents. I know most parents would like to know who their son or daughter is hanging out with. But if they can't communicate with their friends, it's really frustrating. I remember, I hung out with one of my [Chinese] friends, and I couldn't even speak directly to his parents. My friend had to translate. It was really awkward. Admittedly, it'd be a lot easier if the parents were Filipinos because I don't have to explain myself. I know the customs and culture.

Among Filipinos, it was common practice to develop fictive kinship relationships with the parents of their Filipino friends. Within a few encounters, Filipinos were used to addressing their friend's parents as *tito* (uncle) or *tita* (aunt). For most, this was a normal part of the process of developing more intimate ties with their friends. Most viewed the use of formal titles with friends' parents, such as Mr. and Mrs., to be "weird and awkward," and for some, even rude. In this respect, Filipinos were not as inclined to develop familial ties with other Asians' parents as a result of language barriers, which in turn hindered their sense of shared identity with them.

Ironically, Filipinos viewed the role of language differently when it came to their relationships with Latinos, despite the prevalence of bilingualism among the latter. As the two elderly men in front of the market demonstrated, the linguistic overlaps between Tagalog and Spanish made the shared cultural history of Filipinos and Latinos more salient. This was especially the case because they had the chance to hear each other's languages in everyday conversations in Eagle Rock and Carson. In these neighborhoods, Filipinos and Latinos alike were well aware of the numerous words that their languages shared (see Table 4.1). Jon, the hotel manager from Carson, was one of a number of Filipinos who felt a sense of commonality with Mexican Americans because of language. "There's a lot of similarities between Filipinos and Mexicans because there was Spanish colonialism," he said. "With language, there's a lot of Spanish words in Tagalog." His awareness

Table 4.1 Everyday words in English, Spanish, and Tagalog

English	Spanish	Tagalog
HOUSEHOLD		
Table	mesa	mesa
Living room	sala	sala
Chair	silla	silya
KINSHIP		
Uncle	tío	tito
Aunt	tía	tita
CLOTHING		
Pants	pantalones	pantalon
Shirt	camiseta	kamiseta
Shoes	zapatos	sapatos
MEALTIME		
Fork	tenedor	tinidor
Spoon	cuchara	kutsara
Snack	merienda	meryenda
DAYS OF THE WEEK		
Monday	Lunes	Lunes
Tuesday	Martes	Martes
Wednesday	Miércoles	Miyerkoles

of this helped him understand *why* his Latino coworkers at the hotel might have expected him to know at least some conversational Spanish.

Although most Filipinos I interviewed were not necessarily proficient in Spanish, they said that the linguistic commonalities with Latinos helped reduce the language barrier between them, particularly if they were interacting in the neighborhood. Jayson, a registered nurse from Eagle Rock, felt that language created a bond between the two groups:

> A.O.: What's the interaction like between Filipinos and Latinos?
>
> JAYSON: I think we get along pretty well. There are a lot of common lines between the culture and that's why I think we get along pretty well. Filipinos understand Spanish to an extent, but they can get away with understanding Spanish even without a formal background.
>
> A.O.: Do you see Filipinos and Latinos interacting a lot?
>
> JAYSON: All the time! My mom, for example, whenever she goes to the market, she's always like, "Hola, amigo! Hola, amiga!" Because of the similarities in our language, you can communicate in [each other's] native tongue. My mom will say something in Tagalog, and they'll get it. It's common for Latinos to pick up some Tagalog, but I think we can pick up Spanish faster.

Andrea echoed Jayson's feelings about the importance of language. "Every time I'd talk to my parents about Mexicans, they'd always be like, 'They're cool. We have the same language. Why would we fight? We come from the same people.'" Growing up in the south side of Eagle Rock, most of Andrea's neighbors were Latino. She said that her family's basic knowledge of a few Spanish words helped her father develop close friendships with other families in their part of the neighborhood. Their ability to understand each other proved especially important when Andrea's father lost his job during the recession. "A lot of my dad's friends are Hispanic," she said. "He just got laid off a month ago, and he's been trying to find side jobs. Most of his side jobs are with Hispanic people. They help each other out."

Some of the Latinos I encountered during my research reciprocated these sentiments. Many felt compelled to put in their two cents during or toward the end of my interviews with Filipinos if they had inadvertently eavesdropped on our conversations. In Eagle Rock, I conducted many of the interviews at a coffee shop with a decent number of regulars. After one of my very first interviews, I met Lourdes, a Mexican American who had grown up a few blocks nearby. She introduced herself to me and said, "You know, my best friend since I was nine is Filipino, and I always tell her, 'You guys aren't Asian. You guys are basically Mexican. Everything from your last names to the foods.'" Lourdes then brought up language. "You know? I can catch about every ten words in Tagalog," she said. "It's easy to catch the gist of what a Filipino is saying if they're speaking their language." Lourdes explained that this is what helped her become close with her best friend's family and, in turn, what helped her best friend become part of her family. While the commonalities in Tagalog and Spanish were not always enough for Filipinos and Latinos to understand each other completely, the overlaps served a symbolic purpose—the mere awareness of the linguistic commonalities provided the building blocks for Filipinos to develop more intimate ties with Latinos than with other Asians.

Cultural Catholicism

For many Filipinos, the connection between ethnicity and religion was inseparable. When they spoke about what it was like to "grow up Filipino," most referenced activities related to the Catholicism—everything from going to Mass every Sunday to praying the rosary whenever there was a close relative sick in the hospital. Even if they were no longer practicing Catholics, many maintained nominal connections with their religious background. "I still consider myself culturally Catholic," said Diana, a young woman from Eagle Rock who no longer attended Mass regularly. "I'll still make the sign of the cross if I get on the freeway or see an accident. I still have a rosary hanging in my car. Just 'cause I don't go to mass doesn't mean I don't believe in Jesus."

Filipinos felt that Catholicism was a major area of difference between themselves and other Asians. As noted earlier, the Philippines is the only predominantly Catholic society in all of Asia. More than 80 percent of Filipinos, both in the homeland and in the United States, identify as Roman Catholic.[8] In contrast, the number of Catholics in other major sending societies in Asia—China, Taiwan, Korea, Vietnam, India—is negligible (in China, it is less than 1 percent).[9] In fact, the population of *Christians* in these countries does not exceed 30 percent. Granted, there are larger numbers of Catholics among Asian immigrants in the United States; however, no other ethnicity comes close to Filipinos. The next closest group is the Vietnamese, of which only a third are Catholic.[10]

If anything, Filipinos tended to associate Roman Catholicism with their Latino peers, having grown up seeing many Mexican Americans attending their churches. Alma, a librarian from Carson, felt that being Catholic was "more of a Filipino and Latino thing." Alma said she could not remember a single non-Filipino Asian family who had ever attended her parish in Carson. "When you hear Filipino and Latino, you think 'Catholic' automatically," she said. "I don't think of religion when I think of Asians, or if I do, I think Buddha, but not Jesus or Mary."

Alma and others had reason to think that Catholicism was "more of a Filipino and Latino thing." As compared to other Asian countries, the religious landscape of the Philippines resembles that of a Latin American society. There are churches and cathedrals throughout the country that have been preserved since the Spanish colonial period. Beyond these places of worship, Filipinos and Latin Americans prominently display Catholic symbols in their homes, stores, and restaurants. It is relatively common to find images of Jesus Christ, the Virgin Mary, and other Catholic patron saints painted on buildings and vehicles. The Catholic presence in both the Philippines and Latin America is so strong that social movement leaders have used religious iconography to strategically rally support from the masses. Even when Filipinos and Latin Americans migrate to the United States, many maintain close ties to the Catholic Church.[11]

Filipinos had an easy time seeing the strong association between Catholicism and ethnicity for both themselves and Latinos, given where they grew up. Angie, a market researcher from Eagle Rock, spoke about how religion brought the two groups together:

> A.O.: Which group do you feel Filipinos are closest to?
>
> ANGIE: Definitely Latinos. [Being Filipino is] about a lot of that strict Catholic stuff. My parents were very into having saints and the Virgin Mary in our house, and that's just like Latinos. There's a lot of culture and religion intermingled. That's a big similarity.

As Angie's response suggested, Catholicism also shaped family relationships for both Filipinos and Latinos. This was something that Ronald observed from his many years working for his local parish's youth ministry. As a youth ministry leader, he had regular interactions with Filipino and Latino families in Eagle Rock. Over time, he became more and more mindful of the similarities between Filipinos' and Latinos' level of religiosity, which he used to make conclusions about Filipino and Latino family values. "Our family dynamic is very similar with Latinos, especially when it comes to respecting your parents," he said. "Most of my friends are Latino and Filipino, and they're pretty much all Catholic. I'd interact with a lot of my Latino friends' parents that were in the church." Ronald was not necessarily trying to suggest that people of other religions and ethnicities were disrespectful to their parents (although his comments could be interpreted as such). He merely intended to express his belief that Catholicism influenced the family lives of Filipinos and Latinos at his church in very similar ways. As Ronald's remarks demonstrate, it is not that Catholicism in and of itself instills a sense of panethnic consciousness for Filipinos and Latinos. Rather, being Catholic facilitates opportunities for

Filipinos to witness firsthand the cultural similarities between themselves and Latinos. Many Latinos echoed these sentiments, having observed many cultural overlaps with Filipinos at Sunday masses and other social gatherings sponsored by the church.

One Saturday autumn afternoon, I attended a carnival sponsored by St. Daniel's Catholic Church in Eagle Rock, an annual event that kicked off every school year and raised money for the parish's elementary school. The local streets were closed down and the church converted its parking lot into a neighborhood theme park complete with bumper cars and a Ferris wheel. On the perimeter of the carnival were several booths where parents of the elementary school children were selling traditional dishes from their native countries. That afternoon, the two longest lines were for the booths selling Filipino and Mexican food. At the Filipino booth, one could buy a combination plate with Philippine-style *pancit* noodles, chicken *adobo*, and white rice. At the Mexican booth, one could purchase *carne asada* tacos or *pozole*, a tasty Mexican stew with hominy and chicken. The Filipino and Mexican cuisines were a hit, compared to the booth selling "American food"— that afternoon, the carnivalgoers were more about the ethnic options than the hamburgers and hot dogs sold at the "American" booth.

At the carnival, I made my acquaintance with Antonio, a Mexican American who was born in the United States but grew up most of his life in Michoacán. Antonio lived in Pacoima, a predominantly working-class Latino neighborhood in the San Fernando Valley, but he had passed by the carnival on his way to another engagement he had in the area. He had never been to Eagle Rock but said the festivities reminded him of "your typical Latino carnival in Pacoima, even though there are a lot of Filipinos here." I offered Antonio some free meal tickets that an old friend had given to me and I told him to try some authentic Filipino food while he was here.

About twenty minutes later, I noticed Antonio making conversation with an older Filipino man across the carnival grounds. After a few minutes, he made his way back to me with two cactuslike stems in his right hand.

"They have *pitayas* here!" Antonio shared excitedly as he walked back to me. "It's dragonfruit, in English," he clarified. Antonio had purchased the *pitayas* from a fruit vendor at the carnival. After he bought the stems, he said the older Filipino man had approached him with some advice about how to grow them. "Are those *pitayas*?" the man had asked Antonio, who at that point had wondered how this Filipino man knew the Spanish word for dragonfruit. "Make sure to grow them ten to fifteen inches apart so they will grow fruit," the man advised Antonio. At this point, Antonio said he became even more intrigued. "How did this guy know what *pitayas* were? How did he know how to grow them?" he thought to himself. The man explained to Antonio that he had eaten *pitayas* throughout his childhood and that they were a delicacy at five-star hotels back in the Philippines. "I thought they were just a Latino thing," Antonio admitted.

As we were talking, an elderly Filipina woman interrupted our conversation to ask Antonio where he had obtained the cactuslike stems. "Are those *nopales*?" she asked him. Antonio looked perplexed at the Filipina woman's seamless use of the Spanish word for cactus. He told the woman that they were not. "Oh, because *nopales* are good for uric acid," replied the woman, who at this point had hiked up her long dress to show us her swollen ankles resulting from a recent gout flare-up. "I'm going to get *pozole*. It's my favorite," the woman said, before she smiled good-bye and walked away.

"How does she know that?" Antonio asked, seeming puzzled by the Filipina woman's cultural proficiency with "Latino" home remedies. "That's something my mom or grandma would say. Maybe she heard it from one of the Latina ladies," he said, appearing content with his hypothesis.

Antonio finally managed to wait the line out and try the Filipino cuisine. After a few hours of hanging out at the carnival, we parted ways. But before we did so, he shared a few of his revelations from the event:

> You know, at first, I felt like an outsider because I'm not from this church or the neighborhood. But at the same time, I felt I was in a

familiar place because of the setting, the food, the people. The majority was Filipino, but there were *pitayas* and *pozole.* At some point, I
found that I couldn't figure out who was who. The people I saw, their
ethnic background was questionable. I wasn't sure if they were Latinos
or Filipinos.

Antonio's experiences at St. Daniel's carnival illustrated the importance of place. Religion facilitated opportunities for the overlaps between Filipino and Latino cultures to become more salient to those
who occupied these shared spaces. Cultural practices and items that
were once seen as just "a Latino thing" also became "a Filipino thing"
within a matter of a day. Even after spending a single afternoon in
Eagle Rock, Antonio had already begun to develop a shared sense of
peoplehood with the Filipinos that he encountered. Ultimately, for
those who lived in the neighborhood their entire lives, the cultural
similarities between Filipinos and Latinos were a matter of common
sense.

Race, Class, and the Limits of Colonial Panethnicity

When describing his Latino friends and neighbors, Franky made it
clear that they were not "your stereotypical *cholo*-looking [gangster]
ones." None of the Latinos he grew up with was the type who sported
"Dickies, Nike Cortez shoes, plain white T-shirts," and other gang-
affiliated clothing, nor were they the ones who "Bic'd their heads,"
in reference to the practice of using a razor to shave off one's hair
entirely. "Some had shaved heads like me, but they didn't look gang-
sterish," Franky said of his Latino friends, most of whom he had befriended while attending private Catholic school. Living adjacent to
the working-class communities of Glassell Park and Highland Park,
Franky felt qualified to make such distinctions between Latinos who
were middle class versus those who were "more ghetto."

As Franky's comments suggest, Filipinos' relationships with Latinos
vary depending on the context of their interaction. As many others
have pointed out, the cultural similarities between the two groups are

undeniable—Filipinos in Eagle Rock and Carson could easily observe these on an everyday basis. However, the cultural similarities did not always supersede the negative racial stereotypes imposed on Mexican Americans and other Latinos. Not surprisingly, Filipinos were frequently exposed to such negative portrayals through the media, their schools, and at times even their parents, some of whom were overtly prejudiced against Latinos.

Jayson grew up on the border of Eagle Rock and Highland Park, where he frequently encountered both middle- and working-class Latinos. Because of where he spent most of his time, he said he "felt more Eagle Rock than Highland Park." Part of the reason was the ethnic connotations of the two neighborhoods. "When you say 'Eagle Rock,' you think Filipino, but Highland Park you associate with the Chicano [and] Latino crowd." In the end, though, Jayson felt that the "Filipino and Latino population go hand in hand." Echoing his earlier comments, Jayson said, "Culture-wise with the Filipinos getting their background from Spain, we share a lot of similarities with Latinos—importance of the family, importance of parents, and religion. So there are a lot of common lines between the culture."

Nonetheless, despite his affinity for his Latino friends and neighbors, Jayson said his parents imposed a different set of rules depending on the specific group of Latinos he was hanging out with. They tended to be more overprotective when he spent time with his Highland Park friends, more so than with his Eagle Rock friends:

JAYSON: My parents were a little overprotective because of where we lived. If they knew I was with these friends on Hill Drive in Eagle Rock, they wouldn't care if I stayed out longer. But if I were with one of my homies at his house in Highland Park, they would force me to come home earlier even though it's a lot closer to where we live.

A.O.: Was your area around your home dangerous?

JAYSON: Honestly, my parents can never say that they saw something actually happening, like an actual crime. It was a lot about the

> reputation, what you hear on the news, that there are gangs. You
> don't associate gangs with a good neighborhood like Eagle Rock.
> A.O.: So where did they get this association?
> JAYSON: The news and the people in the neighborhood. I hate to say
> it, but when they think of crime, they think of the Latino popula-
> tion because we live in LA. They see the news. If they see bald
> heads, they think something is up. They try to overgeneralize to
> the larger population in the neighborhood.

Jayson felt that his parents had no problem with his Latino friends
who attended his same Catholic school: "Most of my friends that
weren't Filipino were mostly Latino, and my mom treated them the
same way." In Jayson's view, their status as fellow Catholic-school students helped offset some of the stereotypes his mother held related to
Latinos' class status and criminalization.

Michael's father was not nearly as lenient about the friendship
choices of his son. In his early childhood, Michael had grown up with
a single father and both of his grandparents in a mobile home on the
border of Carson and the working class community of Wilmington.
Although his family was now living in a more solidly middle-class
area of Carson, he vividly remembered the illicit activities that happened right outside the front door of their mobile home. When he
lived closer to Wilmington, most of his friends and neighbors were
Latino. However, by the time he was twelve, his father explicitly for-
bade him from hanging out with them and encouraged him to have
only Filipino friends:

> One time I was hanging out with this one Latino friend, and we were
> playing outside of our house. My dad came out and pulled me aside
> and told me, "I don't like you hanging out with the Latino kids." He
> said he didn't want me to get caught up in the wrong crowd. "I want
> better things for you," he said. I was like, "How would hanging out
> with a Latino kid mess that up?" He just reiterated what he said again.
> Funny enough, when I hit puberty, he didn't want me hanging out
> with Latina girls either, just in case you-know-what happened.

To some extent, Michael understood his father's concerns. Some of his Latino friends had older brothers who were in gangs, which in turn prompted their desire to join gangs as well. "They had older siblings who were in that lifestyle, and so they wanted to be in gangs from an early age, I remember," said Michael. He also remembered witnessing drug deals in the grounds of the mobile park as early as age ten. However, in other ways, his father's strictness was also fueled by racial stereotypes he held about Latino young men and women—that they were likely to get into trouble or become teenage parents. In the end, Michael said it was just easier to maintain friendships with his Filipino friends because his father never questioned him when he spent time with them. Ultimately, Michael's proximity to Latinos of a lower socioeconomic status prevented him from developing close ties with his Latino friends and their families, which was a stark difference from the experiences of Filipinos who grew up primarily around more solidly middle class Latinos.

Panethnic Moments

Although Filipinos acknowledged that most people categorized them as Asian, there were a plethora of experiences that prompted them to question this. Viewing race as a culturally based identity, many explicitly disidentified from Asian Americans, asserting that popular constructions of the panethnic category failed to describe their own experiences as Filipinos. For most, the act of selecting a racial identity was an ambivalent experience whether they conceded to the "Asian" label or decided to resist this by choosing "Pacific Islander" as a default option. For Filipinos, Asian American identity did not fit well, particularly when it came to aspects of their culture heavily influenced by American colonialism.

In contrasting the idiosyncrasies of their ethnic culture from other Asians, Filipinos came to realize that they shared more cultural similarities with Latinos. "Filipinos are more Spanish than Asian. Their culture is more influenced by Spanish culture," said Maria, a restaurant server from Eagle Rock. As Maria's assertion demonstrates,

Filipinos negotiate racial boundaries through the lens of culture, and several aspects of their ethnic culture converge with those of Latinos—language, last names, and religion. These cultural markers led many Filipinos to be racialized as Mexican American or some other Latino ethnicity, which in turn prompted many to further distance themselves from other Asian Americans. However, being associated with Latinos was not always a good thing in the eyes of some Filipinos, particularly if they encountered ones who were of a lower socioeconomic status. In situations when Latino identity was criminalized or policed, the potential for Filipinos to develop close social ties with Latinos diminished significantly. As the next chapter emphasizes, the negative racialization that Latinos face in schools, particularly public high schools, has driven an even bigger wedge between the two groups. The cultural links between Filipinos and Latinos are not often salient in the context of high school, particularly in institutions where the racial stratification of the students is most overt. In other words, the rules of race that bond Filipinos and Latinos together do not always extend beyond the boundaries of the middle-class neighborhood.

5 Getting Schooled on Race

JANICE STILL REMEMBERED the first time that race really seemed to matter in her life.[1] When she started seventh grade at South Bay Middle School in Carson, she noticed something different about the clique of girls she used to hang out with in elementary school. Only a year before, their group was evenly split between Filipino and Mexican girls. Within the few weeks at South Bay, however, almost everyone in the group was Filipino—that is, except for Lupe Hernandez, the one Mexican girl left in the crew. Lupe had no reason to change friends; she had hung out with the same set of girls since kindergarten. Janice and her friends certainly had no problem with it. The Mexican girls at South Bay, though, were not as happy with Lupe's choice of friends, as Janice recalled.

"Lupe was Mexican, but she hung out with all the Filipinos and she got shit for it," said Janice. "I always heard people talk about her. Other Mexican girls would pass by her and stare her down. They would say that she's not really Mexican. I even remembered them confront her once. 'Why you gotta be hanging out with all the Filipinos for? Like you think you're Filipino?' they'd say." Most of the time, Lupe would brush things off, according to Janice. Nonetheless, the negative treatment that Lupe received from her Mexican classmates was an indication of how strong the inclination was for students at South Bay High School to self-segregate by race.[2]

To Janice, it made sense that Lupe maintained her friendships with the Filipino girls — she was in all of the same classes with them at South Bay. Lupe and her friends were all part of a special honors program known as GATE, which stood for "Gifted and Talented Education." The GATE students at South Bay had a different teacher, they had an extra tutor, and they would on occasion leave campus for special field trips or educational programs. "I remember they'd take us out of class and to the auditorium to learn more advanced stuff," said Janice. "I remember learning about biology. We dissected animals. They were gearing us toward higher levels of academic work because we were capable." The latter part of Janice's remarks exemplified how the classroom divisions at South Bay precipitated assumptions about students' academic ability and work ethic. Those in the regular classes lacked such privileges and knew it. Sammy, an employee at a tattoo shop, was also a student at South Bay around the same time as Janice but was not in the GATE program. According to Sammy, the teachers "didn't seem to care, and no one was taking school seriously. Everyone just fooled around in class."

This institutionally driven separation of students is known as academic tracking.[3] On the surface, academic tracking sounds like a practical idea. Schools, especially those that are large, separate students into different tracks based on their supposed ability. Proponents of academic tracking argue that more remedial students are able to learn at a pace appropriate to their needs instead of struggling to keep up with their more advanced peers. In turn, these more advanced students are not held back by their slower peers. Sociologists have demonstrated, however, that academic tracking creates a new set of problems, particularly in racially heterogeneous schools. In these schools, academic tracks are almost always stratified by race. As a result, school officials and students alike develop strong stereotypes about the academic abilities and cultural orientations of different racial groups. The everyday happenings within the school further serve to naturalize these racial differences, not to mention the practice of racial segregation.[4] In other words, academic tracking demonstrates the power that social institutions have in shaping everyday understandings of race.

At South Bay Middle School, Filipinos were mostly in the advanced tracks while the majority of Latinos and other minorities dominated the regular tracks. The separation of Filipinos from other minorities shed light on why Janice's friendship circle at school became less diverse and why her friend Lupe might have encountered resentment from some of her Latina peers. These social and academic divisions between Filipinos and other minorities only worsened when the girls moved on to South Bay High School.

Bernard remembered his middle school years quite differently from Janice. Bernard attended St. Thomas Elementary, a small Catholic school on the border of Eagle Rock and Glassell Park. Bernard grew up just a few miles away in a small house, not too far from where many of the other St. Thomas students lived. Like Janice, Bernard's group of friends in elementary school included both Filipinos and Latinos. "We used to call ourselves the *vatos locos* [crazy guys]," he joked, making sure to point out that such implications of gang affiliation were made only in jest. The intimate setting of St. Thomas seemed to cultivate a sense of collective identity between Filipinos and Mexicans. "The Filipinos were definitely up there among the students that did well, but the Latinos would also do well," he clarified. There was no GATE program at St. Thomas. Bernard had essentially shared a classroom with the same set of forty students, whether they were academic overachievers or slackers, from kindergarten to eighth grade. "I tend to grow close to the people I've known for a long time, and I've known these guys for years," he said, speaking proudly of the tight-knit atmosphere he enjoyed at St. Thomas. The sense of family that he felt with his group from St. Thomas was a primary reason Bernard opted to go to Bishop Catholic High School over the more prestigious Jesuit Academy. Bernard joked that Bishop High School's student body was about "99 percent Latino," but a large segment of it was Filipinos. Compared to the ultra-competitive climate of Jesuit Academy, Bishop "was more like a family," Bernard described. "A lot of people came from the same type of neighborhoods. A lot of our experiences were the same."

Although they grew up in different neighborhoods, Janice and Bernard were not very different from each other—their parents worked in the medical field (both their mothers were nurses, in fact), they were both the eldest of three siblings, and both earned excellent grades throughout most of their schooling. They both also grew up around Latinos their whole lives—they had many Latino neighbors on their block, attended Sunday Mass with Latino families, and from kindergarten onward always had schoolmates that were Latino. What was so different about their situations that prompted Janice's group of friends to become divided along ethnic lines while Bernard's group was able to remain intact? Why was the Mexican girl who befriended Filipinos at South Bay Middle School and South Bay High School chastised by her other Latino peers? In contrast, why were the Filipinos and Latinos at St. Thomas Elementary and Bishop High School able to be more of a family, as Bernard described it? Much of the reason has to do with the distinct institutional organization of public versus private schools.

The institutional organization of schools played a pivotal role in shaping the social interactions of Filipinos, as illustrated by Janice's and Bernard's narratives. Not surprisingly, public high schools had significantly more students than private ones. Student enrollment at the local public high schools in Eagle Rock and Carson topped three thousand, about triple the size of the largest private school attended by the Filipinos that I interviewed. The student bodies at public schools were much more diverse in terms of their socioeconomic status and academic performance. For instance, Glenrock and South Bay, the two main public high schools in Eagle Rock and Carson, housed large numbers of low-income and working-class students from nearby neighborhoods. While the majority of students from these public schools earned their high school diplomas, Filipinos who attended these campuses spoke about classmates dropping out as a commonplace phenomenon. In contrast, private schools were smaller and more intimate. Students at these schools were generally from middle-class backgrounds (if not higher), and those who were not were able to attend with the assistance of merit-based scholarships. Most of the private schools that Filipinos attended boasted near-perfect graduation rates, and teachers expected everyone to pursue a college education, no matter their background.

As the educational narratives of Filipinos in Eagle Rock and Carson illustrate, these institutional conditions also influenced the meaning and symbolic value of racial categories within the local school environment. Outside of the school context, racial categories took on more of a cultural significance. Filipinos associated them with ethnic and family traditions, such as food, religion, and language. Within the boundaries of a school campus, however, racial categories also had academic connotations. Race became inextricably linked to intellectual ability, academic drive, and educational ambitions, particularly in public schools that institutionalized academic tracking. In the end, the social construction of racial meanings within high schools greatly affected the way Filipinos negotiated their sense of panethnic identity with other groups on campus.

Same School, Different Worlds: Majority-Minority Public Schools

The student body of South Bay High School was a racial microcosm of the surrounding neighborhood—about half of the students were Latino, and the remainder evenly divided between Filipinos and African Americans, with a small but visible segment of Samoans. Although the student body in its entirety was as diverse as Carson, the two academic tracks at South Bay—honors and regular—certainly were not. Filipinos accounted for the overwhelming majority of students in the honors track. "About 75 percent of the honors track was Filipino," said Rachel, an academic counselor from Carson and alumna of South Bay High School. "The other 25 percent were Latino, with like one or two black students." African American, Samoan, and

Latino students dominated the regular track at South Bay. Rachel, an honors student throughout her years at South Bay, remembered only one classroom experience where the majority of her classmates were African American and Latino. "I was only in one remedial class as a sophomore," she recalled. "They put me in regular geometry with a bunch of seniors, and it was the only time where I had mostly black and Latino students in my class."[5] The correlation between academic tracks and race was so strong at South Bay High School that Filipinos who were not honors students were described by some as "pretending to be black" or "trying to be like a Mexican gangster."

The classroom environments of the honors and regular tracks were vastly different, in terms of not only their racial makeup but also their academic rigor and teacher-student interactions. Jessica, a college senior from Carson, was in the honors track for all four years at South Bay. While most students in the honors track tended to develop their closest friendships with their classroom peers, Jessica was unique in that she also had strong ties with South Bay students in the regular track. As a member of the school's soccer team, Jessica had several teammates who were not honors students. In addition, she also attended South Bay at the same time as two of her "troublemaker" cousins, who were close to her in age. As such, she had multiple opportunities to compare her classroom experiences with those of her peers in the regular track, and she was always shocked at how much they differed.

One of these surprises happened when Jessica and her cousin Jade were at a family get-together and started talking about school. Both of them had Mr. Adams for their junior-year English class, but Jessica was enrolled in the Advanced Placement English course while her cousin was in his regular one. "I had eleventh-grade AP English with Mr. Adams, and it was *hard*," said Jessica. "Every single week an essay would be due, and you would get graded from a one to a ten, with ten being like perfection. He expected a ten every week!" When Jessica tried to commiserate about her stress, Jade's description of Mr. Adams could not have been more different. "What are you talking about?"

Jade would tell her. "We don't do anything in his class. We just sit there and if we *have* to write, we'll just write in a journal." Jessica was amazed that the same teacher that had been the source of her academic stress was merely a "joke" to her cousin. Jessica's experience demonstrated how the academic tracking system at South Bay kept its students "separate, unequal, and unaware of one another."[6]

Jessica said that Mr. Adams and other teachers were rather explicit in the different expectations they held for the two tracks. This became even more evident when she enrolled in a few classes in the regular track during her senior year at South Bay. Jessica intended to take Advanced Placement English literature and calculus in her senior year; she even enrolled in the supplementary summer session math class aimed at better preparing the calculus students for the end-of-the-year examination. However, because of a schedule conflict related to varsity soccer practices in the morning, she had to settle for Mr. Adams's regular senior-year English and a regular calculus course. "Don't expect the same thing as last year," Mr. Adams warned Jessica before senior year began. "They [students on the regular track] can't handle that." In Mr. Adams's advanced class, Jessica remembered having to pen weekly essays and write argumentative responses to classic works in literature. However, her senior-year class with Mr. Adams had none of these stringent weekly assignments. "You could totally see a difference in the way he taught," Jessica said.

Jessica's experience with her senior-year math class was similarly watered down. She had earned an A in the summer calculus course taught by Mr. Morris, who like Mr. Adams, happened to teach both the Advanced Placement and regular versions of the senior math courses. Like her English class that year, Jessica found the regular math class completely unchallenging. "Mr. Morris was teaching totally slow like we were idiots," she said. "And it took him so long to cover the chapters that I had already learned during the summer in like four weeks." Jessica said Mr. Morris was shocked at first to see her in the regular class, but she explained to him her schedule conflicts with soccer. About three months into the first semester, he confronted her. Jessica recalled, "Mr. Morris was all mad. 'You're supposed to be in my AP class,' he said. 'Go change your class because it's pointless for you to be in that [regular] class. You're not going to pass the AP test if you stay in that class.'" After some juggling with her school counselor, Jessica was eventually able to switch back into the Advanced Placement English and calculus courses by her spring semester.

One of Jessica's teachers went so far as to sanction her if she socialized with students who were not in honors. Jessica vividly remembered the warning she received from her studio art teacher Mrs. Becker. Art classes were among the few times where students from both tracks shared a classroom, but even here, the students were segregated. According to Jessica, Mrs. Becker seemed more than willing to facilitate this separation. "If you associate with those people [regular track students]," Jessica remembered Mrs. Becker telling her, "I'm going to give you a B. Even if your work is A work, I'll give you a B if you sit with them. I know you're an AP student, and I know you're capable." Mrs. Becker's attitude toward the regular track students exemplified the pessimism many of Jessica's teachers not only held, but also openly shared with their honors students. With respect to presenting information on colleges, one of the school counselors even told Jessica, "Sometimes we go to the regular classes, but they're not going to listen, so why bother?" It was evident that teachers and other school officials invested more of their pedagogical energies into the students in their more advanced classes while maintaining a more disciplinary outlook on the regular track classes. In the latter, maintaining order seemed like the main objective of the job.

The students in the honors track at South Bay enjoyed a number of other privileges beyond a better classroom environment. They had supplementary college counseling sessions to teach them about their postsecondary options and financial aid. They had the opportunity to go on school-sponsored college visits throughout the state and, for a select few who could afford it, throughout the East Coast. On these trips, the honors students had a number of opportunities to amplify their cultural capital. They visited museums, attended plays and musicals, and took "architectural tours" to learn to "deconstruct the culture" of the city.

Not all students on the honors tracks had the same experiences though. Teachers at South Bay expected Filipinos to be in the honors track; many of them were admitted nearly automatically into the academically advanced pathway after participating in the GATE program during middle school. "We traveled in cohorts in middle and high school," said Rachel, about Filipino students' placement in the honors track. Lia, a writer and college instructor from Carson, graduated from South Bay a few years prior to Jessica. She said that the expectations for Filipinos to be on the honors track were so prevalent that "you'd be looked down upon if you're not in the AP classes because Filipinos are *supposed* to be in the AP classes." Lia felt that the expectation that she was intelligent and hardworking explained why her teachers and counselors were kind to her and more invested in her academic outcomes.

Teachers and students, however, did not always apply the same expectations toward African Americans and Latinos in the honors track. Lia was close friends with Jamal, one of the only two African Americans who took the same Advanced Placement courses that she did in high school. While Lia felt compelled to take honors classes in part because of her ethnicity, she was surprised to find Jamal had the opposite experience. "My black friends make fun of me because I'm in AP," Jamal once confessed to Lia, which she in turn felt was "strange." Interestingly, none of her Latino classmates encountered the same experience with their coethnic peers, perhaps because there was a visible (though disproportionately low) presence of Latinos in the advanced track.

While Lia's African American and Latino classmates in the honors track had distinct experiences with their peers, she remembered a few times when teachers policed their behavior more fiercely relative to her own:

Whenever I would come in late, or turn in an essay late, my teacher would be like, "That's fine." They liked me. They thought I was smart because I was Filipino. But when a black kid or Latino kid did what I did, they'd be sent to detention. The teachers would be on their asses. If I came late to my psychology class, the teacher was like, "Oh hey! Why you late?" I would joke around with him. And then when a black kid did that, he would lock the door.

Lia acknowledged that these incidents were not an everyday occurrence, but nonetheless, she felt that teachers were occasionally harsher to her black and Latino peers. Sociological research on schools has shown how tracking often fosters a sense of entitlement and autonomy among the racial groups that are favored but serves to police and criminalize those who are not.[7] It was telling that Lia automatically attributed teachers' unfair treatment toward her classmates to race, as opposed to gender, even though both examples were about male peers. However, later in our conversation, she did allude to gender differences in how teachers treated students at South Bay. At times, her boyfriend, who was also Filipino, would come late to class and receive the same treatment as African American and Latino boys did. "When he'd come late, he'd get locked out, even though he was Filipino," she said. "Sometimes counselors would recommend the remedial classes for him, which they didn't do for me." Lia's stories were examples of larger trends among minority boys in public high schools beyond South Bay. Teachers are much more likely to be punitive toward misbehaviors of males, especially young men of color.[8] In addition, as compared to their female peers, Filipino young men are more likely to be racialized negatively as troublemakers in ways similar to African American and Latino young men.[9]

The unfair treatment of Lia's high achieving African American and Latino classmates was a by-product of South Bay's racially stratified tracking system. If most African Americans and Latinos were in the regular track courses, which teachers perceived as the least rigorous and most unruly, they were more likely to implicitly and automatically associate black and brown students' missteps as acts of deviance.[10] The self-segregation of students on campus by race was an additional contextual factor that could have influenced teachers' perceptions toward their African American and Latino students, whether or not they were on the honors track. "Everything was segregated," Rachel remembered. "Filipinos hung out in the northeast side of campus. The blacks hung out by the cafeteria, and the Samoans were nearby. All the Latino kids kicked it in a separate spot of the school." This highly segregated campus environment prompted school officials to label many of the conflicts and incidents that happened on the school grounds as racially motivated. And these racially motivated incidents almost always involved the African American and Latino students.

Even though the South Bay High School alumni that I interviewed graduated over the span of a decade (from 1999 to 2009), they all spoke about racial tensions that at times even erupted into physical altercations between students. Many recalled how school administrators would automatically dub these fights between students as "race wars" or "race riots," illustrating how authorities were quite comfortable in criminalizing race issues in the school. Rachel recalled two such incidents that occurred in her senior year at South Bay:

> RACHEL: There was always some kind of tension. When I was there, we actually got locked down twice. People were forced to stay in the classrooms with the teachers, and you weren't allowed to leave until the sheriffs came. We had a really, really big fight. It was between the Mexicans and the blacks.
>
> A.O.: What caused it?
>
> RACHEL: I remember it started as a joke. Someone swatted a milk carton, and then one of the black students hit one of the Mexicans, and then it turned into a huge fight. There were twenty to thirty people fighting. We were put on lockdown because it was a huge fight. The administrators were like, "It's a race riot."

Robin, who was a sophomore at South Bay when these events happened, said that the Filipinos generally tried to stay under the radar. "The blacks at school would sometimes trip [get upset] if a Mexican came around, and vice versa, but if it were me or one of the other

Filipinos that went up and talked to them, they didn't really trip," Robin said. Jacob attended South Bay a few years after Rachel and Robin, but reiterated that school officials did not generally implicate Filipinos in these "race wars." "There weren't really any Filipino fighting or anything," Jacob said. "I wouldn't say that the Filipinos beefed [had conflicts] with the blacks or the Mexicans. If anything, maybe Filipinos would have tensions with other Filipinos, but not with any other groups." The prevalence of conflicts that involved the African American and Latino students help explain why Lia's teachers treated her with such leniency in comparison to their more punitive approach toward her black and brown (and male) peers.

Canonized Model Minorities

Glenrock High School in Eagle Rock also used the academic tracking system. Similar to South Bay in Carson, this practice resulted in divergent classroom experiences for the students in the honors versus the regular tracks. According to Gerald Cruz, a twenty-six-year-old barista at an Eagle Rock coffee shop, the classrooms at Glenrock were as racially divided as those in South Bay. Gerald said this division started as early as middle school:

> In the GATE classes in junior high, unfortunately there were more Asians. I'm pretty sure that they were mostly compiled of Asians and Filipinos in the honors classes in high school. You'll see mostly Asians and Filipinos, and there'll be like one or two Mexicans and like one black person.

Gerald added that education was the primary thing that linked Filipinos with other Asians at Glenrock High School:

> If you were to ask me about Asian culture, I'm stumped. Except for the fact that with Filipinos, it's the same thing with education. You gotta score the highest grade or you gotta be in the top of your class all the time. Asians believe the same thing—education matters a lot. That's not any different from Mexicans because they also believe the

same thing, but the typical Asian is like, "You can't do anything unless your homework is done," or "You can't go out during the weekend unless your homework is done." The parents are always asking if you studied already.

Gerald's story exemplified a common trend in the high school experiences of the young adults I interviewed: Filipinos accounted for the majority of honors students in their middle schools and high schools, which made them like the "typical" Asians. In turn, this reified the idea that Asian identity was synonymous with being intelligent, hardworking, and academically inclined. To be Asian was to be an honors student. By extension, to *not* be in honors was to be "less Asian" or, as Rachel implied earlier, to be more like the black and Latino students. Although such implications were clearly problematic, most Filipinos internalized the cognitive association between academic achievement and racial identity. For many Filipinos, education was often the primary mechanism for identifying *with* other Asians and identifying *as* an Asian American. As one of the women I interviewed put it: "Education's where the similarity with the stereotypical Asian person is. That's about it though." In other words, academic achievement became Filipinos' litmus test for Asian American identity in the absence of other culturally based similarities that more often compel panethnic identification.[11]

"Asian" Educational Values

When I asked Filipinos if they ever identified as Asian, they most often cited education as the primary link between themselves and other Asian groups. Although Filipinos were the primary Asian group in their high schools, some noted the commonalities between themselves and the few other Asian Americans in the school. Because of their academic experiences in high school, many Filipinos internalized the idea that they, along with other Asian groups, had strong educational values. At the same time, Filipinos generally did not disparage Latinos and other minorities in their high schools as being less invested in their education. Rather, they tended to attribute the differences in their academic experiences to the way that families prioritized education.

"As far as Asian cultures are concerned, a lot of them have similar morals," said Rita, a music instructor who graduated from South Bay High School, "I think a lot of Asian parents are strict about studying and not really staying out late. Academics are a core value." Rita compared the academic pressures she felt during high school to those of her Japanese American classmate Lynn:

> I see a lot of commonalities between me and my Asian friend Lynn. Her parents always wanted her to try really hard at school. She was smart. I don't even know why she went to high school 'cause she could have been in college already. Her dad was always so hard on her. Always pushing her more, and that's kind of how my dad is. Our dads would always push us to do better.

Although she did not have much to say about the similarities between Filipino and other Asian *ethnic* culture, Rita said there was an overlap in the *academic* culture of Filipino and Asian families. In her family, it was always assumed that she and her siblings would all attend college—that idea was never up for debate. Although a significant segment of South Bay's student body did not pursue higher education, she said college was the norm among her other Filipino and Asian friends at South Bay High School, even if this meant pursuing community college. As her comments illustrate, Rita's explanation of Filipinos' collective achievement at her high school has to do with culture and family, not the structural inequality built into the social organization of South Bay High School's tracking system.

Cesar, a fellow South Bay alumnus, echoed Rita's belief about Filipino and Asian families prioritizing education differently from other minority families. "I'm not saying that Latinos don't embrace education because all of the Latinos I know have parents that believe education is important," he said. "But I think they prioritize education differently from how Asians do." Throughout his schooling, Cesar said that he and other Filipinos were discouraged from getting a job in high school. "With my parents, they always said, 'Don't work. Just go to school,'" Cesar recalled. "A lot of my Latino friends said they *had* to work even though they also had to go to school." Even though many of his Latino friends were also middle class, he felt that being more solidly middle class allowed many Filipino classmates of his to focus on their academics full-time rather than hold down a part-time position during high school.

The tracking system helped solidify the belief that Filipinos and Asians had "better" educational values than other minorities at the school. The close association that Filipinos made between race and achievement would come out implicitly at times. As Jessica's earlier comment about the honors students being more "capable" demonstrated, the academic tracking system made it easy to internalize the belief that students on the different *tracks* had distinct educational values. Given the fact that academic tracks were racially stratified, it was also easy to subconsciously associate educational values and race. As the educational narratives of Filipinos highlighted, school officials also played a major role in reifying the idea that Filipinos were "the Asian ones" of the school. Dustin, an alumnus of South Bay High School, said that his teachers and counselors viewed Filipinos as the students with the most academic potential. "If we were to talk about racial hierarchies, Filipinos were at the top," he said.

"Filipinos Were the Favorites"

Ronald attended St. Daniel's Elementary, the Catholic primary school in Eagle Rock, but decided to attend Glenrock High School because of financial struggles that his family was facing at the time. His parents had already spent nine years paying private school tuition for him and his two siblings, and moving to Glenrock would allow them to save a significant amount of money. At first, he did not mind the decision because several of his classmates and friends from church had also opted for public school. However, he described his first few weeks as "sobering." Most of the friends he had before Glenrock were from

St. Daniel's, and to the best of his knowledge, they were from middle-class, two-parent households. "I never even knew anyone whose parents were divorced," Ronald said. Glenrock was the first place where he had ever had classmates who not only had divorced parents but also were part of gangs and experimented with drugs. "I'd even see people smoke weed right on campus sometimes!" he remembered.

Like South Bay, the academic tracks at Glenrock High School were racially stratified. Although the majority of students at Glenrock were Latino, only a small proportion of them were in the honors track. Filipinos constituted the second-largest population at Glenrock, but they dominated the honors track. "Filipinos and Asians were the ones in the Advanced Placement classes at Glenrock," Ronald recalled. "In the regular track were the Latino and few black kids at the school. The Latino students weren't seen as the AP students by the general school population." Within the context of Glenrock, many associated the Latino students, regardless of their academic placement, with the gang members and other deviants who sometimes loitered on the perimeter of the campus. "People have a bad impression of Glenrock. There are always old school *cholos* and *cholas* hanging out, and you'd see them in groups outside the school," Ronald recalled. "I was scared." Even though the majority of Latinos at Glenrock were not affiliated with these gang members, Ronald said it was not unusual for students and teachers to subconsciously associate Latino students with them, especially if they were male and dressed in baggier clothing.

Even though he was not an honors student, Ronald said that the teachers and counselors treated him better than his Latino friends who were in the advanced track. Despite his parents' expectations for him to take college preparatory classes, Ronald described himself as a "pretty average" student. "I took a few advanced classes, but I was pretty average," he said. Rather than enroll in Advanced Placement classes, Ronald preferred to dedicate his time to his church youth ministry and graphic design projects that were unrelated to school. "Those classes cut into my time to do other things, like my art, or being more social, or being in youth ministry," he said. Although he had a few Filipino friends who were in the honors track, most of his closest Filipino friends were his classmates in the regular classes at Glenrock. Ironically, Ronald said that the college counselors at Glenrock had high academic expectations for him and his friends, even in comparison to his Mexican friend Mario, who took nearly every Advanced Placement class offered at the school:

> I remember my Mexican friend [Mario] had a really good rank and asked the counselor about college, specifically Stanford. The counselor was pretty discouraging, telling him he probably wouldn't get in. But I remember Filipinos who were ranked lower than him would be told by the same counselor to apply to Stanford. My Filipino friend didn't get in, but my Mexican friend did, and he said the counselor didn't even congratulate him.

Ronald's story about his friend Mario exemplified how strong the correlation between race and academic abilities were at Glenrock High School, even among the school officials. In very opposite ways, race strongly shaped the academic experiences of Filipinos and Latinos. As Ronald's story demonstrates, Filipinos were generally stereotyped as the "honors kids," whereas Latinos were assumed to be less academically ambitious, even if they had the record to prove it. An additional reason that Ronald mentioned that explained Mario's experience had to do with his friendship circles. Mario hung out with other Mexican Americans, according to Ronald. Having such close ties to other Latino boys at Glenrock may have led the counselors to impose a "courtesy stigma" on Mario, even though everything about his academic performance signaled that he was bound to end up at a school like Stanford.[12] In the eyes of school officials, Mario was guilty by association.

Jacob witnessed the same type of favoritism toward the Filipino students at South Bay. This favoritism was easy for Jacob to observe because he was biracial—his mother was an immigrant from the Philippines, and his father was African American. Jacob had transferred to South Bay High School from a neighboring public school to run on the track team. Part of his involvement in sports was his mother's doing. Focusing on sports was his mother's insurance that he would stay out of trouble on campus, especially important given the racially charged atmosphere at South Bay. "My mom would have me playing sports all the time. I was always busy doing something," Jacob said. In this sense, Jacob said it kept him out of the "annual black versus Mexicans fight" that somehow managed to occur every year, sometimes several times a year. Of course, he also noted that such violent eruptions were more sporadic than the norm of everyday life at South Bay. When I asked him about the Filipinos at South Bay, his description echoed the others. "There weren't any real Filipino fights," he said. "They would get along well enough."

While he never found himself in trouble because of his race, being biracial definitely made a difference in his academic experiences. When teachers viewed him as just a black athlete, namely when he would hang out with his black friends, their expectations for him were relatively subpar. Jacob knew that there were social benefits to hanging out with the other black students, but worried that these friendships might hinder his access to academic support in the school.[13] Soon after he transferred, he tried to enroll in three Advanced Placement courses, much to the chagrin of one of his counselors. "A counselor tried to convince me not to take Advanced Placement and instead take a cooking class," he remembered. "He said I would have to learn how to cook and that I couldn't handle too many AP classes." Jacob ended up taking the cooking class because he "didn't know any better." It was then that Jacob started to really notice the difference in the way the teachers and counselors were approaching the Filipino versus the African American and Latino students:

> JACOB: I would say there was favoritism at South Bay. A lot of black and Mexican students wouldn't do as well [as the Filipinos] at South Bay. But I don't think it's their fault. I think they get put in the lower track classes, so they end up with teachers that aren't even expecting them to do well. So they don't care for

themselves, and they don't end up doing well. There's not really Asians in South Bay, but there's Filipinos. So those would be the students that the majority would be in the advanced classes. And that's favoritism right there to me.

A.O.: How would teachers treat students differently in those classes?

JACOB: Higher expectations for the Filipinos. First of all, putting them in more challenging classes. And when you were in the actual room, if there *were* black students—and if I recall, in my AP classes, there'd be two or two and a half if you count me— the stereotype is just that you would expect Asians to do better. That's the stereotype. But in Carson, it's the Filipinos that were considered the smarter ones, so they'd get called on more by teachers or just be expected to get higher grades. The non-honors classes I took, it's like going to two different schools. There might not be books. The teacher just didn't care. It's cool to be dissing the teacher in front of everyone and mess with the teacher. Whoever could be the class clown would be the coolest person in class. It's just a joke.

Jacob's candid account of the classrooms at South Bay exemplified how race could determine one's educational pathway and academic experience. The lower track classrooms, which also happened to include the bulk of the African American and Latino students, were hardly conducive to learning. The divestment of the teachers in these classrooms further exacerbated the problem. In turn, teachers would invest most of their energies in the honors classes, which housed mostly Filipino students with a few select token minorities. Jacob's comments about Filipinos being "the smarter ones" are very telling as well. In the absence of other Asian American students, the group stereotyped to excel in academics, Filipinos *became* the Asians at South Bay High School, and they had the experiences to match.

Eventually Jacob fought his way into the honors track, and at this point, his friendship group shifted almost immediately. Whereas before most of his friends were fellow track teammates, in his latter two years at South Bay, most of his friends were Filipinos from his honors and AP classes. It was not too long after this transition that people started to view his academic abilities differently. Jacob had always wanted to go to college, and he had set his sights for California State University–Dominguez Hills. It was the only college that he knew at the time. "I didn't know the difference between UCs [University of California] and CSU [California State University]," said Jacob, in reference to the two public university systems in California. However, once he was in the honors track, counselors started to see him differently. One counselor, Miss Rawlins, became particularly invested in him:

> "I'm going to need you to go to UCLA," Miss Rawlins said to me. She didn't know anything about me, but she just expected it. Her son went to Harvard. I guess she just trusted me. She had me join this peer counselor program to learn about college. That decision probably saved my life. There were seminars during the summer that taught us about the college application process, about the FAFSA [the federal financial aid program], and what classes to take to get into the good schools. The good students in my mind went to Cal State Dominguez Hills or Long Beach State. I didn't think UCLA was even an option.

Although Jacob was not shy about his naiveté of the college application process, Miss Rawlins was persistent with him. Even after scoring two hundred points below the average SAT score for the top University of California campuses, she insisted that Jacob apply. He was eventually accepted to five of the most selective campuses—Berkeley, Los Angeles, Santa Barbara, Irvine, and San Diego. In the end, he chose UCLA.

As an "outsider-within," Jacob witnessed the drastic differences in how teachers and counselors treated him when they saw him as African American versus when they saw him as Filipino. In the end, joining the ranks of the honors classes helped to reinforce his Filipino (and to an extent, Asian) identity, as he was seen as "less black" than had he stayed in the regular track, where he would have been seen as "just another black kid." He ended up on the winning side at South

Bay, but this did not stop him from openly criticizing the distinct set of expectations that teachers held for their Filipino versus other minority students. "People don't expect you to be anything because you're black, and if people don't expect you to be anything, you're not gonna be as motivated," he said. "The thing is with Filipinos in Carson, people expect you to do well. They expect you to pursue college as a Filipino. I guess it's just different being in that situation."

"Mexicans and Filipinos Are Like Cousins": Majority-Minority Private Schools

Amy and her family moved to Eagle Rock from nearby Lincoln Heights (a neighborhood around East Los Angeles) right before she was about to start high school. Before their move to Eagle Rock, Amy had attended public school, but for high school her mother was intent on sending her to a private institution. Having gone through a messy divorce had made it impossible for Amy's mother to pay even the modest tuition costs for St. Daniel's Elementary, the main Catholic primary school in Eagle Rock. However, by the time Amy was in middle school, her mother and her partner were financially stable enough to send her to a private high school. Although there were no Catholic high schools in Eagle Rock, there were a number within a ten-mile radius for Amy to choose. Amy decided to attend St. Anne's Academy, the same all-girls Catholic high school where many of the alumnae from St. Daniel's happened to matriculate.

Having just moved to Eagle Rock, Amy remembered being anxious about her freshman year at St. Anne's Academy. "Eagle Rock was different for me," Amy said. "I didn't go to Glenrock Middle School or St. Daniel's." Luckily, Amy had some connection to the other girls at St. Anne's because she had attended catechism classes and Sunday masses at St. Daniel's since she was a child. "Eagle Rock was about the church experience," she said. "I never went to St. Daniel's Elementary, but I did go to catechism classes to get First Communion and I even went there to go through Confirmation classes." Because of her church involvements, Amy had no trouble making friends with the other girls in her class—most of her classmates felt like they already knew her because she had been a part of St. Daniel's parish for years, even if they had never gone to school with her.

In many ways, St. Anne's Academy was a far cry from Amy's previous experiences at Dover Middle School in Lincoln Heights. St. Anne's was much smaller, and by consequence, more intimate. There were a thousand students in Dover, as compared to the three hundred students that made up all four grades at St. Anne's. Dover was more racially heterogeneous than St. Anne's, but the diversity was virtually nonexistent within individual classrooms. Dover's student body included a few whites, Latinos, and other Asian ethnicities (though relatively fewer Filipinos). Like other public schools that practiced academic tracking, the students were highly segregated by race, both academically and socially. All of the Latinos were in the regular track classes. Amy was in the GATE program with the Chinese, Vietnamese, Korean, and white students. From what she recalled, Dover seemed more competitive than St. Anne's, even though the students were only middle school age. "I know when I went to school at Dover, I had Chinese friends and Korean friends," Amy remembered. "They [the teachers and other students] would say to us, 'Oh they're getting the As because they had to study because of their families.' It's very stereotypical—the Asians get the good grades." Even though Amy grew up seeing Filipinos as "seeming more Hispanic," she was lumped in with the other Asians because of the tracking system at Dover.

At St. Anne's Academy, the students were not separated either by "ability" or by race. First, the school was significantly smaller, and as such, creating rigid academic tracks did not seem necessary to the daily operations of the school. While there were some Advanced Placement course options, there were not enough for any one student to pack their entire schedule with honors-level classes. In other words, honors classes did not structure friendship groups in the same manner as they did in public schools. Given the size of St. Anne's Academy, it was virtually impossible for students to complete their four years without sharing at least one classroom with every single classmate in her grade. Second, the school administration ideologically seemed dead set against highlighting the ethnic differences in any capacity within their predominantly Filipina and Latina student body. "Ethnic clubs weren't even allowed on campus," Amy said, when I asked her if there was a Filipino club in her high school. Amy said that unlike Dover, the idea that certain ethnic groups academically thrived while others struggled was an entirely foreign concept at St. Anne's Academy.

This was made more evident to me when Cheryl, a fellow alumna of St. Anne's Academy, shared her high school yearbooks with me during our conversation at her house. As we flipped through the black-and-white pages of the yearbook, nearly every photo featured both Filipina and Latina students. Filipinas and Latinas seemed equally represented in most of the campus clubs, student government positions, and sports. Even in the random photos of the lunchroom, the classrooms, and the outdoor hangout spots at St. Anne's Academy, segregation between the two groups appeared to be nonexistent—a stark contrast to the highly balkanized atmospheres at both Glenrock and South Bay High Schools. The last page of the St. Anne Academy yearbook was the most telling. Each year, the St. Anne's Academy yearbook staff dedicated its final page to the ten young women with the highest grade point averages over the four years, including the valedictorian and the salutatorian. On the last page of Cheryl's senior year annual, these were the featured names:

Elisa Gutierrez (Valedictorian)
Cheryl Marquez (Salutatorian)
Maria Contreras
Danielle Macias
Olivia Santos
Evelyn Higuera
Janice Tapia
Jennifer Del Rio
Marisol Torres
Allison Gutierrez

Ten bright young women, ten Spanish surnames, five Filipinas, and five Latinas. The valedictorian, Elisa Gutierrez, was a Latina. Cheryl was the salutatorian. Even from my brief gaze at the young women's photos, it was not entirely clear who was Filipina and who was Latina until Cheryl clarified the ethnicity of each person. In many respects, my inability to distinguish ethnicity among the ten women was a nice metaphor for the everyday classroom experiences at St. Anne's Academy. "I was so close to valedictorian," Cheryl said, "But Elisa deserved it, honestly. She worked really, really hard." Besides a little bit of an "aw shucks" tone, there was no sense of resentment about Elisa having taken the top spot—or about the fact that Elisa had been admitted to a number of highly selective colleges, including UC Berkeley and Stanford. I asked Cheryl if I could peruse her freshman, sophomore, and junior yearbooks just to see whether this level of integration between the Filipina and Latina young women was simply a fluke for Cheryl's senior year. It was not. The images throughout the yearbooks were much of the same, including the final page featuring the top ten women of the graduating class.

Amy did not have her yearbooks on hand but told a story quite similar to Cheryl's. The difference in the racial climate between Dover and St. Anne's was like night and day. Compared to highly segregated Dover Middle School, St. Anne's Academy was more racially egalitarian. "At St. Anne's, all the honors classes are mixed, not monoracial," she remembered. "I actually graduated fourth in my class," Amy said. "But one of my best friends, Sylvia, she was the valedictorian, and now she's at NYU [New York University]. She's Hispanic. My other friend Clarisse Nuñez, she's Hispanic too. She went to UCLA." At nearby Glenrock High School, having Latinos dominate the top spots in the graduating class seemed more anomalous. If it did occur, it was seen as an "exceptional" event, rather than the norm, like it was at St. Anne's. Joey, a neighbor and former classmate of Cheryl's in elementary school who went to Glenrock, said he could not ever remember if there was a Latino valedictorian during his time. "The valedictorians at Glenrock High School were always Asian or East

Asian or white," he said. In contrast, from what I gathered from Amy and Cheryl's narrative about St. Anne's Academy, there was every bit as much of an expectation—from both school officials and students—for the Latinas to excel academically and pursue college as there was for the Filipina students.

Bernard felt that the Filipinos and Latinos shared this same sense of ethnic camaraderie at Bishop High School, the all-boys "brother" school of St. Anne's Academy. Bishop High School and St. Anne's Academy shared many similarities. Although neither was located in Eagle Rock, both schools attracted many of the alumni from St. Thomas and St. Daniel elementary schools in Eagle Rock, most of whom were Filipino and Latino. The student bodies of Bishop and St. Anne's were similar in size, allowing the students to develop more intimate relationships with *all* of their classmates, more so than had they attended a large public high school with thousands of students. It is no wonder, then, that Bernard, Amy, and Cheryl all likened their high schools to a "big family." Although both institutions charged tuition, the costs were modest enough that even working-class and lower-middle-class families could send their children there, which was unlike the case at some of the more prestigious Catholic schools in the area. The generous financial aid options of both Bishop and St. Anne's further ensured that students from more modest socio-economic backgrounds could have access to a private school education without compromising the economic survival of their families.

Outside the halls of Bishop High School, the connection between Filipinos and Latinos did not always exist in Bernard's life. When Bernard was in his early teens, his family moved to a more solidly middle-class area of Eagle Rock, a few miles from the "more ghetto" neighborhood of Glassell Park. Some of the older brothers of his Latino friends from *vatos locos* began to join local gangs. His Latino friends were not themselves in gangs, but they often would receive a courtesy stigma—residents and police in the neighborhood would automatically assume they were gang affiliated by virtue of having siblings who were known gang members.[14] Bernard described how having Latino friends in Glassell Park sometimes even prompted others to see *him* as gang affiliated:

> Actually in Glassell Park, growing up there, it was a little different from Eagle Rock. I used to live across the street from the church, but I remember over there, there used to be a problem with gangs, so I used to be a little wary when I would hang out with friends. We would go play basketball in the church parking lot, and we'd get harassed by dudes walking by. They were Latino guys—Mexican guys from the Boulevard Boys.[15] They'd walk by and ask us where we were from [inquiring about their gang affiliation]. Dudes would come to us all the time. Growing up, most of my friends were Latino, so I guess that's what triggered it, but we were like in fifth or sixth grade. They would ask us what we were doing there. Even our school got tagged up.

As Bernard was reaching his teenage years, his parents started to reprimand him for spending too much time with his Latino friends. "Me and my brother were cool with our [Latino] friends, but my parents didn't see it the same way," Bernard said. "They saw the other kids as bad influences and stuff." However, once Bernard and his family moved to Eagle Rock, his parents' surveillance of him declined significantly, even when it came to new Latino friends he made in the neighborhood. "It was a lot different in Eagle Rock," he said. "The Latino family next door just did things differently, as if they were like white folks—in terms of how they dressed their house, their cars, not speaking Spanish at all." His parents were more accepting of Bernard's friendships with the Latinos who lived next door because of "the way they handled themselves," in reference to their public displays of middle class status and assimilation.

Bernard's childhood experiences instilled the idea that there were "bad" Latinos versus "good" Latinos, and at Bishop High School, most of his classmates were part of the latter group. "The Filipinos and Latinos were never competitive with each other," he said. "There were never any racially motivated conflicts or Filipino and Latino fights." Like St. Anne's Academy, there were honors and Advanced

Placement classes, but the limited options for these courses meant that Filipino and Latino students shared most of their classrooms, for the most part. Since Latinos accounted for the majority of the students, they were well represented in most honors classes at the school. "A lot of the Latino kids did well, and a lot of the Filipinos did well. But there were a lot of Filipino kids that didn't do that well too," Bernard pointed out. Unlike his public school peers, Bernard asserted that there was not as strong a correlation between Filipino identity and academic success at Bishop High School.

Since most of the students at Bishop High School were second generation, the Filipinos and Latinos also bonded over their shared experience coming from immigrant families and communities. "Everyone used to make fun of Mr. Sanchez," Bernard said, regarding one of his teachers who was a Filipino immigrant. "Mr. Sanchez had a super-thick Filipino accent, and that was kind of a unifying point where both the Filipino and Latino kids would mimic him and start clowning." Although he admitted it was not the ideal way to commiserate with his Latino peers, Bernard said that making fun of "FOBs" ("fresh off the boat" Asian immigrants) and "chuntaros" (newly arrived Mexican immigrants) ended up being a source of connection for Filipino and Latino students, many of whom shared an immigrant sensibility because of their close ties with immigrant relatives and neighbors.

Schooled by the Rich White Kids: Predominantly White Private Schools

The vast majority of the Filipinos I interviewed attended predominantly minority high schools, whether public or private. As such, most of them recalled having only minimal interaction with white peers from kindergarten through high school. It would not be until their college years that they would have the chance to interact with whites on a more intimate, everyday basis. However, a few Filipinos attended predominantly white private schools that were further removed from their neighborhoods. For example, after graduating from St. Daniel's Elementary, Ines and Jen both decided to attend St. Augustine's

Preparatory Academy, a co-ed Catholic school in an affluent area of Pasadena, about fifteen miles east of Eagle Rock. St. Augustine's was known to have a more prestigious reputation than either St. Anne's Academy or Bishop High School, but the tuition costs were nearly three times as much (more than $10,000 annually). Given the high tuition, the majority of students at St. Augustine's were from more affluent surrounding neighborhoods in Pasadena and San Marino. Most of these students also happened to be white.

Although a third of the residents in Eagle Rock were white, Ines and Jen grew up with other children of immigrants, most of whom they befriended while attending St. Daniel's. They both came from middle-class families, but it quickly became clear in their first days at St. Augustine that the wealth of their white classmates was on an entirely different level. Having grown up in the "ghetto side" of Eagle Rock around mostly Latino neighbors, Ines and Jen described their freshman year at St. Augustine's as a culture shock. "It was a predominantly white school. I mean, it was like *upper-class* white people," said Ines. "All the kids, they would just turn fifteen, not even sixteen, and their parents would buy them BMWs and Mercedes cars." These class differences made them particularly self-conscious whenever they interacted with their white classmates, especially outside of school:

> JEN: St. Augustine's was a totally different world for me. I didn't really hang out with people at St. Augustine's. And yeah, they were mostly white people. They'd invite me to go out, but I didn't really have anything common with them, so I'd end up hanging out with my friends from [Eagle Rock], who are mostly Filipino.
>
> A.O.: So you *never* hung out with any of them?
>
> JEN: It was mainly with school, like if we had a project together. That's pretty much the only time I felt I hung out with them. I was definitely shy. I didn't want to go out with them and feel like I didn't have anything in common. I was afraid of it being awkward and that there'd just be dead conversation. So I would rather go home right away than hang out.

Beyond the obvious class differences, both Ines and Jen asserted that their white classmates at St. Augustine also had different family values. "My mom was strict. You know, my white classmates could always go to each other's houses and sleep over," said Ines. "They could do all these different things after school like go out, and I couldn't really do those things."

Franky had very similar experiences at Jesuit Academy, a widely well-regarded all-boys institution near Downtown Los Angeles. Like St. Augustine's, Jesuit Academy was more expensive than the private Catholic high schools attended by most of the Filipinos I interviewed. It was also predominantly white, but slightly more diverse than St. Augustine's—nearly half of students were minorities. Filipinos, Latinos, and African Americans were evenly represented in the student body. Every year, Jesuit Academy provided students with a directory with each student's home address, telephone number, and email—all of which was aimed at providing opportunities for the young men to connect or make carpooling arrangements. However, the Jesuit directory also had the unintended consequences of marking people's class status according to which neighborhood they came from. "The white kids would be from rich neighborhoods in LA like Santa Monica, the [Pacific] Palisades, Manhattan Beach, South Pasadena, San Marino," said Franky, "If someone was from that area, you knew they were rich." In contrast, many of the minority student addresses were located in predominantly minority neighborhoods and zip codes, Eagle Rock and Carson included, given the centralized location of Jesuit Academy. Neighborhoods also functioned as a proxy for students' sensibilities about race. "If you were black, but you were from Manhattan Beach, that meant you were whitewashed," Franky remembered.

The racial balkanization of Jesuit Academy was readily apparent in the courtyards of the campus. Like St. Anne's and Bishop, the regular and honors classes at Jesuit were not racially stratified. Franky noted the diversity of his classrooms—white and minority students were both just as likely to be in the regular classes as they were in the

Advanced Placement classes. However, once classes ended, students self-segregated by ethnicity. Using his fingers, Franky drew me an ethnic map of the campus. "The white kids would all hang out by the soccer fields. Then all the black kids would hang out in 'Bro Row.' All the Latinos would be in Chicano corner. And the Filipinos had the island. People called us 'Little Manila.' Even the teachers called it 'Little Manila,'" Franky explained. Teachers' willingness to use these labels signaled the extent to which the racial balkanization of the students was tacitly accepted. Of course, there were a few mixed-race groups of friends—the jocks, the debate team, and the academic decathletes—but in general, students tended to stick to "their own." Students at Jesuit Academy who found their clique beyond ethnic boundaries were sometimes "clowned on," but such jabs were often in jest. From what Franky and other alumni of Jesuit said, such students would never experience the type of harassment that Janice said happened with her friend Lupe, the Mexican girl who was part of the Filipina group at South Bay High School in Carson.

Franky found himself at the butt of such jokes as a member of Jesuit's baseball team, one of the few sports that was predominantly white. All of Franky's close friends at Jesuit were Filipino, and most of them were from Eagle Rock or the surrounding neighborhoods. Franky remembered them giving him a little flack for joining the baseball team. "I'd say I was different because I was the coconut of the group—brown on the outside, but white on the inside," he said with a chuckle. "I was called whitewashed in terms of my personal ability to feel comfortable around people that aren't Filipino—being able to shoot the shit with white people." Nonetheless, Franky was adamant about pointing out how strong the racial and class barrier felt between him and his white teammates on the baseball team, even though his Filipino friends perceived him as comfortable with whites. Franky's white teammates were different from white peers he occasionally encountered in Eagle Rock, who were "inclined to have minority friends." The other members of the Jesuit baseball team "lived in nicer areas, they had nicer equipment, and talked about traveling all the time with the club teams they played with." Franky said he was always aware of these ethnic and class differences. "I was the only ethnic person on the baseball team," he said. "I had my one bat that I kept forever, my cleats that I kept forever, [and] my dinky-ass baseball bag."

Although Franky did his best to bond with his baseball teammates, the ethnic and class barriers proved too difficult to overcome. While his teammates would hang out with each other after practice, Franky retreated back to his Filipino group of friends. It was like living in two worlds. What made things even more challenging was the obvious discomfort his parents had when trying to interact with other parents during his games. Franky recalled the anxiety he felt whenever his parents came to watch him play:

> They [the white parents] had conversations that people with money had—being able to travel, donating this money, going to this [charity] event. My parents always said there was a snobby sense about those parents. I think it affected their opportunity to interact with the other parents because they had nothing to relate to. I remember when they'd come to the game, they would be by themselves. The other parents already knew each other [from club teams].

Even though Franky grew up middle class, the blatant affluence of his white teammates at Jesuit Academy hindered him and his family's ability to build ties across racial lines, something that they were accustomed to doing when he attended St. Daniel's Elementary. Ironically, there were certain reasons Franky's parents would be inclined to befriend the parents of his white teammates. His father was a member of the US military and had served in the Persian Gulf War. His mother had a master's degree in economics and worked as an accountant. Some might argue that his parents' educational background and careers would make it easier to socialize with the mainstream.[16] At the end of the day, neither the middle-class status nor cultural familiarity that his parents possessed was enough to break the ice with the parents of his white teammates.

Learning Race Off the Books

Minus the obligatory mention of slavery or the civil rights movement in their social studies classes, Filipinos in the United States did not learn much else about race from their schoolbooks. Filipinos acquired most lessons about race through their interactions with their teachers, counselors, and classmates both in and beyond the classroom. From these interactions, Filipinos made inferences about the meaning and value of different social categories, including Asian American identity. Given how closely people associate Asian American identity with the model minority stereotype, it is not too surprising that academic performance, not culture, has become a litmus test for who was "really" Asian within the contexts of schools. In majority-minority public schools in Eagle Rock and Carson, Filipinos ended up being the "default" Asian group, given the demographic makeup of these neighborhoods. The tracking system at these schools further crystallized Filipinos' status as the "Asian ones" at both Glenrock and South Bay High Schools. Racial segregation was the norm at these schools, and tracking helped institutionalize divisions both in and beyond the classroom.

In contrast, the lack of academic tracking and the more intimate environment of private Catholic schools did the opposite. In schools like St. Anne's Academy and Bishop High School, the mostly Filipino and Latino student body remained relatively tighter knit. This was also likely a by-product of the homogeneity of the student body. Tuition costs existed but were modest, and so most students were roughly of the same class background. For the most part, everyone was Catholic and came from immigrant families and communities. However, cross-racial friendships were less commonplace at more affluent private schools like St. Augustine's Preparatory and Jesuit Academy. Although both St. Augustine's and Jesuit were similar in size to St. Anne's and Bishop, the more intimate setting did not facilitate the same type of cross-racial interactions between Filipinos and other racial groups, both minority and white. Instead, racial and class barriers were constantly salient in their minds, which prompted them to self-segregate by ethnicity and stick with the other Filipinos.

Nonetheless, as compared with their public school counterparts, even the Filipinos who went to the predominantly white private schools had a more heightened sense of pan-minority solidarity with other students of color. "Hispanics and Filipinos were the only people I really interacted with in schools," said Jen of her classmates at St. Augustine. "More interactions led us to become friends." Franky echoed these thoughts: "With my Mexican friends at Jesuit, you can talk about race. I can joke about Mexicans to my Mexican friends," he said. "I think it's because I grew up with Latinos and have always had Latino friends. Culturally, we have the same type of family values." For the Filipinos who went to public schools, to do such a thing would further exacerbate the inequalities between them and the other minorities. Robin, an alumna of South Bay High School, argued that staying segregated from other minorities was the pragmatic thing to do to avoid conflict. Robin's orientation illustrated why Filipinos who attended public school often felt as if other minorities were "practically invisible," as one alumna from South Bay High School put it. Such a remark spoke to the impact that academic institutions made in shaping the cross-racial relationships of Filipino youth in Los Angeles.

6

"Filipinos Aren't Asian" and Other Lessons from College

THE RULES OF RACE changed in college. The racial and ethnic categories that Filipinos had been accustomed to using in their everyday lives in their neighborhoods and high schools took on new meaning once they entered the halls of university life. Ask Aaron Gonzalez, a graduate of the University of California in Los Angeles. At Glenrock High School, Aaron's alma mater, "Filipinos were the Asian ones," in his words. They enrolled in the honors classes, matriculated to college, and were the canonized model minorities at Glenrock. By the end of his days at UCLA, Aaron came to see Filipinos and Asians as inherently distinct. In his mind, to be Filipino at UCLA was to be a card-carrying member of Samahang (Tagalog for "togetherness"), an undergraduate organization in which the underrepresentation and retention of Filipino students was a mainstay issue throughout its forty-year history. In contrast, underrepresentation was never the story of the "real" Asian Americans at UCLA, long jokingly dubbed the "University of Caucasians Lost Among Asians." Aaron felt that Filipinos weren't part of the acronym. To Aaron, the typical Asian was the politically uninvolved bookworm studiously pursuing a degree in science or engineering. I asked Aaron whether he was overgeneralizing, but my interjection did not sway him much—it was clear how strongly the stereotype of the model minority influenced his opinions of other Asian American students at UCLA.

Aaron was hardly shy about his opinions of the other Asians at UCLA. During his tenure as president of Samahang, one of his primary responsibilities was to be the liaison to the other Asian American student organizations on campus. At one of their meetings, he recalled a "crossing the line" icebreaker exercise that he participated in with the other Asian American student leaders:

> For one of the activities, we all had to stand in a straight line. Then a facilitator would read statements and people had to either step to the right if they agreed, and to the left if you disagreed. One of the statements was "Filipinos are Asian American." I stepped to the left. It must have been weird for people to see me do this since I was the president of the Filipino American student organization.

Though the lone soul to voice this opinion at this workshop, Aaron's sentiments were echoed by Filipinos and non-Filipinos alike not just at UCLA but also at other college campuses. Often times, this "transformation" from Asian to non-Asian in the context of academic life was more process than epiphany. This cognitive shift did not only involve Filipinos and their Asian American classmates—enmeshed in this process were a variety of other actors, from the white sorority girl to the Chicano student activist to the African American biology professor. For many of the Filipinos I interviewed, this change in racial consciousness began on their very first days as new college students.

Freshmen Orientation

When Rachel was accepted to UCLA, she was one of twenty Filipinos from South Bay High School to be offered admission that year. Years prior to her applying, members of Samahang had specifically targeted South Bay as a site for recruiting more Filipinos to UCLA. They feared the number of Filipino undergraduates would dwindle following the 1996 passage of Proposition 209, the California ballot initiative that banned affirmative action at public universities.¹ Rachel was happy to have a cohort of more than twenty South Bay alumni moving from Carson to the UCLA campus in Westwood. Even though it was only about thirty miles away from her hometown, UCLA felt like a world apart from Carson, a neighborhood that "no one ever leaves," according to Rachel. For most Filipinos, Carson or otherwise, their entire social world revolved around the neighborhood, so to up and leave was a big deal. In fact, the majority had pointed out how *resistant* their parents, family, and even friends were to their leaving for college, even if campus was but an hour's drive away. Always one to challenge herself in school and through new experiences, Rachel was somewhat critical of how other Filipinos in her neighborhood got too comfortable with life in Carson, but even she herself admitted she was unprepared for her first social encounters at UCLA.

Rachel's cohort from South Bay had all attended the same freshmen orientation weekend the summer prior to their first year, but because of work conflicts, she had no choice but to attend her orientation with a group of new classmates she didn't know. Besides one other person, everyone in Rachel's orientation group happened to be white. Growing up in Carson, Rachel said she had had little to no interaction with white people for most of her life. The one experience she did have was during a summer leadership program she attended for high school girls across the country, which did not leave her with the best impressions. It was only a weekend long, and she had received a scholarship to attend. About 90 percent of the participants were "upper-crust white girls," and Rachel found herself hanging out with the Latinas. Rachel remembered most of the weekend feeling "super out of place" and wanting to get straight back to Carson. In many ways, her UCLA orientation seemed like déjà vu.

"I vividly remember standing behind three bleach-blonde sun-kissed white girls with their Roxy beach wear, Abercrombie & Fitch, and high-end luggage," Rachel recalled, still reeling from the memory from a decade earlier. "They're talking about soccer camp and how much fun they had, and I'm just standing there thinking, 'Good Lord!

Where am I?' It just didn't feel right," she said. "They dressed differently from I did. They *looked* different from I did." In this moment, Rachel became keenly aware of the socioeconomic and racial privilege that she lacked relative to her white classmates.

From her high school summer program, Rachel had already typecast the "typical" white girl. Freshmen orientation merely confirmed her stereotypes that white girls were not only affluent but also showy about their wealth—in their clothing, life experiences, and social interests. "All the girls wanted to do was go to sorority things, fraternity parties, and none of that felt right to me," Rachel said. "I felt super ostracized for most of orientation." Like other college students of color, being in a predominantly white space amplified Rachel's awareness of her minority status, especially because she grew up around immigrants and other people of color.[2]

Being at UCLA gave Rachel the opportunity to see the full spectrum of socioeconomic difference. Going from a majority-minority neighborhood to a place with such a large and visible population of white students made it easy to conflate whiteness with affluence. The surrounding residential area of the college further crystallized this belief. Multimillion-dollar homes and estates, owned almost entirely by white residents (and maintained almost entirely by Latino laborers), accentuated the association between whiteness and wealth. Whether accurate or not, in Rachel's eyes, the white sorority girls were merely the manifestation of such blatant forms of white privilege. The feeling of being an outsider, coupled with the awareness of class and race that she developed growing up in Carson, made it even more important for her to find a community with other Filipinos.[3]

The first months of college taught Rachel the difference between being wealthy versus middle class. Freshmen orientation only provided the opening lesson. Rachel had requested to live with her best friend from South Bay, a fellow Filipina, and the two were placed in a triple with a white student from Orange County, a region in Southern California known for both its affluence and its conservative political leanings. "Our third roommate was this white girl from Anaheim, and she was—*woo*—something else. Totally different from my experience." Rachel had considered herself middle class and found it odd that her white roommate identified in the same manner. In a way, her roommate's unawareness about the qualitative differences between their middle-class experiences perfectly illustrated the unconscious nature of white privilege.[4]

"Carson folks are middle-class people with a blue-collar mentality," she said, alluding to the glass ceiling and lack of opportunity her college-educated professional parents faced. "My parents, they're not in management, and they've worked in the same positions for thirty years. They clock in and clock out, and there's no point to proving yourself to anybody because you're not going to climb the ladder." Rachel was quick to juxtapose her definition of middle class to that of her white classmates': "My mom may be a nurse, and she makes money, but that money doesn't go to high-end luggage. It goes to all her family members back in the Philippines." Being able to financially provide for loved ones back home was among the main reasons her mother had migrated to the United States in the first place. Like other middle-class minorities, this heightened sense of family obligation that Rachel's family felt was nonnegotiable—to not give back was the equivalent of being "too white" or "too American," in her eyes.[5]

Both her parents' economic situation and rationale for migration help explain why Rachel's orientation toward college seemed so incongruent with that of her white classmates. College was not just about having fun—college was about getting a job. As is the case with many children of immigrants, college served an economic function for the entire family.[6] College was less about the college experience, which Rachel considered a "first-world problem," and more about giving back to her parents and community. Growing up hearing her parents' narrative conditioned her to frame college in this light.

"You go to school to get a job," she said, reiterating her parents' pragmatic view about the function of higher education. "My dad told me, 'You go to school so you can prove to somebody that you know how to learn. So when you apply for a job, they see you can learn, and you'll get a job.'" When juxtaposing this perspective to the images of rich white girls in her orientation and freshmen dormitory, it became clear why Rachel felt that "college wasn't made for people like [her]." For her and other children of immigrants, college was the equivalent of another family obligation. It was both a sign of respect for her parents' migration struggles, as well as the opportunity for her to repay them for all they sacrificed for her and her siblings.[7]

Experiences like Rachel's were often enough for her and other Filipinos to write off having relationships with white people altogether. Of course, Filipinos interacted casually and politely with whites in their classrooms, dormitories, at their jobs, or the gym. However, very few Filipinos remember their white classmates as part of their more intimate activities—throwing parties, eating in the dining hall, or going on dates. Many even joked about white people being "spoiled," "ignorant," and "cultureless." They assumed all white people were privileged, often times the default assumption for many people of color.[8] Only one Filipino spoke about having a mostly white group of friends in college, which in turn prompted his neighborhood friends in Eagle Rock to dub him a "coconut"—brown on the outside but white on the inside. Yet even he saw himself as the "weird Filipino." In other words, racial integration hardly bought Filipinos the opportunity for actual social incorporation, especially on a campus with more than twenty thousand undergraduates where anonymity was more the norm than the exception.

Erik's memories of his first few days at UCLA were much like Rachel's. "College was a culture shock! I had never seen so many white folks in my life. It was crazy," he said. The social world Erik entered his freshman year of college was a far cry from the "bubble of people of color" that he was accustomed to both in his hometown and high school. "I felt out of place because it was something so new and so different," he remembered. "Everywhere I turned, there was a white person."

By Erik's own admission, his upbringing was rather comfortable. His parents were both working professionals who also owned a small but thriving restaurant in the San Fernando Valley, located about a ten-mile drive northwest of Eagle Rock. Being middle class, however, hardly prepared Erik for the social norms of his white classmates. Having grown up on the border of middle-class Eagle Rock and working class Highland Park, he was dumbfounded with their lack of street smarts:

> One thing I wanted to talk about that was very shocking to me was that they would just leave their shit around. That may seem like a small thing to you, but it blew my mind! Near the dining hall, they would just leave their shit and start stacking their shit on top of each other's, and I was like, "What the fuck?" Back in Eagle Rock, if you did shit like that, it was gone as soon as you turned your back. That's when I was like, "What *is* this place?" There was no way I would just leave my shit out like that.

Erik's thought process was directly shaped by the continued presence of illicit activities he witnessed growing up in his side of Eagle Rock. Although he himself grew up in a nice house, there were gangs and graffiti within a three-block radius of his childhood home. Even at UCLA, a place he viewed as a "white-dominated institution," he maintained a certain awareness of street life and street smarts—a cultural trait that distinguished middle-class people of color from middle-class whites. Although he viewed UCLA as an affluent university, he was quick to point out that this did not necessarily make the campus immune to the type of crime he saw growing up.[9] Ultimately, Erik's remarks about his first year at UCLA demonstrate that middle-class status did not automatically mean that one could feel comfortable in white social spaces.[10]

Similar to Rachel, Erik described his freshmen orientation as a mess, especially the advising session he received on the last day. "It was bullshit," Erik said. "My orientation counselor was this white girl who didn't know what the fuck she was talking about. I ended up taking some random German literature class my first quarter because of her, and I'm thinking, 'She didn't know what the hell she was doing.'" This being Erik's first time going to school with whites, there was a certain suspicion and reluctance that he developed about his white classmates after his interaction with his well-meaning but culturally unaware white counselor. It is often the case that college students of color possess a cultural mistrust with white counselors, particularly if they had little to no social interaction with whites prior to entering college.[11]

Given the racial makeup of their respective neighborhoods, it was not surprising that children of immigrants, such as Erik and Rachel, did not find it easy to blend in with their white classmates, regardless of how Americanized their upbringing actually was. Growing up in the majority-minority neighborhoods of Eagle Rock and Carson, they never had to learn how. In a "bubble of people of color," as Erik put it, their social well-being never depended on their ability to be accepted by whites. It was not uncommon for Filipinos in Los Angeles to be socialized within minority middle-class "segments" of society that were, for all intents and purposes, separate from the white middle class.[12] As both their stories show, minority and white middle-class individuals felt that they functioned under a different system of logic when it came to their families, communities, school life, and property.[13]

This lack of experience interacting with whites was what made college such a culture shock for Filipinos, particularly for those who went to campuses with large numbers of white students. As such, many Filipinos gravitated toward an ethnic niche within their campus as early as their first few weeks as college freshmen. The idea of children of immigrants assimilating into different spheres of society is hardly a new concept. Sociologists of immigration even have a term for this phenomenon—*segmented assimilation*—but they have used this framework mainly to describe how children of immigrants integrate into different neighborhood contexts. What the narratives of Filipinos demonstrate is that segmented assimilation also occurs in the arena of higher education, especially if that space is racially and ethnically heterogeneous.

Confronting Asian American Identity

At the University of California campuses, white students were not the only source of angst for Filipinos. Filipinos also voiced their dismay at the "sea of Asians" in their college. Although they acknowledged that Filipinos were "technically considered Asian," most had always considered themselves distinct from other Asians. "Whenever I filled out a form at school, there was always a Filipino box and an Asian box," said Arvin Manalo, a graduate of UC San Diego, "Why would I ever check 'Asian' then?" The irony of university life was that there were several social institutions that aimed to foster a shared sense of Asian American identity, from student organizations to Asian American studies courses. Instead, the social landscape of the college campus often reinforced the distinctions that some Filipinos already held between themselves and other Asians.

In both Eagle Rock and Carson, Filipinos accounted for more than 80 percent of the total Asian population. For the vast majority, Filipinos were also the predominant Asian group in their high schools. However, at many of the University of California campuses, East Asians dwarfed the population of Filipinos, even though the latter have constituted the largest Asian subgroup in the state for the past two decades. Even though the populations of Chinese Americans and Filipino Americans in the state are roughly the same, Chinese American students outnumbered Filipinos by a ratio of four to one. This disparity is even greater at the more selective campuses.[14] For example at UC Berkeley, the flagship and most competitive of the UC campuses, Chinese Americans outnumbered Filipinos by a ratio of nine to one. One in five freshmen entering UC Berkeley in the fall of 2013 was Chinese American. In contrast, Filipinos accounted for a mere 2 percent of the total freshmen class that year, a proportion that paled even in comparison to the number of Korean, Vietnamese, and South Asian first-year students.[15] These patterns run consistent across many of the other UC campuses, particularly at the most highly selective ones.[16]

"I guess subconsciously I had this idea that every Asian was Filipino, since Filipinos don't necessarily all look the same," said Dustin, an alumnus of UCLA. It was not until his first year at UCLA that he thought that seriously about the heterogeneity of Asian Americans. Being from Carson, the only times he had ever interacted with other Asian ethnicities were when he traveled to nearby Torrance and Harbor City, both of which he described as being "whiter" and having a "more privileged" income bracket than his neighborhood. In a similar way that Rachel and Erik did with whites, Dustin came to associate other Asians at UCLA with affluence and privilege, which he said deterred him from making friends with other Asians on campus. In certain instances, Filipinos described other Asians as the de facto "white" students on campus because of their disproportionately high numbers. Many transposed some of the same cultural perceptions they had about whites toward their Asian peers. In fact, whenever respondents would talk about the "students of color" on campus, they almost always excluded the Asian students.

Andrea grew up in the "'hood side" of Eagle Rock, bordering the working-class Mexican American neighborhood of Glassell Park. She described everyday life around her parts as more gritty—gangsters and graffiti were simply part of the backdrop growing up where she did. In this respect, moving from the hood side of Eagle Rock to UC Irvine was unsurprisingly a "culture shock." The city of Irvine itself is incredibly affluent. The median family income easily tops $100,000, making it one of the richest cities in America. In 2014, the Federal Bureau of Investigation crowned Irvine the safest American city for the tenth consecutive year.[17] The overwhelming majority of Irvine residents are white and East Asian. The campus's manicured appearance was a reflection of the picturesque surrounding community, a quality Andrea was not too fond of. "Where I came from, it was dirty. Here, it was hella clean," she said. "I didn't hate Irvine, but I was just bored of it. I came from something that was so lively and different to something that was mundane."

Throughout our conversation, it became evident that Andrea conflated her Asian classmates with the affluent Asian Americans that lived in the surrounding community. She would seamlessly talk about the Asians in Irvine in one breath and then the Asian Americans at her school in the next. "Everyone in Irvine is Asian, and they're all in their own little bubble," Andrea said. Even though she had her criticisms of her more solidly middle-class friends in Eagle Rock, Filipinos regularly interacted across racial and class lines. "When I think of the other Asians, I see them as more conservative or hanging out with themselves. But when you see the Filipinos, they get along with the Mexicans, the blacks, and even sometimes whites like there's no cultural barrier," she said. "Other Asians? They just stick to their own kind." I knew Andrea was generalizing, and I knew that this line of thinking was both reductionist and problematic. Nonetheless, it was interesting to see how dominant this narrative was among the Filipinos that I spoke with, especially those who attended college at the University of California campuses. In the end, a pan-Asian community was not the niche where Filipino college students usually found a home.

Discovering Differences

Although Filipinos did not find themselves embedded within Asian American organizations and social spaces in college, they did point out that they had more frequent casual interactions with Asian Americans on campus than in their neighborhood environment. Often times, their encounters reified their stereotypes about whites and Asians, even for Filipinos who developed close intimate ties through their classes, dating relationships, or extracurricular involvements.

Before college, Filipinos were used to being typecast as the "good students." However, encountering other Asian Americans made them realize how laissez-faire they and their families actually were about their everyday educational lives. After high school, Jen moved from Eagle Rock to Northern California to attend University of the Pacific, a school with an excellent undergraduate pre-pharmacy program. The makeup of the university's student body was a challenging adjustment, given that most of Jen's friends before college were Filipino and Mexican. "My school [University of the Pacific] was predominantly Asian and white. And by Asian, I mean Vietnamese and Chinese," she said, adding that she had never met a Vietnamese person until moving to college. In her first year, Jen was randomly assigned to live with a Vietnamese American roommate, who happened to be in the same pre-pharmacy program.

"My program was comprised mostly of Vietnamese and Chinese. It was, um, interesting," Jen said, implying the novelty of attending school with other Asian students. College was Jen's first real opportunity to compare her experiences with other Asian Americans. What stood out to her most were the differences in their academic habits:

> My roommate was Vietnamese, and she was very strict and always very stressed out. She was very driven, and she was always pushing me because I wasn't *as* driven. She'd always say, "Jen, stop watching TV! We have to study!" I noticed that her other Vietnamese friends were also the same way—very goal oriented and driven.

Given her limited interactions with other Asians prior to college, situations like these became particularly impactful for how Jen began to conceptualize Asian American identity. Jen came to associate academic overachievement as a distinctly Asian trait—one that her Vietnamese and Chinese classmates possessed but that she and her Filipino peers did not. Comparing their academic habits also opened the door for Jen to point out cultural distinctions between Filipinos and other Asians. Jen felt the difference in their academic lives had everything to do with culture. "Asian parents are strict. Filipinos' aren't," she argued. "When I look at my roommate and my classmates, I just never felt like I was Asian." At the University of the Pacific, Vietnamese and Chinese students set the rules of Asian American identity. In the end, Jen never felt that she ever fit the criteria.

Jayson, one of Jen's former classmates from elementary school, had a similar experience as a student at UC San Diego, even though his campus boasted much larger numbers of Filipino undergraduates. In high school, Jayson said his parents were relatively uninvolved in his academics. "My parents never meddled that much. I brought home good grades, so they didn't ever pry. They pushed me to put in the effort, but they said to just try my best." He said he was "shocked" when he heard stories his East Asian classmates shared about the parental pressures they felt during high school:

> If you look at Chinese and other Asian parents, the kids are at a chokehold to their parents. I mean, Filipino parents are strict, but Asian families tend to be a lot more hardcore with regulating their kids. I had a friend from college who was a girl. Plus she was the eldest. Her parents were very overprotective, and she told me that they made her go to Chinese school. Between going to American and Chinese school, her parents basically had her on lockdown. She said it was always hard for her to go out because her parents had her on a schedule! Her parents were always telling her, "You gotta study."

Jayson was not trying to dispute the importance of education within Filipino families. Valuing a college education was something he believed that Filipino and other Asian families shared. Rather, Jayson was making a distinction between Filipinos' and Asians' academic *behaviors*, not their educational attitudes. Like Jayson, most Filipinos were taken aback at the degree to which the parents of their Asian classmates meticulously managed the ins and outs of their academic lives. The prevalence of the model minority narrative on their respective campuses further crystallized this stereotyped version of Asian American experiences in higher education. With the exception of the few who enrolled in ethnic studies courses, Filipinos rarely took the opportunity to question their preconceived notions of other Asian Americans.

There was a commonplace narrative among the people I interviewed that Filipino parents prioritized familial social obligations over academics while other Asian parents did the opposite. Many pointed out that the other Asian Americans they knew would often commiserate about their parents' push for them to attend the best colleges possible, no matter the distance from home. In contrast, Filipinos more often spoke about their parents' tendency to hold them back from educational opportunities that were located too far away from home. Mikey, a native of Eagle Rock, said his dream since high school was to pursue a science degree at UC San Diego. However, Mikey's mother had other ideas about her son's academic ambitions:

> Before I even applied to college, my mom was already brainwashing me to want to stay home. I just compromised with her by not applying to Berkeley. I remember how excited I was when I got into UCSD's program because it's so competitive. When I told my mom about it, all she said was, "When do you hear from UC Irvine?" That was her reaction!

Fortunately, Mikey held his ground and accepted the offer to UC San Diego. However, even as he was packing his bags for San Diego, a mere two-hour drive from his parents' home, his mother remained persistent, going so far as encouraging her son to renege and attend the local community college instead. Mikey was appalled. "When she suggested I go to a two-year, I was like, 'No way! Are you serious?'" Whenever Mikey shared this story with his Chinese and Korean classmates at his school, the most common reaction was disbelief. "You're kidding me," Mikey recalled them saying. "With [Chinese and Korean] parents, it's the exact opposite." Although Mikey strongly resisted his mother's coercion, he was more the exception than the rule. Nearly a third of the Filipinos I interviewed spoke extensively about holding themselves back from educational opportunities they wanted to pursue out of fear of "disappointing" or "financially burdening" their families. Because of these concerns, only a few even considered applying to colleges that were located out of state. Interestingly, educational scholars have shown that despite having parents who are college educated and middle class, Filipinos were significantly less likely than other Asians to apply to prestigious and private universities.[18]

Joey was among a handful of Filipinos who openly expressed frustration with this pattern. "My parents were the exception from other

Filipinos," he said. "They'd actually get me out of going to family gatherings when I was in college by telling everyone I was studying." As a biological science major at UCLA and then a medical student at UC Davis, he talked about how the number of Filipinos in his classes dwindled with each passing year. By his first year of medical school, he was just one of three Filipinos in his entering class. In contrast, the proportion of East Asians in his classes seemed to increase from college to medical school, giving him multiple opportunities to compare his story with theirs. It was only then that he saw how different Filipino parents were from other Asians in terms of their orientation toward school.

Before college, Joey had considered himself the quintessential model student. While at Glenrock High School, he attended after-school tutoring programs and took an SAT prep course taught by college volunteers. He was proud to have been accepted to UCLA, his dream school. According to Joey, few others at Glenrock had even bothered to apply. However, his pride in his accomplishment waned when he compared his experiences to those of his Chinese American girlfriend and her friends. "She had friends who went to Stanford [and] Harvard. UCLA was my dream school, but for her and her friends, the UCs are the backup schools," he said. Joey realized that his dream school was one that his girlfriend and her Asian American friends felt they merely "ended up" at when they were not accepted to Ivy League institutions.[19] For Joey, his girlfriend's and her friends' "cultural tastes" in colleges served to create a symbolic boundary between Filipinos and other Asians.[20]

Among Joey's neighborhood friends, no one had ever even considered going to the East Coast, let alone attending an Ivy League school. Some of his Glenrock classmates even discounted the University of California schools because they were either "too far" or "too expensive." Joey attributed the difference in Filipinos' and Asians' college aspirations to class and family. "I don't wanna stereotype [Asians], but they all have nice houses, nice cars, and grow up in Asian middle-class suburbia," he argued. "My girlfriend, she's Chinese, [and] her

mom was always helping her out with school, on her projects." Joey
and other Filipinos reiterated their surprise at the amount of supplemental educational resources their Asian peers received in high school
courtesy of their parents. Not a single Filipino had even considered
enrolling in established SAT preparation programs, such as Kaplan
or Princeton Review, noting such things as "unnecessary" expenses.
In contrast, it seemed to them that SAT courses and tutors, and even
supplemental college counseling, were the norm for other Asians.
Again, we see how powerful the model minority stereotype is in shaping a problematic understanding of Asian American identity within
higher education.

Finding a Niche

For most Filipinos, encountering whites and other Asian Americans
en masse in their college campuses was a sudden shift that most said
they were not ready for. In new situations, people often rely on physical and behavioral cues to determine the appropriate "script" for an
interaction.[21] For example, after many years of schooling, students
automatically come to understand the individual in the front of the
classroom as the teacher, to whom they act with respect and defer-
ence. Upon encountering an elderly person on the street, people know
instinctually to greet them politely as "Ma'am" or "Sir." In the context
of a (heterosexual) date, a man may abide by the rules of chivalry and
open the door for a woman he is courting, a phenomenon sociologists
have called "doing gender."[22]

Race functions in a similar fashion. Not surprisingly, one of the
most common go-to physical cues, besides gender, is race.[23] Immigrants might spot someone on the street who looks like them and
subsequently start speaking in their native tongue. People might also
determine whether someone belongs to a certain racial group on the
basis of the way that person speaks, acts, or dresses.[24] There are also
countless stories of people using racial markers to negatively stigma-
tize others, both consciously and unconsciously.[25] Racial cues trig-
ger racial stereotypes that in turn can lead to negative consequences,

from racial profiling by the police to housing and job discrimination. These split-second acts of racialization can even turn deadly, as evidenced by the cases of Amadou Diallo in 1999 and Trayvon Martin in 2012, two young black men killed by white men who instinctually associated blackness with criminality.[26]

Within the racial context of college, Filipinos realized that they had little to no "practice" interacting with whites and Asians. "Carson was so diverse, even though it was 0.00001 percent white people," Lia noted about her neighborhood and schools. Given the racial demographics of Carson, it was not too surprising that Filipinos from there often commented on their lack of exposure to whites. However, even among Filipinos from Eagle Rock, where a third of residents are white, interactions with whites were minimal. "I never hung out with white people," said Ines, which was all the more telling given that she attended a predominantly white private Catholic school. If anything, the whites in Eagle Rock had to assimilate to the people of color, according to Franky. Filipinos' encounters with other Asians in either neighborhood were also minimal, given that they were the predominant Asian subgroup.

As a result, many Filipinos, particularly those whose social lives moved from the neighborhood to the university, opted for more familiar territory and joined the Filipino undergraduate organization on their campus. "I joined Samahang on my first day," said Roseanne, a teaching assistant from Carson, about her freshman year at UCLA. "We're in a place where there are so many ethnicities there, so we have to be with other Filipinos to feel comfortable in this environment." Amid the chaos of rigorous academic courses and new racial encounters, the Filipino organization became home. In an environment that "wasn't made for Filipinos," as one respondent put it, they could at least make sense of the happenings within their ethnic niche. For example, at UC Berkeley and Stanford, the colleges with the most geographically diverse group of Filipino students, the Filipino undergraduate organizations reach out to high school students recently accepted to the campuses to welcome them to the *pamilya* (family).

Many of the Filipino organizations within UC campuses immediately recruit Filipino freshmen for their big sister–big brother mentorship program. It was commonplace for Filipino students to apply kinship titles, such as *ate* (big sister) and *kuya* (big brother), when referring to the more veteran members of the group. Filipinos noted that use of fictive kinship titles was commonplace within Filipino student organizations, but they felt it was uncommon among other Asian American organizations on their campuses.

After his disastrous advising experience at orientation, Erik met Cynthia, a fellow Filipino student in her junior year at the time. Cynthia oriented Erik to life at UCLA in a way that was more conducive to students of color. "She took me to the Community Program Office, where all the African Americans, Mexicans, and Filipinos hung out," he said. "It was kind of refreshing—and rewarding. I felt like she got me. I felt like she cared. It was the first time I *wanted* to be there [at UCLA]." Through his Filipino big sister, Erik finally found a niche where his ethnic identity and comfort with talking race actually had some social cachet.

Status Change

Rachel's decision to join Samahang had to do largely with her need to understand her feelings of marginality on campus. One of her primary sources of anxieties had to do with seeing what happened to her cohort from South Bay High School. Although she was initially excited to start UCLA with an entire crew from Carson, her enthusiasm quickly turned into worry after seeing her closest friends drop out of the university:

> College was a difficult experience for us—coming out of Carson to a place where the minority is the majority, and the majority is the minority. Retention was a big thing. There were more than twenty of us from Carson, but most of us didn't graduate. One of my good friends dropped out and she was a really good student. I think her family even encouraged her to do that. Another one was dismissed

for poor grades. A lot of folks were premed or engineering and that wasn't a good fit. My roommate was in danger of being dismissed in her first year. It was like we just weren't ready to be here. . . . It was very discouraging.

Within many of the UC campuses, attrition of Filipino undergraduates was a constant concern, especially at more highly selective institutions like UC Berkeley and UCLA. At these institutions, many of the activities of the Filipino organization were organized around dealing with the change in status that many felt, going from model students in their high schools to "at-risk" undergraduates.

Their racial encounters, combined with their newfound underrepresentation on campus vis-à-vis the "real Asians," made many Filipinos second-guess their academic abilities. These conditions not only exacerbated the typical anxieties and insecurities that came with being a college student—they also infused them with racial undertones. As a mathematics major, a course of study no Filipinos he knew pursued, Jacob always felt that he was representing his ethnic community:

I feel intimidated to ask questions. In one of my classes, for example, there were twenty-two whites, sixteen Asians, and then me. You know, if I ask a question, I am representing my whole race right now. "What if I say something stupid?" I think. Why should I have to feel like that when none of *them* feel like that. They don't know. They don't have to worry about that stuff. I feel like I'm always aware of the racial situation that I'm in.

As Jacob's remarks suggest, the academic environment of college reifies the boundaries *between* Filipinos and other Asians. Experiences like these reinforce Filipinos' perception that other Asians were the model minority and therefore more "authentically Asian." Despite the problematic nature of this belief, Filipinos often use the model minority narrative as a litmus test for Asian American racial authenticity. Because Filipinos regularly juxtaposed what they saw as a thriving Asian (and white) student body to their academically struggling ethnic community, demarcating themselves from the other Asians became a rational thing to do.

Academic outreach programs were central to the organizational mission of many Filipino undergraduate organizations. Educational outreach and retention programs were as important as programs that promoted cultural exploration. At both UC Berkeley and UCLA, Filipino undergraduates have operated and maintained organizations to increase the numbers of Filipino students, facilitate their academic and social adjustment, and assist with the balance between school and family obligations, all in an effort to deter attrition. "I noticed that lots of Filipinos struggle at UCLA," said Rachel. Rachel then spent the last three years of college volunteering as an academic counselor for Samahang.

After finishing her degree, Rachel was hired by the university's minority retention center to work specifically with Filipino undergraduates. After an additional five years working on retention issues, she concluded that much of the problem lay in the disconnection between Filipino students' familial expectations and academic conditions:

> Filipinos would get dismissed all the time. They weren't able to connect their classroom experiences to their lives. They were trying to get this type of science degree, but they didn't know how to put in the time to cut it. Many didn't even know why they were going to school. Many were so unhappy with their classroom experiences that they'd do anything to distract themselves. They'd get overinvolved with the Filipino organization because that at least had to do with their real lives.

Rachel also attributed Filipinos' academic shortcomings to the extreme emphasis that parents placed on attending familial social obligations: "Family is always a responsibility. It's always an obligation. They always make *that* a priority. I think it's the biggest influence on Filipino education." She noticed a clear pattern in the academic outcomes between the Filipino students whose parents "allowed" them to live *and stay* on campus, versus those whose parents coerced them into going home every weekend, even during major exam periods. Filipinos felt that other Asian families prioritized academics above all else. In contrast, they felt that Filipino parents cared about academics only to the extent that it did not deter relationships with family. Ultimately, this narrative played a role in the way Filipinos viewed their racial position vis-à-vis other minority groups on campus.

Politicized Ethnicity

Before college, the meaning of being Filipino for many was sometimes nominal. For some, being Filipino meant having a large extended family, being Catholic, or eating rice with a spoon and fork rather than a fork and knife—in other words, nothing particularly idiosyncratic to Filipino history or culture. Despite growing up around other Filipinos, there were essentially no social institutions, beyond the family, where Filipinos could learn about their ethnic culture. The minority of respondents who attempted to explore their culture more formally—by joining Filipino dance troupes or taking Tagalog lessons— encountered resistance from parents and friends. "My parents were too concerned with us being American," said Grace, referring to her parents' belief that being "too Filipino" would somehow limit their ability to move up in their adopted country. "Learning Tagalog would be a waste of your time," they had said to her. "Learn Spanish instead. At least you can get extra pay." Friends did not help the cause either. Most have vivid memories of US-born Filipinos making fun of each other if they spoke Tagalog or spoke English with a Filipino accent.

This dynamic changed dramatically in college. By their young adult years, many Filipinos were anxious to embrace their ethnic heritage, especially if they found their niche in the Filipino organization on campus. College changed the meaning, as well as the symbolic value, of what it meant to be Filipino. Filipino pride was not entirely foreign; most remember their coethnic peers acknowledging their ethnic identity without hesitation. They simply did not know much about it in terms of history. "People were 'proud' to be Filipino, but it had no depth to it," said Lia about her peers in Carson. "They would wear

'Pinoy [Filipino] Pride' gear, but it didn't *mean* anything. It was just about being part of the cool kids." Once Filipinos became part of the campus ethnic organization, they developed a more politicized sense of Filipino identity within the university context, especially given the prevalent narratives of Filipino underrepresentation and attrition. On campus, Filipino identity became synonymous with political and social consciousness.

"I think what made me really embrace my heritage was going to the social justice events sponsored by Katipunan [the Filipino organization at UC Riverside]," said Julian, a native of Eagle Rock. "Being Filipino wasn't just about hanging out and rehashing your neighborhood experiences. They cared about *real* issues. They rallied for Filipino American veterans' rights. We had Pilipino Culture Night, which helped people learn about Filipino history, culture, and language. It was everyone's chance to learn about themselves in ways that we never could before."

Pilipino Culture Nights, better known as PCNs, are annual showcases sponsored by Filipino student organizations throughout the country. Entirely student-produced, PCNs are Broadway-like productions that integrated a mosaic of cultural artistry—traditional Filipino folk dances (both indigenous and Spanish), hip-hop, chorus, and a capella—that all revolved around a set of story lines that pertained to some quintessential "Filipino American experience." PCN story lines typically explored such themes as immigrant assimilation, intergenerational conflicts, discovering one's roots, racial discrimination, and family dynamics, often culminating in some epiphany of cultural embrace. PCNs involved anywhere from fifty to more than a hundred student volunteers, many of whom spend nearly half a school year developing scripts, rehearsing songs and dances, building sets, and creating costumes. Many months and thousands of hours later, these students proudly debut their springtime show to an audience of their parents, relatives, fellow students, and local community members, who in turn greet them with flowers and regalia comparable to a typical graduation ceremony.

In addition to being an opportunity for cultural exploration and community building, PCNs also implicitly set the parameters for what it means to be "authentically" Filipino at the university. In an effort to solicit laughs and applause, producers of PCNs shoot for content they believe will resonate specifically with a Filipino audience. However, such decisions also have the potential to marginalize certain members who cannot relate to the story arc. "I have friends who aren't Catholic, and so they couldn't relate to all the religious references that were in the PCN," said one young woman. "She ended up feeling more uncomfortable, if anything." Some students were put off by the overly politicized tone of the PCNs. "The PCNs always talk about protesting some cause, but not everyone has the time to do those things," said Andre, referring to his Filipino friends who were busy working, taking care of parents or kids, or more committed to preparing for graduate school. "People always talk shit about the people who don't do PCN, saying shit like, 'They're not really down or really Filipino,'" he added. At times, some who were put off by the Filipino student organizations at their college used their neighborhood "street cred" as a rationale for not being involved. "I'm from Eagle Rock. I don't need to be in an organization to prove how Filipino I am," said Andre, who opted to spend his free time as an undergraduate preparing for the medical school entrance exam.

Rachel was also critical about the way Filipino student organizations, particularly during "PCN season," hindered their academic performance. Already disturbed by the attrition of her peers from Carson, she observed over the years the negative impact of being *too* involved. "That's when all the Filipinos go on academic probation," she noted about the months leading up to the PCN show. "The Filipino organization can become an academic distraction for folks that are in leadership. They ended up staying longer because they always had to withdraw from classes." Having practices of twelve hours or longer until dawn in the weeks preceding the big show are par for the course—they are essentially a rite of passage for many Filipino students, who often use participation in the PCN as a barometer for whether one is really "down" for the Filipino community. Despite her criticisms of Filipino student organizations, Rachel also came to realize the role of the university curriculum on Filipino underperformance and attrition, especially in her years as the director of the Filipino retention program. "I think Filipinos are generally unhappy about their classroom experience, and so they'll look for anything to distract them," she said. "They'll get involved things that are closer to their real lives than their academics because they [can't] connect school to their actual lives."

In the end, most had fond memories of their years of involvement with the Filipino student organization on campus. It provided an important space to find community and critically engage the meaning of Filipino identity in ways not afforded to them previous to college. Ultimately, the politicized meaning of Filipino identity influenced how Filipinos understood how they fit within the racial landscape of the university context.

From Pan-Asian to Pan-minority

Filipinos' status as both an underrepresented group and a politicized presence on campus affected how they viewed their ability to build connections with other groups. Stories like Rachel's and Erik's demonstrated how the sudden shift from model to "at-risk" students alienated Filipinos from their white and Asian peers. The activist and outreach efforts that grew out of Filipinos' relative sense of underrepresentation further distanced them from their white and Asian classmates, whom they would characterize as more privileged and, by extension, politically unaware. Of course, some Filipinos spoke about encounters with struggling white students or politically engaged Asian American student activists, but they referred to such individuals as anomalies to the collective whole of their group. As such, many Filipinos felt self-conscious and uncomfortable whenever they were in social settings that were predominantly white or Asian.

In contrast, Filipinos' social status within the campus allowed them to build rapport with other underrepresented minorities on campus, particularly with Latinos and African Americans. Many Latino and African American undergraduates at the University of California came from neighborhoods where their respective ethnic community had a strong presence. The most active and visible African American and Latino students also tended to be from predominantly minority communities because such neighborhood origins augmented their "street cred" and authenticity with their ethnic community on campus.[27] In this respect, Filipinos found themselves commiserating with African Americans and Latinos about the shared experience of moving from communities where they constituted a visible presence to a campus where they felt like "the representative" of their people. Erik spent several years volunteering for the Filipino retention program at UCLA, where he was able to see the similarities in Filipino, African American, and Latino educational experiences. "We were literally the group in between the African Student Union's and MEChA's [the Chicano–Latino student organization] retention project," he said, adding that their close proximity provided numerous opportunities to share "war stories" about life at UCLA.[28]

Another by-product of underrepresentation on campus was the racial stratification of college majors, something that Filipinos, African Americans, and Latinos all related to. No doubt, students of all racial backgrounds drop out of the most competitive majors on campus, such as the engineering and premed tracks. However, when whites and Asians dropped out of these tracks, there were still ample numbers of them in the major. In contrast, Filipino, African Americans, and Latinos all had disproportionately high rates of attrition from the science and engineering fields. "The narrative of Filipino students dropping out of the sciences was so common that it seemed to be featured in the PCN plot line every year," said Janice, one the few Filipinos in her year who managed not to drop out and to finish her degree in biological sciences. "The stereotype was that the *real* Asians were all science and engineering majors, but when it came to Filipinos, they were all in the 'social justice' majors like sociology," she said. In this respect, college majors functioned similarly to the academic tracking system in high school. The larger proportion of Filipinos in the liberal arts majors meant they were more likely to share classrooms and thus have more face time with their African American and Latino peers, especially because the buildings that housed these majors were physically separate from those housing the science and engineering departments.

Filipinos' neighborhood origins also facilitated their interactions with other underrepresented minorities, especially with Latinos. Having lived alongside Latinos (and with African Americans, for those from Carson), Filipinos possessed a certain level of proficiency with the experiences and sensibilities of other minority groups, which constituted a form of minority cultural capital.[29] As such, they had a level of access to social spaces within the college context not often afforded to whites and other Asians. Amid the culture shock he felt at UCLA, Erik spoke about the relief he felt being assigned to a Latino roommate in his predominantly white and Asian dormitory: "I was fortunate to have one of my roommates, this Mexican guy from Norwalk. We knew what it was like growing up in a Mexican area and going to school with Mexicans. Filipinos and Latinos just gelled," said Erik. "They even say I talk like a Mexican." Erik's cultural familiarity and racial performance made it easy for him to blend in with the Chicano students at campus, some of whom did not realize he was *not* Latino until he explicitly mentioned his Filipino heritage.

Having grown up with Latinos in Eagle Rock became an important form of social cachet for Alex, who attended Brown University, on the East Coast. At Brown, there were a large number of East Asian American students and a relatively smaller, but visible population of Latino students. Throughout his four years, there were practically no Filipinos who attended the university. When he moved to Brown, Alex first assumed he'd find his niche with the other Asian students, but he said, "It just never felt right." Instead, he found he was more comfortable with his Puerto Rican and Dominican American peers. He had this realization when he was invited to a party thrown by the Latino organization on campus:

I never felt out of place at the party, even though it was all Latinos. Funny enough. My one friend who was half Mexican but looked more white and was from like a bougie [rich], all-white town got flack for being there. They kept calling him "white boy." But with me, a bunch of the guys would come up to me and be like, "Oh what? You're Filipino? It's practically the same thing [as Latino]. We all got punked by Spain anyway, right?" Most of my friends in college ended up being Latino because they were the next-closest thing to Filipinos.

Alex was able to relate to many of the cultural experiences of his Latino friends—growing up in a neighborhood where Spanish was spoken, dealing with his parents constantly asking him whether he was going to Mass every Sunday, and feeling like they were "the only one" in their college classes. Moreover, Latinos at his school were quick to invoke the history of Spanish colonialism of Filipinos as a means of promoting a shared sense of peoplehood.[30] These were the building blocks of his closest friendships at Brown. In addition, because of his ability to code switch between the vernacular of urban men of color and "standard" English, it never seemed strange to others around him that all of his friends were Latino. In fact, most people at the university assumed that Alex was Latino until he told them otherwise (in part, because his last name was Aguilera).

Oddly enough, Alex said his friend Nathan had a totally different experience at Brown, even though he was part Mexican American. While Nathan had other Latino friends, Alex said Nathan found it far more difficult to become part of the Latino community at the college because he lacked the same cultural sensibilities and background that Alex possessed. Nathan had a "white" last name (Andrews), did not know a lick of Spanish, and could not relate to the cultural references the other Latinos made about growing up in an immigrant neighborhood. He also "looked more white" than Alex, which made his attempts to speak Spanish more laughable to the other Latinos. In contrast, Alex's ability to casually converse in Spanish (and his knowledge of Chicano slang) gave him a greater level of access to Latino social circles at Brown. "They even included me and the few other Filipinos in their organization's events," said Alex, "We [Filipinos] were even collaborators for the big '1898–1998 commemoration' that the Puerto Rican students sponsored to celebrate a hundred years of freedom from Spanish colonialism."

The political slant of Filipino student organizations at most colleges also facilitated a sense of connection even with Latinos who had had minimal interactions with Filipinos. Jorge, a Mexican American from a working-class community in California's Central Valley, joined MEChA, the largest Chicano student organization at UCLA, in his freshman year of college. Through participating on educational outreach programs, he developed close friendships with several members of Samahang:

> JORGE: MEChA and Samahang are sister organizations. We were always in the student activities center and constantly interacting with each other.
>
> A.O.: What was that like?
>
> JORGE: Their [Filipinos'] vibe, it was so much like us. The Filipinos remind me so much of home and my friends back home. I tried to analyze it before and I think the reason is because historically, the Philippines was conquered by the Spanish. Mexico was too and so our cultures are like a mixture of cultures. Our vibes are so similar. I don't know how to explain it. It's like second nature. Talking to Filipinos is like talking to someone back home. It's in the way we speak, the words we use, [and] our taste in music.

Many Filipinos and Mexican Americans spoke about the ease of interacting with one another because of an "unspoken" and "natural" connection, even if one could not necessarily explain it. Often times, being involved within student organizations like MEChA and Samahang allowed both Filipinos and Mexicans to become more keenly aware of their shared history of Spanish and American colonialism, which in turn became the explanation for these connections they "just knew" were there, a sense of commonality they "just felt instinctually."

For both Filipino and Mexican American students, their involvement in their respective ethnic organizations opened the door for historical and cultural similarities to become more salient.

The interactions between the members of MEChA and Samahang also influenced how Jorge understood Filipinos' standing with other Asian Americans:

> A.O.: Do you think that the Filipinos were like the other Asian American students at UCLA?
>
> JORGE: Not really. I don't see it. To me, Asians stick to themselves. Like when I see someone who looks Asian, I can tell right away if they are Filipino based on their voice, if they are more quiet, or if they're in their own space. Filipinos I can tell because they are very loud and down for their community.

Similar to the remarks made by Filipinos, Jorge's perception of other Asians was that they were more ethnically insular and more bookish, illustrating how his schema about Asian American identity was closely tied to the model minority stereotype. Such comments highlighted how the racial context of the university influenced the way Latinos' perceived Filipinos' racial position vis-à-vis other ethnic minorities on campus.

Ethnicity Off Campus

Unlike his peers who went away for college, Vince never experienced the same dilemma of worrying about whether Filipinos were "authentically" Asian. In fact, he never thought much of the question until I asked him about it specifically—a stark contrast to Filipinos like Erik and Joey, who were both also from Eagle Rock and had very strong opinions about the issue. Vince had even attended the same high school and church as Joey. Both had grown up wanting to be in the medical profession. How, then, did Vince and Joey come to have such different perspectives about Filipinos' racial position relative to other Asian Americans?

Much of the reason had to do with the way their academic lives were organized after high school. Upon graduating from Glenrock High School, Joey immediately went on to UCLA to pursue his degree in biology. At Glenrock, Filipinos dominated the honors classes. In contrast, Filipinos were "nowhere to be found" in the science classes at UCLA, even though many of his large lectures included upward of three hundred students. Throughout his four years as a biology major, all Joey could remember was that other Asians were able to hold their own while Filipinos could not. In fact, the numbers of Filipinos in the science majors seemed to drop with each passing year. In Joey's eyes, the "real Asians" were the ones who could cut it out academically in the toughest of science courses. By this measure, Joey felt that he and his other Filipino classmates were not "really Asian," at least within the context of UCLA.

Vince took many of the same courses as Joey at Glenrock. He also had grades good enough to go to any UC campus, even one as competitive as UCLA. "Three of my friends who had lower GPAs and fewer activities ended up at UCLA," he said. When it was time to apply to college, however, Vince's family had experienced some major financial difficulties. The eldest of four boys, Vince had watched his family go from financially stable to barely making ends meet. For two and a half years, his mother had been the sole breadwinner, as his father had struggled to find a stable job. "At the time, I had a job and I paid for most of my own expenses. I didn't want to spend sixty bucks a pop to apply to the UCs," he said. "I thought I'd just go to Cal State LA and pay $1,500 a quarter. It's cheaper. I don't know if you get the same education, but you get the same degree."

While Joey spent years as a student organizer for Samahang on campus, most of Vince's free time revolved around family. "I'm really close with my parents. I'm a big-time mama's boy," said Vince. A major reason he chose to study at Cal State LA after high school was to stay close to his parents and his three brothers. "Cal State LA was only thirty minutes away by side streets, and I was thinking I'd only be spending a little on gas each week," he reasoned. Vince also shifted his academic major from biology to nursing, which would allow him to contribute to the family household income sooner than a career in medicine. "Nursing wasn't my first choice, but I knew I wasn't gonna get a job with something like theater arts," said Vince, referring to the major he would have selected if he based his decision solely on passion.

Because most students at Cal State LA were also commuters, Vince developed few close ties with his peers in college. Throughout his undergraduate years, he was on campus only for class, rarely opting to attend events on campus, even ones sponsored by the Filipino student organization. Most of Vince's close friends were other Filipinos from his high school and his church. Given that he rarely encountered other Asians, Vince had little to say about them:

A.O.: What would you say your racial identity is?

VINCE: Filipino American, most definitely. That's who I am. I don't try to be something I'm not. My friends know their roots too. They don't try to stay away from it. They don't try to claim they're something else.

A.O.: What about if you're filling out a form and Filipino isn't on there?

VINCE: [Pauses] Hmm. I would pick Pacific Islander. [Longer pause]. I guess I never really thought about it.

In the end, Vince was indifferent about the choice between the Asian and Pacific Islander box—both had minimal resonance with his own sense of identity.

In contrast, Joey developed very strong feelings about which of these two categories he would select on a form:

A.O.: Do you ever identify as Asian American?

JOEY: No. I go by Filipino. I feel weird saying Asian American. I actually put Pacific Islander on my medical school apps. After UCLA, I check the disadvantaged box in everything.

A.O.: What do you see as different between Filipinos and other Asians?

JOEY: Filipinos are disadvantaged, but being Asian American is not seen as a disadvantage in higher education. The model minority myth, I apply to East Asians. I apply the immigrant dreams stereotype to Filipinos.

Joey's strong sentiments stemmed from his feelings of being marginalized in the courses dominated by his Asian American peers. He acknowledged that people saw him as Asian, but he never felt a sense of panethnic consciousness or solidarity with other Asians. Vince, in contrast, never really had to reflect on his identity beyond Filipino because his social world remained centered on his neighborhood context. Unlike Joey, whose social world transferred over to the UCLA campus, Vince never had to reconfigure the rules of race he had in his mind.[31] For him and other Filipinos who opted to commute to college, selecting Asian or Pacific Islander as their race was an unproblematic choice, even if it was the default option. Their lack of interactions with other Asian ethnicities meant that their status as Asian Americans was never really contested. As such, it made sense why Vince and other commuters had little need to question whether Filipinos were "really" Asian American.

College Racialization

Filipinos who left their neighborhoods to attend college found themselves in a new racial context. Much of their social lives before college revolved around their families and neighborhood friends, most of whom were Filipino as well. Upon entering the halls of the ivory tower, Filipinos met people from different ethnic and socioeconomic backgrounds, which forced them to confront their preconceived notions of race and class, based largely on their experiences growing up in middle-class minority neighborhoods.

Once their everyday existence moved from the neighborhood to the college campus, the rules of race changed. Filipinos became socially invested in a new environment where they were no longer the predominant Asian American group on campus. Whites and Asian Americans were the most visible groups, and Filipinos found themselves in the unfamiliar territory of being an underrepresented minority group. Confronted with this new reality, many found a home and community in the Filipino undergraduate organization on their campus, a place where they could be Filipino and explore Filipino identity without fear of feeling stigmatized. For many, the Filipino student organization provided the only space where their Filipinoness had any cachet. In contrast, Filipino identity felt like a liability not only in the classroom but also in settings where whites and other Asians dominated the social landscape.

Instead, the politicization and underrepresentation of Filipinos at many campuses gave them grounds to develop a shared consciousness with other underrepresented minorities. Although the educational arena once reinforced social boundaries between Filipinos and other minorities (via the racially stratified tracking system), they could empathize with each other's sense of marginalization and isolation vis-à-vis the whites and Asian on campus. Their status in the university system facilitated a shared narrative—feeling like the "only one" or the "representative" in their classes, navigating the fine line between their academic obligations and staying "down" with their community (both on campus and at home), and staying mindful of their social obligations with family back home. In addition, involvements in student organizations allowed Filipinos, and Latinos, to become more aware of their shared history and culture.

Filipinos whose social lives did not relocate to the college campus tended not to exercise the same reflexivity about race. For the most part, they remained separated from the campus communities and organizations that might force them to rethink their sense of racial membership. In the end, there were few social situations where their sense of Asian American identity was questioned, let alone threatened, given that their social lives remained firmly rooted in their families and neighborhoods.

7 Racial Dilemmas

WHEN IT CAME TO ETHNIC and racial identities, location was everything. The significance and meaning of Filipino identity often depended on social and institutional context. Being Filipino in the neighborhood was about family, whereas being Filipino in high school was about being a model student. The meanings that Filipinos applied to racial categories were similarly fluid. They might have associated Asian American identity with being less culturally assimilated into their neighborhood contexts and in another moment characterize Asian American identity as being the science geek perfectly acclimated to the academic rigors of college life. Filipinos might equate Latino identity with being family oriented and "super Catholic" in their neighborhoods, and then in the same breath associate it with being an "at-risk" student in the public school in the next town over. Just as the meanings of ethnicity and race were a matter of location, they could also be a matter of life stage. The meaning and symbolic value that Filipinos applied to their ethnic identity, as well as different racial categories, evolved from childhood to adolescence to young adulthood. The story of Eileen Aquino, a second-year medical student from Carson, demonstrates how the evolution of these meanings has much to do with the changing impact of ethnicity and race throughout the course of her personal and academic life.

Life in the Neighborhood

When Helen and Edwin Aquino moved to Carson from the Philippines, they were determined to create the perfect life for their children. Eileen was their firstborn of their three children. Both of her parents worked in health care. Like many other Filipina immigrants, her mother was a registered nurse. Her father, in turn, worked as a profusionist, a medical specialist who keeps the heart and lungs alive while physicians conduct cardiac surgeries. They both worked long hours, not only to make ends meet but also to create an image of success for their young children growing up. In many respects, her parents were her motivation for wanting to enter the medical field. Eileen said she knew pretty early on that she wanted to one day become a doctor.

Eileen's lofty ambitions had humble beginnings in what she called "backyard science." As a young girl, she spent many weekends accompanying her father to the beach, which was a short twenty-minute drive from their house. Eileen described her father as a strict man, and she remembered how much she loved their trips to the beach because they were among the rare moments growing up when she felt her dad was most relaxed. "I loved it," she said. "Back in the day, I was kind of scared of my dad, so maybe I loved it because I got to spend time with him." Amid the stress of working long hours, the beach trips were Mr. Aquino's opportunity to be his daughter's teacher. "I loved the ocean, and he explained everything to me," Eileen remembered fondly. "'These are sea urchins, these are sea anemones,' he'd say. He'd talk about the moon and how the tides are dictated by the lunar cycles. He'd talk about how certain animals in the tide pools are special because they can live in places that had no sun. He talked about how when it's low rise, they're exposed to the sun, and they adapt. I loved it because it was all this cool science stuff."

This love of science, coupled with the slight fear she had of her father, seemed to be a combination that served her well in school, especially since her parents were not always around when she was growing up. Both her parents worked more than forty hours a week. She remembered her mother's twelve-hour daily shifts from seven in the morning to seven at night, a schedule quite typical of many in the nursing profession. Since her parents were usually working when she was finished with school, most of her afternoons were spent at her grandparents' house. Unlike the strict gaze she felt with her father, it was not as difficult to sneak away from her grandfather to her friends in the neighborhood, most of whom were Filipino as well. "We had a lot of freedom," she said. "During that time when you're in that adolescent stage, you're messing around, hanging out after school, talking about boys, meeting boys, walking around, eating fast food."

Considering how unregulated her after-school regimen was, Eileen managed to pull off good grades. Again, part of the reason she did so had to do with her fear of being reprimanded. "I feel almost lucky," Eileen admitted. "What I mean is that out of all those friends, I was the smart one. I was the one who got good grades and straight As. I got in trouble if I got a B. My dad didn't yell at me necessarily, but he would call me out and say, 'Why didn't you get an A?' even in elementary school." Although her parents were not necessarily always around to motivate her in school on a daily basis, all Eileen had to do was look at her surroundings to realize how much her parents were dedicated to the well-being of her and her siblings. "We lived in a really nice house. It was two stories, had a beautiful backyard. My dad even had a BMW," she remembered. "We looked good." With the outward display of the American middle-class dream came the expectation that Eileen and her siblings would fully dedicate themselves to their schooling. "All throughout our lives, they've always had that value that all we had to do is go to school. Don't work, don't do anything, just go to school," said Eileen. From her point of view, this was a belief that was "typical among Asian families."

Having a nice house did not always shield Eileen and her siblings from trouble in the neighborhood. One of the distinctions that sociologists have made between white and minority middle-class communities is that the latter are more likely to regularly encounter criminal activity in their neighborhood, such as drug and gang activity. This distinction has much to do with the sustained connection that middle-class minorities have to people in nearby low-income neighborhoods, where illicit activities are commonplace daily occurrences.[1] This was especially relevant in the first home where Eileen grew up. While she said her neighborhood was "not crazy dangerous," she still remembered seeing gang members on occasion hanging out at her neighbors' homes. "Across the street from my house, one of my elementary friends was killed in a drive-by shooting," she remembered. "He was Mexican. He was a year older than me. Damn! That was a block away from my house! His brother was actually the target. His brother was the one in a gang." Her brother often quipped about the irony of their living situation: "Our house is so nice. It was in a cul-de-sac with a bunch of new model homes. Once you walk outside though, it can be *ghetto*," she remembered him saying to her. Beyond this incident, Eileen herself never really encountered any major trouble. Nonetheless, it was notable that she saw the occasional gang presence as part of the landscape, even in a relatively peaceful middle-class neighborhood like Carson.

Learning the Rules of Race

Within her first weeks at South Bay Middle School, Eileen knew that race was something she had to take into consideration. Like many of her counterparts from Carson and Eagle Rock, Eileen pointed to middle school as the first time where she and her classmates felt pressure from their peers to partition their friendships along racial lines. Prior to sixth grade, hanging out with her classmates who were Mexican or African American or white did not seem like a big deal. However, once she stepped onto the South Bay Middle School campus, interracial friendships became newsworthy. Sometimes they were even taboo. Eileen remembered one Latina friend in particular, Tania Roldan, who received a lot of flack for hanging out with a group of Filipina girls at the school. It was not long before Mexican girls at the school publicly derided Tania for being a "wannabe" who thought "she's Filipino and too good for the Mexicans." I got the sense from Eileen that at South Bay Middle School, it was less of a headache to maintain a group of friends in which everyone was of the same ethnic background.

In retrospect, Eileen felt that her teachers exacerbated the racial segregation among her classmates. It was evident from the start that teachers treated the Filipino students as the smart ones, as the ones with the most academic potential, as the ones who were the least likely to cause trouble. South Bay Middle School's tracking system helped further separate the students by race, although of course, the system was aimed to compartmentalize the students based on their skill level. Filipinos occupied the majority of the desks in the gifted and talented education classes; African Americans and Latinos remained in the regular or remedial classrooms. "When I was at South Bay Middle School, the Filipinos were the Asian ones," she said. Like many other Filipinos, Eileen felt more than comfortable using *Asian* as an academic descriptor rather than a cultural one, especially in the context of school.

It would not be until after college that Eileen would realize just *how* racially segregated South Bay Middle School actually was. "Recently, I looked up the demographics of my middle school, and it's like 62 percent Hispanic!" Eileen said, with a bit of surprise in her tone. "It was 18 percent Filipino, 10 percent black, and then 2 percent Asian and 2 percent white, and the rest, other." It seemed as if these numbers were newsworthy to her, even though she was a decade removed from middle school by this point. I inquired whether she was aware of her school's demographics at the time she was actually in middle school. "Well, I can't really say. I can't really say I felt that or experienced that because I was in this bubble," she said, in reference to being tracked in the honors classes. "I think there was such a divide. Mexicans were practically invisible to me." As I did in most other interviews, I asked Eileen whether she could give me an example of how teachers treated Filipinos, relative to the other minorities at the school. While she felt it to be true, Eileen had a little trouble conjuring up an example precisely because of the racial segregation at South Bay. "I can't even compare how teachers would treat the Mexican students," she said. "We just weren't in the same classes together." Eileen was not alone in this. Among most of the Filipinos who went to public school, there was a lack of consciousness about Mexicans' academic experiences in the tracking system. This awareness was par for the course for Filipinos, who possessed a certain privilege during their middle school and high school years by being dubbed the "smart ones" by their teachers and counselors.

When Eileen graduated from South Bay Middle School, her parents opted to send her to St. Adrian's High School, a diverse private Catholic school in nearby Torrance. While Eileen would have encountered similar racial hierarchies had she attended South Bay High School, the interracial dynamics of St. Adrian's were much different. "I didn't know the specific demographics, but at St. Adrian's, we embraced this idea that we were diverse," she said. "I think it was pretty even—black, white, Latino, and Asian, and granted all the people identified as Asian were Filipino. So I think the whole 'Filipino and Asian are synonymous' carried on." Eileen recalled that students still self-segregated along ethnic lines a lot, but that these divisions did not correlate with any overt special treatment from school administrators: "You could see that it was segregated, but we were more happy-go-lucky about it. It wasn't all like, 'You belong here and you belong there,' like it was in public school." St. Adrian's had a unique strategy to ensure that students interacted across racial lines—it banned ethnic-based student clubs. The principal and other administrators felt that such organizations reinforced ethnic separation. "When I was at St. Adrian's, the interesting thing is that they didn't allow for ethnic student groups," she recalled. "Like, you can't have a Filipino club. You can't have an African American club. They thought it promoted segregation." At the time, Eileen had mixed feelings about the campus policy. On the one hand, she felt that it was "bullshit," but on the other, she could sympathize a bit with the school's desire to not codify racial difference. Years later, though, Eileen felt that such policies were a farce that only nominally celebrated this idea at St. Adrian's: "Oh, we're so diverse and we all get along."

Looking back, Eileen remembered some subtle distinctions in how students of different racial backgrounds were perceived. While St. Adrian's High School did not have a tracking system, the Advanced Placement classes served as a litmus test for determining who were the "hard workers" of the student body. Eileen took as many Advanced Placement (AP) courses as her schedule would allow, and so it was no surprise to anyone at her school when she was accepted to UC Berkeley, one of the most selective and prestigious public universities in the country. However, when an African American classmate who took no AP classes also received an acceptance letter to UC Berkeley, other students at St. Adrian's were quick to dismiss her accomplishment, including Eileen herself. "I remember this black girl in my high school, and she was in none of my AP or honors classes, but she got into UC Berkeley," said Eileen. "I remember thinking to myself, 'What the hell? Why did *she* get in? She didn't take advantage of the AP and honors classes.'" Eileen's friends were similarly judgmental when she brought up her black classmate's acceptance to Berkeley. "Not to hate or anything, but why did she get in?" she remembered asking her friend. "Affirmative action. It's because she's black," the friend told Eileen, without an ounce of hesitation. At that point, however, Eileen had yet to experience any major setbacks in her own pathway to becoming a doctor. This all changed once Eileen stepped foot into the classrooms of UC Berkeley.

The Road to Berkeley

Eileen's journey to UC Berkeley was nothing short of serendipitous. During high school, she had no intention of applying to the school. For most of her high school life, she had her heart set on going to UC San Diego, a campus known for its world-renowned science programs. It did not hurt that the campus was only about a two-hour drive south from Carson: Eileen admittedly wanted to stay close to her siblings and parents. The day she planned to mail her application, her mother happened to ask her where she was applying. "I applied to UCSD and UCLA because it was close, but Berkeley was not," she said. "My mom was like, 'Why don't you check the box for Berkeley?" Initially, Eileen refused to oblige her mom's suggestion. "I don't want to waste forty bucks," she remembered saying. "It's just a box. You'll never know until you try, and it's only forty dollars," her mother persisted. "It was an accident!" Eileen admitted of her decision to actually apply.

Beyond that specific moment, her parents' attitude toward her college ambitions was quite laissez-faire. "Honestly, that was one of the few times that my parents were involved in my decisions," Eileen said. I asked Eileen whether her mother's insistence had to do with the fact that UC Berkeley was consistently ranked as one of the nation's top college. It was not. Her mother had just heard about two other girls in the neighborhood from South Bay High School who had gone to Berkeley a few years prior. In fact, like other Filipino parents, Eileen's father had preferred she attended nearby UCLA, from which she had also received an acceptance. In the end, both her mother and father left it to her. "My parents always trusted me," she said. In May of her senior year of high school, Eileen chose UC Berkeley for college.

Unbeknownst to Eileen, the racial context of UC Berkeley would look dramatically different from the schools she had attended back in Los Angeles. While Filipinos were "the Asian ones" for the first eighteen years of her life, this was certainly not the case at UC Berkeley. Filipinos students were underrepresented, meaning that their proportional representation at the campus was lower than that within the larger state. In 2000, the year that Eileen entered UC Berkeley, 135 of the 3,735 incoming freshman—a mere 3.5 percent—were Filipino. Chinese Americans, whose population in the state was roughly the same as Filipinos, had nearly six times the number of incoming freshmen at Berkeley.[2] In that year, a number as meager as 135 even seemed like an accomplishment by some measures. Five years prior, the number of Filipino incoming freshmen was less than half that figure. Only fifty-eight of the first-year students were Filipino, which was just over

1.5 percent of the freshmen class. For comparison's sake, there were nearly *twelve times* as many Chinese American first-year students. Although Filipinos were not as underrepresented as Mexican Americans and African Americans, it was easy to see why Filipino undergraduates *felt* underrepresented, especially because many came from neighborhoods and schools where they were the dominant Asian American population.

This message of Filipino underrepresentation was embedded within the language of the Filipino student organizations that had recruited Eileen to come to UC Berkeley once she was officially accepted. In the spring of her senior year of high school, Eileen had visited the Berkeley campus and attended an event sponsored by the Filipino undergraduate recruitment and retention organization. She distinctly remembered the skepticism she felt when the Filipino students spoke candidly about the underrepresentation of Filipinos at the campus. There was one icebreaker activity in particular that provoked her aversion:

> You know what's funny? When I was recruited to UC Berkeley, they asked us this question during an activity: "Who do you mostly identify with besides Filipinos? Blacks, Latinos, Asians, or whites?" And I remember at the time thinking to myself, "Well, duh, Asian. How could you even ask that question? That's a stupid question."

Of course, the question made little sense for Eileen at the time. She was from Carson, where more than eight of every ten Asian Americans were of Filipino heritage. However, her tune would quickly change once she joined the sea of premed students in the fall of that same year. Within her first few weeks of college, her lifelong love for science would be put to the test—and along with that, her sense of Asian American identity.

Am I *Really* Asian? Not at UC Berkeley

Like most other aspiring premeds, Eileen never thought twice about enrolling in a biology class in her first semester at Berkeley—that is, until she stepped foot into the classroom for the first time. Everything was different from the more intimate classroom settings at St. Adrian's High School. As was the case in most public universities, the classroom seemed enormous. There were hundreds of students, many premed as well, who were enrolled in the class with Eileen. Not surprisingly, the feeling of anonymity in the large lecture hall made it difficult for her to connect with the professor. After all, Eileen felt there was not much that would distinguish her enough from the other students in the class to spark up a conversation with the professor. She even questioned her ability to maintain a conversation with the professor. Unlike most of her classmates, she had not taken a single Advanced Placement science course during high school. During her time at St. Adrian's, the school did not offer them.

Not having taken AP Biology was not the only thing that distinguished Eileen from her classmates. Although there were many other Asian American freshmen in her biology class, Eileen felt she could not relate, even though she had always identified as Asian growing up. From where she sat, it seemed that most of her classmates were East Asian or South Asian. There were very few who were Filipino. She had never really thought much about the differences among Asian American groups—after all, Filipinos were the Asian ones in Carson—but being in this class prompted her to have a change of heart: "I couldn't connect with my fellow students, and at the time, I couldn't admit this, but I felt like I couldn't relate." Part of the difficulty came from her perception that the other Asians were more ethnically cliquey. "I just felt like all the Chinese students stuck together, and all the South Asians stuck together," Eileen said. "Who could I stick with? There weren't a lot of Filipinos in science. I mean, there were some, but for some reason, I didn't gravitate to them. I just felt really isolated." At this point in our conversation, Eileen began to cry. Even nine years after the experience, the memory of feeling isolated in her biology class still managed to overwhelm her. It would be the first of many science classes in which she would feel this same way.

It was not just the ethnic differences with her classmates that provoked her emotions. Eileen's classroom experiences on the premed track were incredibly rocky. For the first two years, Eileen struggled to get a C in most of her science courses—she did swing a B here and there. It did not help that Eileen felt homesick for much of her freshmen and sophomore year at UC Berkeley. At the time, Eileen's parents were experiencing financial difficulties. Her father had been on disability for some time as the result of an injury at his job. Even more difficult was the fact that her younger brother and sister had recently come out as gay, which was a difficult thing for her parents to accept. On the nights that most of her classmates were preparing for midterm examinations, Eileen often found herself mitigating conflicts between her parents and her siblings, even though she lived nearly four hundred miles away from home. "What happened was that I did poorly in science," she said, tears flowing from her eyes at this point, "I think because I felt really shitty. I don't think I can even describe to you how crappy I felt being unsuccessful in science and feeling that I couldn't really connect with anyone in science."

I began to notice that there was something compelling about the *way* she told her story. Sitting in front of me was not a young woman crying because she felt entitled to good grades. This was a young woman who was shedding tears of frustration and sadness about being one of the few Filipinos in the sciences. Maybe I recognized something in her story seeing as how I was one of just a handful of Filipino sociology graduate students (and now professors) in the entire country. There was something in her story that triggered an awareness of my own feelings of isolation, and I began to cry myself.

As a nineteen-year-old sophomore, Eileen struggled to understand why she was doing so poorly in her sciences classes. "This is where my biases come out," she said. "The Chinese and the Indian students were the ones doing well. That's how I perceived it. They were the ones who were smart. They were getting the As." She laughed a bit at her own willingness to engage in such blatant stereotyping. Regardless, those were the genuine thoughts she was having at that time. I asked her whether she could at least bond with the few Filipinos that were in her science classes. "There weren't a lot of Filipinos in the sciences, and the ones that were there didn't do well. Most of the Filipinos I knew had to retake their classes over," Eileen said. The lack of Filipino role models only made her more conscious of their collective struggles in the sciences:

> EILEEN: At the end of the day, there weren't a lot of Filipinos who were academics, and there weren't a lot of Filipinos who were physicians. Filipinos are not overrepresented in those areas. They're *underrepresented*, and that's why I felt, "Am I Asian or am I not?" Because I know in terms of Chinese Americans, they're overrepresented in the sciences and in medicine, for the proportion that they represent in the population at least.
>
> A.O.: So you questioned whether you were Asian?
>
> EILEEN: In middle school and high school, Filipinos were the model minorities. If you're Asian, then you're probably smart, you're probably good at math, you're probably good at science. I had an identity crisis when I was in Berkeley. Like am I *really* Asian? When people would joke about Berkeley, they would say, "It's so Asian. There are so many Asians at Berkeley and they're all doing science. Oh, MCB [molecular cell biology majors]? It's mostly Asian, and they're all doing well." Well, that wasn't me.

Eileen's assessments of Filipino underrepresentation were accurate. At the time she was at UC Berkeley, there were only two Filipino American faculty members in the entire university.[3] The academic marginalization of Filipinos in turn made her question her identity as an Asian American, something she had never done prior to arriving at UC Berkeley. The experience of not doing well in the sciences, both by herself and by her fellow Filipinos, was incongruent with the broader stereotypes of what it meant to be Asian American at UC Berkeley. In turn, this inconsistency prompted her to raise questions about the way she had conceptualized her own racial identity.

Amid these struggles, Eileen found some solace with the larger Filipino undergraduate community at Berkeley, who outside of the science departments, appeared to be a thriving, visible presence on the campus landscape, particularly among the organizations of students of color. She joined several Filipino student organizations, including one that specialized in supporting those who wanted to pursue careers in health. She participated in the annual Pilipino Culture Night as a dancer, which gave her the opportunity to perform Filipino folk dances for the first time in her life. Eileen's involvement with the Filipino groups on campus, whether they were working on political activism or educational outreach to high school students, provided an outlet—at least on a social level. They "got it" when she explained she had to be there for her parents and her siblings, even if that meant spending long hours on the phone instead of studying for midterms. They were her family away from family.

In contrast, getting involved with the Filipino organizations on campus felt like a double-edged sword. While her friends in the Filipino clubs provided Eileen with much needed emotional support, they offered very little on the academic front, particularly as a science and premed student. There were even a few moments when Eileen felt that her involvement deterred her academic progress. The discourse and the culture of the Filipino organizations on campus were not necessarily conducive to doing well in the sciences. "I was talking to another Filipino student in the sciences once, and we were talking about how in college, all the Filipinos are doing all this social justice and humanities stuff, but they're not doing science," Eileen said.

While her friends in the humanities and social sciences could integrate their classroom experiences with their involvements with the Filipino club's social activism, the same could not be said for the Filipinos in the science and engineering majors. Attending a protest on behalf of Filipino World War II veterans enhanced the political knowledge of the Filipino history major. Tutoring and outreaching to high school youth in the local Bay Area was good experience for Filipinos intending to become teachers. Going to spoken-word events in nearby Oakland helped the Filipino ethnic studies major understand the role of cultural expression in social activism. In contrast, none of these "typical" activities sponsored by the Filipino organization necessarily enhanced Eileen's experience as a biology major. In addition, the logistics of the science major, particularly early morning classes and lab assignments, made it all the more challenging for Eileen to participate in these activities in the first place. Eileen acknowledged that her friends were supportive on the surface, but when she could not attend these events, there were moments when they also passive aggressively voiced their discontent. "They were always like, 'Oh, Eileen's in the library again,' and they were kind of hating on that. She can't hang out because she's in the library," Eileen said, mimicking the sarcasm she observed from other Filipinos. I asked her whether she cared or brushed off the sarcasm. "I did care. I felt kind of bad when I was in the library. I felt they didn't understand what I had to do to do well in the science classes," she said. She conceded, however, that she did her best to stay involved in the programs sponsored by the Filipino student organization even if the events had little to do with enhancing her progress as a science major. According to her, the Filipino club on campus was "the cool thing to do" and what "Filipinos were supposed to do."

Participating in the annual Pilipino Culture Night—a musical production in the spring semester—was one such major rite of passage that Filipinos were "supposed" to do. At UC Berkeley, Pilipino Culture Nights involved nearly a hundred Filipino undergraduate students each year, from scriptwriters to actors, singers, musicians, dancers, stagehands, and artists. The production narrated one main story line about Filipino American history and contemporary issues, all threaded together with dramatic dialogue, comedy, song, and dance. Often, the story line was about the "typical" experiences of Filipino young adults, such as intergenerational conflict, rediscovering one's roots, or dealing with racial discrimination. The amount of work entailed was overwhelming for not only Eileen but also all of the students involved in the production. One of her friends who worked as an academic adviser for the Filipino retention center made a somewhat truthful joke that "PCN season was when all of the Filipino students see their grades suffer." To make matters more challenging, Eileen said that her PCN responsibilities, even in the minor role of being a dancer, were almost always mutually exclusive from their academic obligations. As the night of the big show approached, it was custom for the dancers to rehearse for long hours after their classes. Very often, they would run through dance routines several times over until four or five in the morning. In the final two weeks, these types of practices were held three to four times a week. So while most Filipinos, including Eileen, found the PCN experience culturally fulfilling, they also found it emotionally draining. "You have to be dedicated. You have to show up," Eileen said. To drop out of the PCN midproduction would compromise one's social standing in the Filipino community at UC Berkeley, perhaps even worse than having never signed up in the first place.

Part of the mission of the PCN productions was to showcase the real-life experiences of the Filipino students at UC Berkeley. Ironically, Eileen never felt that her story—the story of a struggling Filipino science major—was ever reflected in the story arc of the PCN shows:

> There's this theme reflected a lot in PCNs, and it reflects the frequent dialogue of Filipinos in college. The story is always of "my parents want me to be a doctor or my parents want me to go into science, but no! I want to pursue sociology!" There's this culture of defecting from science. So what do you do if you actually want to pursue science or pursue medicine? If you're watching the PCNs and the Filipino club dialogues, how does that make you feel as a science Filipino? . . . The theme in a PCN is always the parents asking their children, "Why don't you become a doctor?" or "Why don't you become an engineer?" And the story is always, "No, I want to do what I love." I felt left out because I wanted to be in science. That's what I had to do to be a doctor.

This culture of "defecting from science" made it difficult for Eileen to relate to other Asian Americans on campus. Eileen distinctly remembered an awkward conversation she had with a Chinese American classmate after taking an exam for her molecular cell biology class. Her classmate approached her after the exam to commiserate about the woes of being a molecular cell biology (MCB) major, known to be among the most rigorous majors in the university. "You know how it is for us Asians. When we go to Berkeley, we do molecular cell biology," her Chinese American classmate said to her. Eileen was surprised by the comment. "I was in disbelief!" she said. "She said that comment like, 'Oh, you know how it is.' As if it were typical for Filipinos to major in MCB. Well, I wish that were the case for me, but that was a total assumption." Again, the mismatch between the academic experiences of Filipinos and other Asians on campus prompted Eileen to seriously question whether she was "truly" Asian American.

The Irony of Asian American Studies

In the midst of her academic struggles, Eileen had heard about Asian American studies from a classmate at UC Berkeley early on in her college career. Before college, the idea of studying Asian Americans in the actual classroom was a foreign concept. Beyond the nominally celebrated Black History Month, her previous schools did not do much to encourage the exploration of the history of Asian Americans, Filipinos, or immigrants in general—an odd trend in a city where the vast majority of young students come from immigrant families and communities. "You *have* to take Asian American studies. I learned so much about myself," her classmate told her. "The idea just stuck," Eileen said. Although she did not know much about what they entailed, Asian American studies courses seemed like a good idea. In those spaces, Eileen's life experience had real academic value, something that she was not at all privy to in any of her science courses.

Eileen could still remember her very first assignment in her very first Asian American studies class. "We had to interview an immigrant, so I decided to interview my dad," she said, implying that the choice was an arbitrary one. "That's when I found out that he was a physician!" For the first eighteen years of her life, Eileen had no knowledge of the fact that her father had even attended medical school, let alone had practiced medicine in the Philippines for a number of years before migrating to the United States. For most of her life, she had thought that he was a lab technician who worked his way up to being a profusionist. However, the reality was that her father had experienced occupational downgrade, a widespread phenomenon among immigrant professionals who hold their advanced degrees and licenses from their home countries.[4] Unfortunately, the American medical establishment did not recognize her father's medical license from the Philippines. In turn, having a family to support made it even more challenging for Eileen's father to find time to prepare for the rigorous exams needed to become a board-certified physician in the United States. Learning that her father was a physician who could no longer practice medicine instilled a greater sense of determination in Eileen to not give up on medicine, despite her continued struggles in her science classes.

Eileen decided to pursue more courses in Asian American studies, and she learned more and more about the harsh realities of structural inequality that affected minority groups beyond her family. With each class she took, she found herself reflecting and reinterpreting the life experiences she had before UC Berkeley. "We learned about ideas of power and the need to level the playing field. I learned through Asian American studies classes that we have a lot of subtle biases, and those are just as bad as [biases] that are overt. I think that's where I started to unlearn and look at the times I've been racist or biased," said Eileen. She then called herself out on the way she mischaracterized the accomplishment of her African American classmate in high school. "As a matter of fact, I was very racist in high school. Oh my God, I feel so horrible about the way I judged her," she confessed. "I'm so glad I unlearned that." Another major reason that Eileen was now able to commiserate with the classmate she once dismissed was her own ability to know what it felt like to be "the only one." With the help of the ethnic studies curriculum, Eileen began drawing parallels between her the difficulties she faced in her science courses at Berkeley with the experiences of her African American and Latino classmates back in St. Adrian's High School and South Bay Middle School.

What was ironic about her Asian American studies courses, however, was that they made her feel more distant from other Asian American groups on campus. When Asian American activists rallied to establish Asian American studies college classes, one of their main intentions was to cultivate a sense of shared peoplehood among the different national origin groups. Asian American studies courses intended to draw attention to the shared experiences of racism faced by Chinese, Japanese, and Filipino Americans, who prior to the 1960s had not commonly seen themselves as part of the same racial collective.[5] For Eileen, her Asian American studies courses sometimes had the opposite effect—they occasionally made the cultural differences between Filipinos and her Asian American classmates more salient. When she walked into her first Asian American studies classroom, she looked at her classmates and found that the majority of them were of East Asian descent, not Filipino. "When I went in, and started going to these classes with Chinese people for the first time, I thought, 'Whoa, wait a minute. Are *they* Asian or am *I* Asian?" she remembered. I inquired why she did not feel a sense of connection with her other Asian American classmates:

> A.O.: Why couldn't you both be Asian? Why couldn't you be under the same umbrella?
>
> EILEEN: I can't pinpoint what it is. My friend Lynette put it perfectly. She had the same feeling about Asian American studies. She said, "I felt that there was a difference between those who were Chinese and those who were Filipino. It just *felt* different. I think because a lot of the 'Asian American experiences' that we read about in our class talked about language. The other Asians would talk about their parents only being able to speak Mandarin or Vietnamese and having to be the mediator between two cultures—*that* was the Asian American experience. But I felt that

wasn't the case for me. I was like, 'You know, my parents speak English just fine.'"

Eileen and her Filipino classmate Lynette took Asian American studies because it gave them the opportunity to learn about themselves and their own history. Eileen's assignment to interview an immigrant exemplified how these spaces allowed her to explore her Filipino identity in ways her previous schooling did not allow. However, as Lynette suggested, exploring Filipino history identity did not necessarily translate into embracing Asian American identity. In many respects, her East Asian classmates implicitly essentialized Asian American experiences in such a way that made Eileen feel boxed out, especially when it came to being bilingual or bicultural. "I get the idea of not feeling fully Asian or fully American, but I just didn't feel it in the same way the Chinese students felt it," Eileen admitted. "There was just something different."

For Eileen, both her science and Asian American studies courses seemed to work in conjunction to deter her from identifying with other Asian Americans. By failing to excel in her science courses, Eileen fell short of the "model minority" stereotype that was often applied to other Asian Americans of other ethnicities at UC Berkeley. At times, she overheard other Asian American students speak candidly about the academic differences between Filipinos and other Asians. "I knew a Thai guy who had gone to school with Chinese and Koreans, as well as Filipinos," Eileen said. "We talked about this issue several times. He told me that he wouldn't have liked me if he met me back when we were in high school. He said all of the Filipinos growing up were the cool Asians. They were into dance. While the *Asian* Asians were all doing SAT prep." Observing the differences in Filipinos' and other Asians' educational lives made Eileen more cognizant of the cultural differences between them. She eventually started to attribute the educational differences to culture:

The Asian stereotype that the other Asians talked about had to do with their parents. "My parents were always watching over me, and they were always on my back," they'd say. I mean it was school first with my parents, and it was important and all, but it wasn't like they were on my back like making sure I was in my room, in the library, and that I would get private tutoring, SAT prep, making sure I took all the SAT classes possible. I didn't get the coaching that the Asian stereotype got.

Eileen noted that this narrative was "typical" among the other Chinese and Korean American classmates in her Asian American studies classes. The more she heard such stories, the more she came to view Asian American identity as an inaccurate descriptor for herself and other Filipinos.

Becoming a Person of Color

At UC Berkeley, race seemed omnipresent in Eileen's classes and her extracurricular involvements. It even shaped the way Eileen viewed her chances of becoming a doctor. Early on in her college career, the outlook was pessimistic. With subpar science grades, Eileen knew by her second year that her grade point average was far below that of the typical medical school applicant. "I got As in Asian American studies, but I got a D in calculus and a C– in organic chemistry," she said. Even one of her academic counselors at UC Berkeley tried to dissuade her from pursuing medicine. "You know, Eileen? You're a freshman, and you know it looks like you didn't do so well in your science classes. Maybe science just isn't for you," her adviser said, with a tone seemingly riddled with more condescendence than concern. "Wow," Eileen thought to herself. "I really took it to heart." Many years later, the irritation on Eileen's face seemed as fresh as the day she first heard these words. "Looking back, she should have just asked me if I was going to tutoring or whether anything was going on at home," she continued. "Or maybe she should have asked what my science background was and whether I took AP [science] classes. I would have said no. That's what she should have done."

Despite feeling discouraged from her counselors, Eileen persevered through the rigorous requirements of the biology major. In her third year, she met Professor Howard Reed, an African American endocrinology scholar. Professor Reed's class was the first place where Eileen felt she really belonged in the major, largely because of Reed's unique teaching style:

> I loved the class. He was a great teacher, and he had such a different approach to teaching. He was personal. We were learning about the hormone systems of the human body, and he would talk about his daughter, and how she couldn't pee in the desert because of the endocrinological systems that hindered urine. I also knew his research was socially relevant—about how pesticides affect the reproductive systems of frogs. He said he used to consult for the company that made the pesticides, but when he found these results, they tried to shut him up, and he was a scientist who fought against the big bad guy.
>
> It totally changed how I approached my studying. I felt more connected. I felt like I could connect with him. Like for me, family was important to me, and obviously, his family was important to him. He talked about how he integrated research with his family and social justice. He talked about his wife, who's Korean, and how when they were married, they disowned her because he was black. I was so personally connected to Professor Reed and his story.

Prior to meeting Professor Reed, Eileen had always seen family and social justice as incongruent with science. Professor Reed debunked this, and he placed race and diversity issues at the front and center of his class discussions in ways Eileen did not think possible before.

Eileen excelled in his endocrinology class, and Professor Reed invited her to enroll in a graduate seminar in her junior year at UC Berkeley. She continued to do well in class, and midway through the semester, Professor Reed emailed Eileen to become part of his research team, a position that would have been coveted by most other undergraduates in the major. However, Eileen never responded. She was too intimidated to respond to Professor Reed's invitation, and she feared that he would "discover" that she was less intelligent than he had perceived. "Oh my God, is he for real?" she thought. "Does he really want me? I got scared. I didn't follow through with him. He had to be wrong about me. He had to have had this wrong impression of me. I was so sure that he had made a mistake that I never followed up." Throughout most of career at Berkeley, Eileen had seen herself as the "dumb one" in all of her science classes. It would be an entire year until she would encounter Professor Reed—at her college graduation.

At her graduation ceremony, she spotted Professor Reed. He was dressed in his doctoral gown and hood. Seeing Professor Reed, an African American professor dressed in professorial regalia, Eileen had an epiphany. "He had such an impact on my academic career," she said. "I never thought scientists could be like Professor Reed, and I admired him. So I approached him, and I told him how much his invitation to work in his lab meant to me, and how sorry I was that I never followed up." Professor Reed's response was something that Eileen would never forget. "You know, Eileen, when you didn't respond, I just thought you weren't interested. If you want something, you have to go for it. You have to fight for it." Professor Reed gave Eileen a second chance, and she spent the next year working as a researcher for his endocrinology lab.

Eileen's experience in Professor Reed's lab helped her earn admission to San Francisco State University's master's program in biology. There, she began working with Professor Magdalena Rios, a Latina biologist and close colleague of Professor Reed. Meeting Professor Rios represented another turning point for Eileen. With the exception of Professor Rios, Eileen said many of her professors were patronizing at best. "The white faculty [at Berkeley and San Francisco State] had good intentions, but treated [students of color] like we were a charity case," Eileen said. "They were so paternalistic." Professor Rios's mentorship was different. "You're going to be a scientific researcher," Professor Rios often told Eileen, "I'm not going to give you grunt work. I'm going to give you work that is for a budding scientist because one day, you're going to be me, if not better." As Eileen's mentor, Professor Rios gave her opportunities to conduct and present research, but at the same time, she also taught Eileen how to navigate the science world as a woman of color whose credentials and abilities would constantly be called into question by her peers. As a Latina from an immigrant family herself, Professor Rios also made sure to value Eileen's connection with her family as an asset of support rather than a distraction from her academic success. "I appreciate how she knew me not only as a graduate student but also personally as a minority student who had family, parents, brothers, and sisters that I had issues with," Eileen said. "She helped me stay on track toward earning my degree, even though my family didn't always understand what I was doing." The three years of mentorship that Eileen received from Professor Rios made a world of difference. Eileen graduated from San Francisco State with nearly a 4.0 grade point average, and she was recognized as one of the four most outstanding graduate students in the College of Science and Engineering.

In the absence of Filipino role models in the science and medical field, Eileen turned to Professor Reed and Professor Rios. Everything about their respective narratives resonated with her experiences as a science major at UC Berkeley and an aspiring physician—the need to incorporate the everyday needs of their families into their daily work life, the need to infuse social justice for the community into their careers, and the feeling of being "the only one" amid a crowd of white and East Asian scientists and doctors. As she moved further in her education, Eileen came to identify more strongly with African American and Latino mentors and peers than with the Asian Americans she encountered—a stark shift from her racial orientation during high school. This distance that she felt with Asian Americans grew even greater once her pathway to medical school officially began.

Racial Dilemmas in Medical School

With her master's degree in hand, Eileen set her sights on applying to medical school. Applying to medical school was a grueling experience by virtue of its inherent competitiveness, especially for someone like Eileen who wanted to stay in California. For instance, the medical schools at Stanford, UCLA, and UC San Francisco—three of the top programs in the state—each receive more than seven thousand applications annually, and fewer than 4 percent of applicants are admitted each year.[6] Despite her initial optimism, Eileen's journey to medical school was a struggle from the very beginning.

Shortly after her final year of her master's program, Eileen took the rigorous MCAT examination, the medical school entrance exam that most prospective applicants spend more than a year preparing for. In her first attempt, Eileen earned a score of 28, which placed her in the 60th percentile of all MCAT test takers. Although her score was not highly competitive—it was well below the mean score of incoming students at most medical schools—it was not a deal breaker either. She hoped that her extensive research experiences and her passion to pursue community health would give her an edge in the process. Unfortunately, in her first attempt at applying, Eileen's best outcome was a position on the waiting list at UC Irvine School of Medicine.

Eileen was heartbroken. She decided to forgo her application for the following year and dedicate a full year and a half to preparing for the MCAT examination. During her time off, she held an office job that would give her the freedom to study for the MCAT and to conduct additional research on how to successfully craft her medical school application. Having been interviewed at programs as prestigious and competitive as UCLA and UC San Francisco, Eileen tried to maintain her composure in spite of the devastation of being rejected. "I got wait-listed at UC [Irvine] and I interviewed at really prestigious universities, so I knew I was on the right track," she said. Eileen contacted the medical schools at which she interviewed, requested feedback, and her reviewers unanimously agreed that her biggest shortcoming had been her MCAT score, which fueled her motivation to study even harder than the first time she took the test. In her second attempt, Eileen made a remarkable improvement—her score increased by six points to a 34, which placed her in the 92nd percentile of MCAT test takers. After this incredible feat, she felt ready to give her medical school dreams another shot.

However, Eileen encountered new dilemmas from the moment she filled out her medical school application. In the year before she applied a second time, she did some research on acceptance rates of Filipino medical school applicants. The statistics did not paint an optimistic picture. When she was applying the second time, Eileen sifted through the Medical School Admissions Requirement (MSAR) data, published by the Association of American Medical Colleges. According to the MSAR, about 20 percent of medical school students were Asian American, which was more than double the number of African Americans and Latinos combined.[7] However, when she disaggregated the proportion of Filipino applicants, she found that they were sorely underrepresented. "I went so far as to break down the numbers of Filipinos versus Korean, South Asian, Chinese, Vietnamese on the MSAR and on the census," she said, with a look of frustration. "I looked at our numbers to see if the percentages matched. We were disproportionately lower." Among Asian American medical students at the University of California, only 6 percent are Filipino, even though Filipinos constitute a quarter of the Asian American population in the state.[8] There were significantly more medical students who were of Chinese (33 percent), Indian (18 percent), Vietnamese (12 percent), and Korean (12 percent), despite the fact that Filipinos outnumbered all of these groups. In other words, the statistics were clear that Filipinos were an underrepresented group, at least with respect to medical school.

Unfortunately, the Association of American Medical Colleges thought differently. Given the statistics she shared with me, I asked Eileen how she felt about choosing "Asian" as her racial background on the medical school application. It was evident on her face that this experience aggravated her a great deal, even retrospectively:

EILEEN: God! I still feel very frustrated with that [having to pick a race]. I remember there was one secondary application that I had to turn in for a school, and it asked, "Are you an underrepre-

sented minority?" And I was like, "Hell, yeah," because Filipinos are underrepresented in medical schools. And then when
I clicked "yes," it prompted me to select from this drop-down
menu, and of course, Filipino was not there. I tried every which
way. I looked for an "Other" option, and there wasn't one, and
eventually I had to go back and click "no," and say I'm not an
underrepresented minority.

A.O.: What did that do to you?

EILEEN: It was frustrating. I just had to click "no" and say, "That's
not what society defines me as." And although I know the truth, I
have to be OK with that.

Eileen's anger with the mere task of selecting her race exemplified the
dissonance that she felt with the racial category of "Asian." Although
just a few years earlier Eileen had never questioned her status as an
Asian American, her difficulties in the educational pipeline, particularly as an undergraduate, prompted her to think otherwise. At different moments, Eileen acknowledged that not all Asians were stellar
in their academics, but throughout our conversation, it was evident
that the stereotype of the model minority overwhelmingly colored her
notion of what it meant to be Asian American.

Fortunately, in her second attempt, Eileen was able to earn a place
at the UCLA School of Medicine. As the MSAR statistics suggested,
she was one of only a handful Filipino medical students in the program. Asian American medical students constituted nearly 40 percent of the student body at the UCLA School of Medicine,[9] but Eileen
could count the number of Filipinos on one hand. "There are only
three Filipinos in my class of about 165 students," Eileen pointed out.
"In the class above me, there's only *one* out of like 180 students. And
we're in *California*. This is *UCLA*." It was hard for Eileen to mask
her disappointment. The Filipino presence was negligible at a medical school located in the city with the largest settlement of Filipinos
in the entire country. Despite the lack of Filipino medical students,
Eileen found her community with the PRIME program, a specialized

track for those interested in working with underserved communities. With the exception of one white student, the other members of
PRIME were Latino and African American, many of which were from
working-class backgrounds.

As was tradition with the PRIME program, Eileen began outreaching to premed undergraduates of color at UCLA. She spoke at career
workshops and activity fairs that focused on recruiting underrepresented minorities into the health professions. It was in her second
year at UCLA that she encountered a small group of Filipino undergraduates who were interested in pursuing medicine. Eileen attended
an event sponsored by the various premed organizations on campus.
"There was the Latino pre-health organization, the Asian pre-health
organization, and the Pilipinos for Community Health [PCH]—
notice how there's always a separate Filipino one," she said, emphasiz-
ing Filipinos' choice to have a club autonomous from other Asians.
There, Eileen met Karen, a Filipina undergraduate student who was
manning the PCH booth. Eileen noted that the young Filipina premed
could hardly comprehend that a fellow Filipino could be an actual
medical student. "Are you Filipino?" Karen asked Eileen, who excitedly respond affirmatively. Karen could not contain her enthusiasm.
"You're so rare. I never see Filipino medical students!" she told Eileen,
"Can I talk to you? Can I be your friend? Is it OK if I email you so we
can get coffee and talk? You're like my idol now!" For Karen, meeting
Eileen was like finding a needle in a haystack. "I kid you not. That's
what [she] really said to me," Eileen felt the need to qualify.

Eileen met a handful of other Filipino premed students through
Karen, and she said she got in the habit of meeting with them every
quarter just to touch base about their progress. For her, being a mentor was important because she never had a Filipino mentor herself.
"When I was at Berkeley, out of all the Filipinos who said they were
premed, there were only two others besides me that I know followed
through with it." Eileen wanted to make sure that her new mentees did
not fall through the cracks in the same way countless other Filipino
aspiring premeds did. "Most Filipinos I meet that are premed say they

want to try nursing first and then pursue medicine," she said. "But that never actually happens. They're completely different training programs." That Filipinos would say this was not surprising—nearly all the Filipinos I interviewed said that their parents at one point had pushed them to pursue nursing as a career. Because of this, it became increasingly important for Eileen to provide Filipinos who want to pursue medicine with accurate information about the different career pathways in health. "I spin a little bit of 'haterade,' and I let them know that their parents don't know what they are talking about because they didn't go to school here," she said.

Eileen's involvement with PRIME and other forms of community outreach also influenced the way her medical school classmates viewed her, especially when it came to racial identity. At the start of her second year at UCLA, Eileen struck up a conversation with Claire, a white classmate of hers, about how they spent their respective summers. "I had spent the past summer doing global health research in Peru . . . because I really wanted the opportunity to learn Spanish," she said. When she mentioned this, Claire felt compelled to interject. "Oh my God, Eileen, for some reason I totally forgot that you're Filipino," Claire told Eileen. "In my head, I was like, why is she trying to learn Spanish? Doesn't she speak Spanish already?" Eileen found the incident amusing but not too surprising. "I think she forgot because I'm involved in PRIME, and most people who feel strongly about serving minority communities are black and Latino," she hypothesized. "I do talk a lot about outreach and advocacy, and that's usually associated with black and Latino, I guess." Eileen's association with PRIME and underserved communities signaled "Latino" to Claire. Eileen also suspected that her Spanish surname and close group of Latino friends were part of the constellation of factors that influenced Claire to instinctively see her as a Latina, instead of a Filipina or an Asian American.

Evolving Identities

Eileen's story exemplified how race was about more than mere physical characteristics. The way she situated herself racially within the larger society had to do with her ability to connect her own personal experiences with those of a larger community. Although her sense of Filipino identity remained consistent, her connections to other racial communities shifted dramatically from high school to college to medical school. Being one of the high-achieving Filipino girls in high school made it logical to identify as an Asian American. However, her academic difficulties as a science major at UC Berkeley forced her to question her status as an Asian American. Her identity dilemmas throughout her undergraduate years highlighted how much schooling experiences influenced her racial orientations. Over time, she found it became more logical to connect both her experiences and those of other Filipinos with other historically underrepresented minorities, especially Latinos and African Americans. As she continued through the pipeline toward medical school, the distance between herself and other Asians only grew larger.

In my last conversation with Eileen, she was happily preparing for her wedding. For the past five years, she had been dating Diego Santiago, whom she had met at a Starbucks while en route to a John Legend concert. In fact, the first time Diego saw Eileen in that coffee shop, he thought she was Latina, which was a major part of why he approached her in the first place. Diego too was from an immigrant family, although his was originally from Mexico, not the Philippines. And even though her parents had their stereotypes about "typical Mexican guys," many of the cultural overlaps helped mitigate any initial discomfort they might have had with Diego. The Aquino and the Santiago families got along well, with their shared religion providing a helpful icebreaker for the two clans to get to know each other. "We're both Catholic. We're both family oriented. I think it helped," Eileen said. "Religion makes it easy for my parents. They told me that if he is at least the same religion, that would make things easier." Most of their friends tended to forget that they were an interracial couple. "Friends say that Diego looks Filipino and that I look Latina," she said. Eileen shared a few photos of her and Diego, and I could not help but concur.

What Eileen's story highlighted best was the distinct set of rules that Filipinos used to conceptualize Asian American and Latino identity, respectively. Often, the litmus test for Asian American identity revolved around school, while the equivalent test for Latino identity centered on culture and family. After our conversation wrapped up, I wished Eileen the best for her medical career, her upcoming wedding, and her new life with Diego. She too reciprocated my well wishes for both my own career and romantic life. A few minutes later, Diego picked her up from the downtown Los Angeles coffee shop where our interview took place. I introduced myself and made a bit of friendly small talk before we finally parted ways. Before I left, I took a last glance at the married couple to be, happily enjoying each other's presence. As I watched Eileen and Diego walk away, I realized something—it was the ordinariness about Filipino-Latino relationships that I had always found to be most remarkable.

8 Panethnic Possibilities

ONE FATEFUL AUGUST morning in 1993, a twelve-year-old boy accompanied his mother to meet a man she said was his uncle. The mother told the young boy that he would travel thousands of miles with this uncle, even though he had never met this relative before in his life. Their journey would take them to the United States—San Francisco, to be specific—and the young boy would start a new life in the home of his mother's parents, his grandparents. It was no surprise that the first few months were hard. Although he had known English before coming to America, he was not totally fluent in American slang, which sometimes prompted some awkward moments in his new American school. There was a moment when one of his new classmates greeted him, "What's up?" Taking the salutation too literally, the young boy replied, "The sky," and the other kids broke out laughing.[1] Rather quickly though, the young boy became acclimated to his new life, and he began to excel in school. His mother's American dreams seemed to be going according to plan.

This all changed when the young boy turned sixteen and became a young man. One afternoon, he tried to do what millions of other American teenagers do when they reach this milestone age—get a driver's license.[2] He made his way to the DMV, waited his turn in line, and handed the clerk his green card. Moments later, the course of his life would take an unexpected turn. "This is fake," the clerk informed him. "Don't come back here again."[3] The young man was scared. From his perspective, his green card looked identical to the ones carried by millions of immigrants living across the United States. He soon learned, however, that his green card was not issued by the US government; it was purchased by his grandfather, who for nearly all of his life had been the provider for him and his mother ever since his father left them when he was barely three years old.[4] Despite this incident, the young man still felt as American as any of his classmates at school. In his eyes, US citizenship was not a prerequisite for feeling like an American. Nonetheless, citizenship was something he strived toward—it was something he felt he would earn by following the American ethos of hard work.

"I've tried [to earn my citizenship]," he said. "Over the past fourteen years, I've graduated from high school and college and built a career as a journalist, interviewing some of the most famous people in the country. On the surface, I've created a good life. I've lived the American dream."[5] In reality, the young man's self-assessment was a modest one. After high school, he worked tirelessly with his teachers to secure scholarships from organizations that did not inquire about immigration status so he could attend San Francisco State University (undocumented immigrants were not eligible for government-sponsored financial aid). Throughout his time at San Francisco State University, he took on menial jobs at the *San Francisco Chronicle* and did some freelance writing on the side. Eventually, he built a portfolio of work that earned him internship offers at the *Wall Street Journal*, the *Chicago Tribune*, the *Boston Globe*, and the *Washington Post*. He chose the *Post* and moved to nation's capital.

In many ways, the career that he built as a twentysomething exceeded what many average Americans accomplish in a lifetime. He had penned stories for national outlets about everyone from Allen Iverson to Mark Zuckerberg to Hillary Clinton. He had written extensively about the HIV/AIDS epidemic in Washington. He had written about the role of social media in the 2008 presidential election. Before his thirtieth birthday, he and his team at the *Post* won a Pulitzer Prize, one of the highest honors in the journalism profession. What should have been one of the happiest days of his life, however, ended up being one of the worst. On the day he received word of the award, his grandmother called him on the telephone. She was not calling to congratulate him though. "What will happen if people find out?" she asked her grandson. All he could do was weep.[6]

In June 2011, the anxieties, fears, and constant evasions of truth became too much for the young man to handle. That month, he penned an article for the *New York Times Magazine* titled "My Life as an Undocumented Immigrant," in which he came out as an undocumented immigrant:

> I learned that no amount of professional success would solve my problem or ease the sense of loss and displacement I felt. I lied to a friend about why I couldn't take a weekend trip to Mexico. Another time I concocted an excuse for why I couldn't go on an all-expenses-paid trip to Switzerland. I have been unwilling, for years, to be in a long-term relationship because I never wanted anyone to get too close and ask too many questions. . . . I'm done running. I'm exhausted. I don't want that life anymore.

After revealing his undocumented status to the nation, the young man has since become a household name. He joined campaigns to help advance federal immigration reform and the DREAM Act, which would give young undocumented Americans a pathway to citizenship. He founded Define American, a nonprofit organization dedicated to educating the American public about undocumented immigrant issues. With the sponsorship of CNN Films, he produced a film based on his experiences, *Documented*, which has been screened at colleges and film festivals throughout the nation. One year after the *New York Times Magazine* article was published, his face graced the cover of *Time* magazine, and he became one of the most widely recognized figures in the undocumented immigrant movement.

For his commitment to this movement, the young man has been told countless times by strangers, "Go back home to Mexico."[7] There was only one problem, however—he had never once in his life been to Mexico. How could he have been born there? "I did not anticipate the level of how many people use the word illegal and Mexican interchangeably," he told a reporter for the *Nation*. "Just assuming that somebody who is Latino or somebody who is brown is Mexican and then making the assumption that he appeared illegal."[8]

The young man, better known as Jose Antonio Vargas, is not Mexican. Vargas was born in the Philippines, which means that he is a Filipino.

I often wondered to myself, how did a Filipino become one of the most popular faces of a social movement most often associated with Latinos? Vargas has never once hidden his Filipino background, yet managed to carve out a space within the Latino public sphere. On the *Huffington Post*, where Vargas once worked as a journalist, many of his articles are categorized under the category "Latino Voices." As mentioned, others constantly mistake Vargas as a Mexican immigrant. Vargas shared on his Facebook page that he had been told to return to his "home" country of Mexico a record thirteen times in a single day.[9] He himself has provided a partial explanation as to why. "My name—Jose Antonio Vargas—cannot scream 'Latino' any louder," he wrote in another Facebook post.[10] It is this constellation of factors that has allowed Vargas to become a national leader for one of the biggest Latino political issues of our time.

* * *

For more than a decade, I have ruminated on this question: "Are Filipinos really Asian American or Latino?" The evolving nature of racial identity suggests there is no definitive answer to this puzzle. Still, my curiosities persist. Will Filipinos continue to remain part of the Asian American collective, or will the cultural differences between them and other Asians prompt them to disassociate completely? As the political clout of Latinos in the United States expands, will Filipinos make moves to "become" Latinos or at least shift their panethnic allegiance to Latinos? Even if they do, could Latinos ever consider including Filipinos as legitimate members of the larger Hispanic community (especially since Filipinos are not generally fluent in Spanish). The lack of an obvious answer has also forced me to ponder whether either question is even worth asking.

At the end of the day, I think it is. I have spent much of the past decade using my sociological imagination and research training to explore this puzzle, and the resulting conversations I have had with friends and strangers alike have convinced me of its importance, despite no guarantees for a definitive answer. Filipinos are sometimes perceived as Asian, and sometimes they are not. Filipinos are sometimes mistaken as Latinos, and other times they are not. The impact of this racial ambiguity extends far beyond the realm of Filipinos' identity development. Let's consider some of the ways in which Filipinos' racial experience might affect other aspects of their lives, such as their physical health, romantic relationships, educational prospects, and economic future.

The Color of Health

Marvin Ramos, a thirty-four-year-old Filipino physician, recounted a recent experience he had at his annual physical. At the end of his checkup, Marvin peeked over his doctor's shoulder as he was filling out his chart. He noticed that his doctor listed his race as Hispanic. Marvin interjected. "I asked him why he did not list me as Asian," Marvin said. At first, Marvin thought his doctor might have mistaken him as Mexican, given his racially ambiguous phenotype and his Spanish last name. Studies show that medical personnel, including doctors, often mistakenly categorize Filipinos as Latino because they rely on surnames as a proxy for race.[11] However, upon probing further, he discovered this was not the case—the doctor knew he was Filipino. "Filipinos' patterns of heart disease and diabetes are more like Hispanics than Asians. The way your families eat is more like Hispanics. That's why I listed you as Hispanic," Marvin's doctor explained. Most likely, his doctor's assessment was based on anecdotal evidence from his encounters with patients. Nonetheless, we might expect that the diagnoses and treatments that Marvin's doctor gives his Filipino patients are based on his perception that Filipinos and Latinos share the same risks for disease.

There were other moments when I have seen how Filipinos' racial ambiguity might affect their health outcomes. When I was still a graduate student at UCLA, I recall an afternoon when Asian American student organizations on campus were attempting to recruit more Asians for the National Marrow Donor Program Registry (NMDP). According to the NMDP, the availability of Asian American and other minority organ donors remains disproportionally low.[12] This means that Asian American and other minority cancer patients have much more trouble than whites in finding matches for organ transplants. In response to this shortage, an Asian American fraternity at UCLA decided to reach out to the campus population to increase the representation of Asian potential donors. While eating lunch on campus one day, I watched members of this fraternity pass out flyers to random passersby. Within minutes, however, I realized that their outreach efforts were not random at all. Members of the fraternity were giving flyers only to individuals who were of Asian descent, that is, those who *they* thought were Asian.

There was one major problem. Whenever Filipino students passed by, the fraternity members (who were mostly East Asian) rarely handed them a flyer. I myself conducted a little experiment of my own and walked by the fraternity members at least four times, and each time, I was not handed a flyer. Given that organs are most likely to match when donors are of the same ethnic background, the inability for these Asian American men to recognize Filipinos as potential bone marrow donors would have proved most devastating for Filipinos suffering from cancer, who at this moment were not fully benefiting from the outreach efforts of an health organization dedicated to serving the needs of all Asian Americans.

The Color of Love

For much of American history, interracial relationships were illegal. As recent as the early twentieth century, Filipinos and other people of color were legally banned from marrying white women.[13] Although antimiscegenation laws are off the books today, Filipinos and people of color sometimes view interracial relationships as a challenging endeavor, whether they partner with whites or someone from another racial group. People in interracial relationships sometimes find it difficult to relate with each other's families because of language barriers or religious differences.[14] Other times, the parents of the interracial couple might have deep-seated racist views of their children's partners, which in turn might push them to put a stop to the relationship.[15] Depending on the racial attitudes of the local context, interracial couples might even encounter hostility from total strangers.[16] In the end, when it comes to interracial relationships, there are usually two things happening: a blurring of ethnic boundaries between the two groups involved and some level of external acceptance (whether it be from the family, the community, or at least the surrounding society).[17] The challenges involved with interracial relationships help explain why sociologists have found that "Hispanics and Asians display strong marital affinity for individuals from the same broad racial category, even if marriage patterns are not from the same ethnic group."[18]

On the basis of this hypothesis, Filipinos should most likely partner with other Asians if they opt not to date or marry someone of their same ethnicity. However, Figure 8.1 shows that they do not. In a study conducted by the University of California, researchers asked second-generation Asian Americans about the ethnic or racial background of their partners. My analysis of their data contradicts sociologists' predictions about interracial marriage—that is, if you assume that Filipinos are Asian. In Los Angeles, one in five Filipinos has a Latino partner. In contrast, less than 3 percent of other Asians partner with someone of Latino descent. In fact, Filipinos are twice as likely to partner with a Latino than they are with a non-Filipino

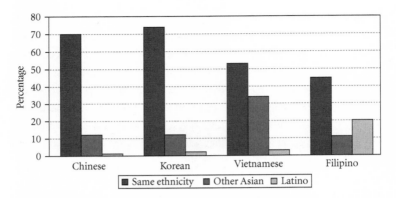

Figure 8.1 Ethnicity/race of respondent's partner, second-generation Asian Americans in Los Angeles by ethnicity (*n* = 526)

Source: Immigrant and Intergenerational Mobility in Metropolitan Los Angeles Survey, 2004.
Note: Sample size for each group: Chinese (119), Korean (133), Vietnamese (109), and Filipino (165).

Asian. In my previous study of Filipinos in San Diego, another predominantly Latino city, I discovered a similar pattern. Among the Filipinos who were married, one in four had a Latino spouse. In comparison, only about 10 percent of Filipinos in San Diego had married another Asian American.

What do these romantic partnership patterns tell us about Filipinos' position in the racial landscape of Southern California, a region where the Latino and Asian populations are rapidly growing each year? To borrow the language of intermarriage studies, Filipinos' romantic relationships patterns suggest that the cultural barriers between themselves and Latinos are thinner than those between Filipinos and Asians.[19] The interracial relationships of Nelson and Eileen mentioned in the earlier chapters of this book help explain why. Filipinos and Latinos had "ethnically linked symbols" such as religion, family, and Spanish last names that made their partnerships make sense to them, to their families, and to the outside world.[20] Filipinos felt more culturally fluent with Latinos than with other Asians, as exemplified by Nelson's angst about dating a Vietnamese American woman. The ethnically linked symbols between Filipinos and Latinos helped Eileen's parents overcome some of the negative stereotypes they might have held about Mexican men so that they could get more comfortable with her fiancé Diego. Nonetheless, further exploring the qualitative differences between Filipino-Latino and Filipino-Asian relationships would teach us about not only their racial proximity to other groups but also the qualitative differences in the process of blurring ethnic boundaries.

Stereotype Threat or Stereotype Promise?

The impact of race is so powerful that it can affect a student's academic performance without him or her even realizing it. Social psychologists have proved that even asking a simple demographic question about race before taking a test has the potential to affect the test outcome.[21] However, asking a question about race prior to a test, something social psychologists call "priming," has been shown to affect academic performances in both negative and positive ways, depending on the racial group being tested. When primed about race, African American and Latino students seem to do worse on tests (stereotype threat), whereas Asians tend to do better (stereotype promise).[22] Considering the variety of ways that Filipinos are racialized, especially within schools, how would this psychological phenomenon play out for them? Would Filipinos experience stereotype threat or stereotype promise?

Consider the following interview excerpt from the book *Academic Profiling*, by Gilda Ochoa, a sociology professor at Pomona College. In her research, Ochoa spent countless hours interviewing and hanging out with students at "Southern California High School," a public school comprising Latinos (mostly Mexican) and Asian Americans (mostly Chinese). The general consensus among the teachers—as well as the students—was that the Asian Americans were the high achievers, and the Latinos were either average or below average, with a few exceptional cases. While there were just a few Filipino students at the school, they were not always seen as Asian American. This became evident when Ochoa interviewed a small group of young men at the school:

> RAUL: Mr. Johnson [a school administrator], the remarks he makes to certain students makes him a dick.
>
> MARCOS: Yeah, he told me, "I'm surprised you could afford the prom."
>
> NICK: He picks on people who look like troublemakers, like Mexicans, gang members, skinheads.
>
> TRAVIS: He goes after Mexicans and blacks.
>
> RAUL: He told me and my black and Filipino friends, "I'm watching your group."[23]

Although Raul did not explicitly label his Filipino friend as "Latino," his comments highlighted where Filipino students fell on the spectrum between the high-achieving Asian American students and the lower-achieving Latino students. While this was the only mention of this Filipino student in Ochoa's book, it would be fair to presume that this type of racialization by teachers would only hinder this young man's academic promise. Educational researchers have shown this to be the case when Filipinos attend school with East Asian students. In these school contexts, teachers stereotyped their Chinese American students as intelligent, hardworking, and college bound. In contrast, Filipinos were pegged as gang members and were often encouraged to take remedial or vocational courses that did not facilitate their pathway to college.[24] Although the racialization of Filipinos in these studies seemed harsher than those profiled in the previous chapters, there is still a common thread between them: context shapes whether Filipinos are perceived as legitimately Asian American.

The psychological research on stereotyping and academic performance suggests that there might be a strong association between identifying as Asian American and educational attainment later in one's life. In my earlier research on Filipino students in San Diego, I found this to be the case. Filipino students who did not identify as Asian

Americans during high school were less likely to have their bachelor's degree by their midtwenties.[25] It would be premature to argue that the relationship between Asian American identification and college graduation was causal, but these patterns signal the possibility that Filipinos could be primed as either Asian or Latino, which in turn might lead to divergent educational outcomes. Future studies might consider whether the racialization of Filipinos as non-Asian minorities in schools may help explain why Filipinos are underrepresented in the nation's most competitive colleges and graduate school programs. As a previous chapter noted, Chinese students at the University of California–Berkeley, the flagship campus of the UC system, outnumbered the number of Filipino students by a ratio of nine to one, even though the latter is the largest Asian population in the state.

It's All in the Name

People sometimes ask me whether Filipinos who "don't look Latino" or who "look more Chinese" are racialized as Latino in the same way as those who are racially ambiguous. I admit that I did not systematically code for people's phenotype as more or less Asian (or Latino), nor did I feel appropriate in asking people to categorize their own phenotype in such a manner. It would be a faux pas for me as a researcher to ask Filipinos whether they thought they looked "more Mexican" or "more Chinese." Given the tremendous heterogeneity within these groups, I did not want to contribute to such essentialist notions of racial identity. Nonetheless, I found it intriguing that some Filipinos who described their look as "more Asian" still spoke at length about being mistaken as Mexican. After a while, it dawned on me. In the digital age, people are becoming less dependent on face-to-face interactions and more accustomed to electronic correspondence. When people communicate with each other via emails, online classrooms, or professional social networking platforms, they become less dependent on phenotype to make conclusion's about others' racial identity. When it comes to online correspondence, it's all in the name.

There have been a number of academic studies, news articles, and blog posts about the way names serve as a proxy for race.[26] In October 2014, José Zamora conducted his own experiment to see whether names really mattered for one's job prospects. Each week, José sent his résumé to hundreds of job posts online, and each week, his efforts yielded few responses. However, after dropping a single letter from his name and becoming "Joe Zamora," the responses began flooding in.[27] It is fair for José (a.k.a. Joe) to assume that the change in response had to do with his original name sounding too Latino for comfort. Latino names were not the only ones discriminated against. Employers and even professors have been known to be less responsive to correspondences from "minority sounding" people, whether they were Latino, African American, or Asian.[28]

As the case of Jose Antonio Vargas demonstrates, however, we should not assume that the consequences of having Spanish last names are always bad. In his case, the surname Vargas likely grants him a certain amount of legitimacy among Latinos in this country—at the least, it gets his foot in the door. My own name, Ocampo, has proved nothing but an asset at the institution where I teach. Cal Poly Pomona is a Hispanic-serving institution that ironically has an underrepresentation of Chicano and Latino faculty. When I first arrived at Cal Poly, I overheard students express their enthusiasm about "the new Latino professor in the department" (in reference to me). Surely, as a first-time professor anxious about his very first academic job, this enthusiasm and immediate rapport worked to my advantage. Even when I openly shared that I was Filipino, my Latino students seemed to view it as nothing more than a technicality. In the absence of Latino professors in the department at the time, I was, according to one of my first students, "the next best thing." Several years into the job, there are always at least a few Latino students who approach me in the middle of the term to express their surprise that I am not "really Mexican." Thankfully, this new bit of information has not seemed to disappoint any of my students too much, at least to the best of my knowledge.

* * *

After a decade of thinking and researching about the experiences of my community, one thing seems clear—when it comes to race in America, Filipinos break the rules. The objective of this book has not been to push for categorizing Filipinos as either Asian American or Latino. At the end of the day, neither the Asian box nor the Latino box fully captures the complicated nature of Filipino Americans' history and contemporary experiences. Rather than belabor the question of Filipinos' racial identity choices, this book has aimed to highlight their panethnic moments—the situations in which they feel a sense of collective identity or "we-ness" with some other group outside their ethnic community. As illustrated by the experiences of everyday Filipinos like the ones profiled in the previous chapters or more well-known Filipinos like Jose Antonio Vargas, these panethnic moments can have either positive or negative consequences, depending on the situation in question. My hope is that by developing a better understanding of Filipinos' racial experiences in America, those reading this book—from academics to community activists—will have a clearer sense of how to address the social problems that continue to hinder the full inclusion of the Filipino American community within the imaginary of American society.

Acknowledgments

I NEVER WOULD HAVE THOUGHT that my random musings about Filipino identity in my freshman year of college would have somehow evolved into a book a decade and a half later. There were countless moments when I felt like giving up on this project, but fortunately, the love and support from my mentors, friends, and family helped me reach the finish line.

Thank you to my professors from the Comparative Studies in Race and Ethnicity program at Stanford University. Having grown up in a strong Filipino family and community, I remember how frustrating it was to be one of the few Filipino students at Stanford. There were times when being the only Filipino in my classes led me to doubt my abilities, but the CSRE faculty played a major role in helping me develop my intellectual confidence. Dawn Mabalon's unwavering commitment to Filipino American studies inspired me to pursue a career as an academic. I thank Rudy Busto for encouraging me to write every final paper on Filipino American experiences—in all nine of the classes I took with him. His belief that Filipinos were "Pacific Latinos" helped me see that my own ideas on Filipino identity were not too far off the mark. I am also grateful to Anthony Lising Antonio, who validated the importance of studying Filipinos, even when the structure of the academy tells us that we are not a community worth studying. Thank you also to David Palumbo-Liu, Monica McDermott, and Christine Min Wotipka for their support during and after my time at Stanford.

I am thankful for the mentorship that I received while at UCLA. Min Zhou encouraged my passion for pursuing a Filipino project from the beginning. I thank Min for being an inspiration and candidly sharing her own challenges, even though most know her as an internationally renowned scholar. Rubén Hernández-León, Mignon Moore, and Jerry Kang have been great role models for me, especially in showing me how to share my work with audiences beyond the academy. I want to thank Vilma Ortiz, Roger Waldinger, Melany de la Cruz-Viesca, Cesar Ayala, Cherie Francis, Mark Sawyer, Victor Bascara, and Wendy Fuijnami for their support during earlier stages of my career.

I am so proud of my brothers and sisters from the UCLA Department of Sociology. Thank you to David Cort, Nancy Yuen, Leisy Abrego, Katy Pinto, Kristen Schilt, Veronica Terriquez, and Desiree Juarez for helping me navigate my way. I am grateful for all the laughs and memories shared with Christina Chin, Celia Lacayo, Amada Armenta, Jooyoung Lee, David Medina, and Laura Orrico. My deepest gratitude goes out to Anthony Alvarez, Sylvia Zamora, Erica Morales, Elena Shih, and Forrest Stuart for spending countless hours celebrating all of my important milestones and comforting me on the days that weren't so bright. Thank you for being my best friends at UCLA and in life in general.

Thank you to my fellow Filipino trailblazers in academia, especially Robyn Rodriguez, Sarita See, Faye Caranon, Jason Perez, Rhacel Parreñas, Paul Ocampo, and Kris de Pedro. I want to say a special thanks to Liz Pisares, who wrote a brilliant essay about Filipino identity that inspired me to pursue this work back when I was in college. I am also grateful to Grace Kao, Kimberly Kay Hoang, Karthick Ramakrishnan, Jody Agius Vallejo, Dina Okamoto, David Leonard, John Skrentny, David Fitzgerald, Tanya Golash Boza, Zulema Valdez, OiYan Poon, Hyeyoung Kwon, Prudence Carter, Jennifer Jones, Lorena Castro, Abigail Andrews, Anthony Peguero, and Linda Trinh Vo, whose feedback and questions seriously elevated the quality of this project. Thank you to C. J. Pascoe for being the personification of a brilliant scholar who never fails to exhibit kindness. I owe a great deal to Kerry Ann Rockquemore for the transformative impact she has had on my career and life. Becoming part of the National Center for Faculty Development and Diversity team has truly been a privilege.

I want to thank my colleagues and students from Cal Poly Pomona. I have shared so many laughs and amazing conversations with Anjana Narayan,

Stacy McGoldrick, Faye Wachs, Alex Morales, and Leticia Keenan. Mary Yu Danico has provided invaluable mentorship and friendship from the moment I was hired for the job. Thank you also to David Horner, Laurie Roades, Sharon Hilles, Jenny Huyler, Diane Slusser, and my other colleagues in the department for their support. I am grateful to have such incredible students at Cal Poly. Working with them has made me a better researcher, teacher, mentor, and writer. Thanks to Archi Silva, Jose Cuchilla, Alejandro Zermeno, Andrea Lavilles, and Audrey Aday not only for helping with this research but also for making my job that much more enjoyable.

This book has benefited from the feedback and support of several organizations. From UCLA, I am thankful to the Graduate Division, the Department of Sociology, the Institute of American Cultures, the Asian American Studies Research Center, the Chicano Studies Research Center, the Southeast Asian Studies Center, and the Institute for Research on Labor and Employment. Thank you also to the UC Pacific Rim Research Program, the UC Office of the President, the Haynes Foundation, the American Sociological Association, the Association of Asian American Studies, the Latina/o Studies Initiative, the Cal Poly Pomona Office of the Provost, the UC Merced Department of Sociology, the UCSD Center for Comparative Immigration Studies, and the University of Pennsylvania Asian American Studies Program. I appreciate the feedback received from *Ethnic and Racial Studies* and the *Journal of Asian American Studies*, which published some of my preliminary findings from this project.

Shannon Gleeson has been an amazing friend throughout the writing of this book. People often describe writing a book as a lonesome process, but I had the joy of writing this book alongside Shannon as she was working on her second. It has been such a pleasure working with my editor Jenny Gavacs, as well as Frances Malcolm and Kate Wahl from Stanford University Press. I am grateful for their enthusiasm and support, and I thank them for pushing me to be unafraid to write for an audience beyond academia. Thank you also to Wendy Roth for her faith in my work and for putting me in touch with the press. I thank Emily Bautista, Bianca Angeles, Armand Gutierrez, and Gabriel Sanchez for their research assistance at different stages of the project. Rudy Guevarra and Rick Baldoz were kind enough to provide such insightful feedback on my chapters in the final stages of the writing. I am grateful for the young Filipino Americans who shared their stories with me. Though the conventions of research prevent me from thanking you by name, please know that your stories have made an impact on the lives of countless Filipinos, who rarely get the chance to read about themselves.

I owe so much to my friends and family, especially Elmer Manlongat, Nelson Donado, Eddie Gonzalez, and Tony Ochoa. Daniel Soodjinda has been the best person to experience these first years of professor life with. I feel lucky to have the love and support of Joseph Cipriano, my adventure buddy, who always encourages me to aim high but also keeps me grounded when my head is in the clouds. Thank you also to the Cipriano family for always making me feel like a part of your home. Filipinos are often stereotyped as having families that are way too close, constantly gossiping, and always eating, and I'm blessed to have a family that fits this script. I am grateful for the love from the Ocampo and Crisostomo sides of my family. Thanks to my cousins, aunts, and uncles from Club Tondo for being my rock of support. I am still inspired by the lives of my late grandparents—Vicente Ocampo, a fighter for social justice; Angeles Ocampo, a loving grandmother; and Loreto Crisostomo, the most resilient woman I've ever known and one of the two women who raised me. Thanks to them for keeping watch over me from above.

Finally, I want to express my most heartfelt thanks to my mom and dad, to whom this book is dedicated. Honestly, I feel like I am only beginning to scratch the surface of knowing the love and support you have given to me these past thirty-four years. Looking back, I am definitely grateful for all the big things—putting a roof over my head, providing for me, and sending me to some really great schools. However, what I always think about most are the ordinary moments that we've shared—the laughs in the car, the meals at the kitchen table, and doing nothing more than being together at home (at our respective TVs, of course). I'm so blessed to have parents who accept me for everything that I am. I am grateful that I've inherited my mom's ability to empathize with people no matter who they are, and I'm so thankful for my dad's unwillingness to settle for anything less than the best for his family. Thank you both for reminding me to stay hungry but also to never be ungrateful for all of my blessings. I pray that I make you proud with the way I live my own life. I love you both very much.

Appendix

Reflections on the Research

FOR THIS BOOK, I interviewed eighty-five Filipino American adults (between the ages of twenty-one and thirty) who had grown up and were currently living in Los Angeles. All of the respondents were second generation, meaning that at least one of their parents was born in the Philippines. The majority of them were born in the United States, but a small segment of them migrated before the age of eight. I chose to recruit my interviewees from two middle-class, multiethnic neighborhoods in Los Angeles—Eagle Rock and Carson. At the beginning of this research, many sociological studies had looked at children of immigrants in communities of color that were low income.[1] I specifically targeted Filipinos from Eagle Rock and Carson because I was interested in the creative ways that middle-class people of color strategically navigated race in their social and institutional environments, a relatively newer topic of interest within sociology.[2] Even though most of the Filipinos were middle class, the majority noted that there were subtle intraclass differences within the neighborhood on the basis of where one lived. To account for these nuances, I recruited both Filipinos from the more affluent parts of the neighborhood and those who lived on the border alongside working-class communities. Given the complexity of identity, I made sure to include Filipinos with different educational pathways and cultural involvements. Some Filipinos went to community college and stopped there; others were in graduate school. Some Filipinos participated in Filipino student organizations during high school and college; others rarely frequented such spaces because of competing obligations and priorities. In other words, I wanted to include "everyday" Filipinos and not only privilege the perspectives of those who were more highly educated and deeply embedded in ethnic organizations, who tend to be overrepresented in studies of race.

The Latinos of Asia is all about the way that Filipinos in Los Angeles experienced ethnicity, race, and panethnicity in their everyday lives. Like many sociologists, I spent many years fine-tuning my theoretical understandings of these concepts before embarking on the research, and this is what I came with. *Ethnicity* generally refers to the cultural practices—language, traditions, and history—related to the immigrant homeland.[3] Many sociologists use ethnic identity as a proxy for national origin. *Race* has to do with larger umbrella categories that are unique to the US context: white, African American, Asian American, and Latino.[4] Some sociologists characterize race is an imposed identity that entails the physical characteristics and behaviors that mark one's background; however, other researchers, with whom I tend to agree, have demonstrated that race is as much a self-ascribed identity as ethnicity.[5] More often than not, race is a product of both choice and ascription. Finally, *panethnicity* entails the conscious effort of individuals from different ethnic backgrounds to establish and cultivate a united identity, such as Asian American or Latino.[6] While panethnicity often implies choice, there are also moments when panethnic identification happens more subconsciously.[7]

None of these eighty-five individuals shared these precise understandings of identity, which presented some interesting challenges to my research. One of the first lessons I learned is that Filipinos (and most people, for that matter) do not spend much time distinguishing the concepts of ethnicity, race, and panethnicity. In fact, Filipinos often conflated ethnicity and race in our conversations, and the majority have never even heard of the word *panethnicity*. For example, when I'd ask, "What do you consider to be your racial identity?" I would expect an umbrella category like Asian American. However, the vast majority said "Filipino" without an ounce of hesitation. While helpful in my analyses, invoking sociological terminology was essentially useless during my interviews.

If I wanted to get anywhere with my respondents, I had to temporarily divorce myself from the conceptual meanings of ethnicity, race, and panethnicity that I had spent years in my doctoral program trying to understand. I learned to take a stealthier and more inductive approach to uncovering Filipinos' conceptions of identity. Most people had a strong sense of what it meant to them to be Filipino. My strategy was to ask questions that allowed me to uncover the cognitive mapping rules that Filipinos had in their minds regarding race—something that University of British Columbia sociologist Wendy Roth terms a *racial schema*. What were the different characteristics and criteria (e.g., phenotype, language, culture, history) that went into the constellation of Filipino identity in their heads?

The other major part of my research was to see how Filipinos fit themselves within the American racial hierarchy. Unlike immigrants of yesteryear, this was not a matter of black versus white; in an immigrant metropolis like the Los Angeles, Filipinos wrestled with other labels, like "Asian American" and "Latino."[8] In fact, they wrestled more with the latter categories than the former. To see how Filipinos related to these categories, I asked questions that unpacked Filipinos' racial schemas about these other minority communities. Similar to the Filipino question, what were the different characteristics that helped them decide who was—and just as important, wasn't—Asian American or Latino? As the research progressed, I became particularly interested in the way Filipinos related to Asian and Latino identity, not only because these were the two groups they encountered most frequently in their everyday lives but also because of their strong historical and cultural connections with both groups.[9]

Racial miscategorization was a constant theme of discussion among Filipinos. Filipinos frequently talked about the way their sense of identity collided with how others perceived them. Elizabeth Pisares, a UC Berkeley English doctorate and friend of mine, is among the few people I know who has written explicitly about how Filipinos constantly mess with people's racial mapping rules, yet the experiences of "looking Asian but having a Spanish last name" or "looking Mexican but identifying as Asian" came up time and time again during my conversations.[10] The idea of a segment of Asians identifying with Latinos forced me to seriously reconsider some of the major arguments in the field of immigration studies.[11] Namely, why would a middle-class group like Filipinos identify with a panethnic community that tends to be negatively stigmatized by the larger society? Also, why were they *disidentifying* from Asian Americans, a group that is often portrayed as upwardly mobile and successful? Throughout my interviews, I kept asking myself, how is this story not getting any airtime in sociological research?

For nearly all of the Filipinos I interviewed, the answer had to do with colonialism. This response prompted another methodological issue—how does a researcher address a topic as loaded as colonialism in an interview? Social scientists have written about the way that historical colonialism structures the sending society and the patterns of migration to the United States, but this was something totally different.[12] This was colonialism as narrative. I never brought up colonialism during the interviews. However, when respondents did talk about it, I listened carefully to the way colonialism shaped how they negotiated panethnic boundaries. As one might expect, colonialism was not a salient theme in every aspect of their lives. As such, I also paid special attention to whether the association between colonialism and identity was mitigated by other factors, such as their schools, neighborhoods, and class issues.

Of course, the Filipinos whose stories fill the pages of this book are not representative of all Filipinos. There are Filipinos who come from working-class backgrounds or who come of age in other regions of the country with very distinct racial contexts from Los Angeles. In places where there are fewer Filipinos, they might have a greater inclination to identify as Asian American so that they are racially legible to the people around them. In locations where the Latino presence is minimal, the probability of a colonial panethnicity developing between Filipinos and Latinos is probably lower. Nonetheless, this study provides lessons for understanding how Filipinos and other children of immigrants negotiate competing, often contradictory, notions of identity to determine their racial position within their local environment as well as the broader society.

Notes

Chapter 1

1. Bliss, Catherine. *Race Decoded: The Genomic Fight for Social Justice.* Stanford, CA: Stanford University Press, 2012, 1. The first quote is from a speech by former President Bill Clinton in which he is reiterating the findings of Craig Venter, an American biochemist and geneticist, and Francis Collins, an American geneticist and director of the National Institutes of Health. The second is from Francis Collins from his 2001 publication in the journal *Cancer*, which he coauthored with Monique Mansoura. Collins, Francis S., and Monique K. Mansoura. 2001. "The Human Genome Project: Revealing the Shared Inheritance of All Humankind." *Cancer* 91.1: 221–25.

2. Espiritu, Yen Le. *Asian American Panethnicity: Bridging Institutions and Identities.* Philadelphia: Temple University Press, 1992.

3. Bonus, Rick, and Dina Maramba. *The "Other" Students: Filipino Americans, Education, and Power.* Scottsdale, AZ: Information Age Publishing, 2013; Chiang, Mark. *The Cultural Capital of Asian American Studies: Autonomy and Representation in the University.* New York: New York University Press, 2009; Ocampo, Anthony C. "Are Second Generation Filipinos 'Becoming' Asian American or Latino? Historical Colonialism, Culture, and Panethnic Identity. *Ethnic and Racial Studies* 37.3 (2014): 425–45; Rondilla, Joanne. "The Filipino Question in Asia and the Pacific: Rethinking Regional Origins in Diaspora," in *Pacific Diaspora: Island Peoples in the United States and Across the Pacific*, ed. Paul Spickard, Joanne Rondilla, and Debbie Wright, 56–66. Manoa: University of Hawai'i Press, 2002.

4. This figure includes both legal residents (approximately 3.5 million) and undocumented immigrants (approximately 300,000). US Census 2010; Golash Boza, Tanya. *Race and Racisms: A Critical Approach.* New York: Oxford University Press, 2014.

5. Pisares, Elizabeth. "Do You (Mis)Recognize Me?" in *Positively No Filipinos Allowed: Building Communities and Discourse,* ed. A. Tiongson, E. Gutierrez, and R. Gutierrez, 172–98. Philadelphia: Temple University Press, 2006.

6. Hayward, Mark D., Samantha Friedman, and Hsinmu Chen. "Career Trajectories and Older Men's Retirement." *Journal of Gerontology, Series B: Psychological Sciences and Social Sciences* 53B.2 (1998): S91–S103; Lareau, Annette. *Unequal Childhoods: Class, Race, and Family Life.* Berkeley: University of California Press, 2011; Portes, Alejandro, and Ruben Rumbaut. *Legacies: The Story of the Immigrant Second Generation.* Berkeley: University of California Press; New York: Russell Sage Foundation, 2001; Portes, Alejandro, and Ruben Rumbaut. *Immigrant America.* Berkeley: University of California Press; New York: Russell Sage Foundation, 2006; Zhou, Min, and Yang Sao Xiong. "The Multifaceted American Experiences of the Children of Asian Immigrants: Lessons for Segmented Assimilation." *Ethnic and Racial Studies* 28.6 (2005): 1119–52.

7. Bulanda, Jennifer R., and Susan L. Brown. "Race-Ethnic Differences in Marital Quality and Divorce." *Social Science Research* 36 (2007): 945–67; Carter, Prudence. *Keepin' It Real: School Success in Black and White.* New York: Oxford University Press, 2005; Waters, Mary, and Tomás Jiménez. "Immigrant Assimilation: Current Trends and Directions for Future Research." *Annual Review of Sociology* 31 (2005): 105–25.

8. Block, Jason P., Richard A. Scribner, and Karen B. DeSalvo. "Fast Food, Race/Ethnicity, and Income: A Geographical Analysis." *American Journal of Preventative Medicine* 27 (2004): 211–17; Kao, Grace. "Asian Americans as Model Minorities? A Look at Their Academic Performance." *American Journal of Education* 103.2 (1995): 121–59; Kao, Grace, and Marta Tienda. "Educational Aspirations of Minority Youth." *American Journal of Education* 106.3 (1998): 349–84; Leonard, David J., and C. Richard King. *Commodified and Criminalized: New Racism and African Americans in Contemporary Sports.* Washington, DC: Rowman and Littlefield, 2011; Portes and Rumbaut 2001; Warikoo, Natasha. *Balancing Acts: Youth Culture in*

the Global City. Berkeley: University of California Press, 2011; Wolf, Diane. "Family Secrets: Transnational Struggles Among Children of Filipino Immigrants." *Sociological Perspectives* 40.3 (1997): 457–82.

9. Alim, H. Samy. *Articulate While Black: Barack Obama, Language, and Race in the U.S.* New York: Oxford University Press, 2012; Baugh, John. *Beyond Ebonics: Linguistic Pride and Racial Prejudice.* New York: Oxford University Press, 2000; Feliciano, Cynthia, Rennie Lee, and Belinda Robnett. "Racial Boundaries Among Latinos: Evidence from Internet Daters' Racial Preferences" *Social Problems* 58.2 (2011): 189–212; Ochoa, Gilda L. *Academic Profiling: Latinos, Asian Americans, and the Achievement Gap.* Minneapolis: University of Minnesota Press, 2013; Robnett, Belinda, and Cynthia Feliciano. "Patterns of Racial-Ethnic Exclusion by Internet Daters." *Social Forces* 89.3 (2011): 807–28; Pager, Devah. *Marked: Race, Crime, and Finding Work in an Era of Mass Incarceration.* Chicago: University of Chicago Press, 2007. Waldinger, Roger, and Michael Lichter. *How the Other Half Works: Immigration and the Social Organization of Labor.* Berkeley: University of California Press, 2003.

10. Wilson, William Julius. *The Declining Significance of Race: Blacks and Changing American Institutions.* Chicago: University of Chicago Press, 1980.

11. McDermott, Monica. *Working Class White: The Making and Unmaking of Race Relations.* Berkeley: University of California Press, 2006.

12. Jaret, Charles. "Troubled by Newcomers: Anti-Immigration Attitudes and Action During Two Eras of Mass Immigration to the United States." *Journal of American Ethnic History* 18.3 (1999): 9–39, at 28.

13. Foner, Nancy. *From Ellis Island to JFK: New York's Two Great Waves of Immigration.* New Haven, CT: Yale University Press, 2000.

14. Ignatiev, Noel. *How the Irish Became White.* New York: Routledge, 1997, 49.

15. Ignatiev 1997; Roediger, David. *Working Towards Whiteness: How America's Immigrants Became White.* New York: Basic Books, 2005; Takaki, Ronald. *Strangers from a Different Shore.* New York: Back Bay, 1998.

16. Jiménez, Tomás. *Replenished Ethnicity: Mexican Americans, Immigration, and Identity.* Berkeley: University of California Press, 2010; Warner, Lloyd W., and Leo Srole. *The Social Systems of American Ethnic Groups.* New Haven, CT: Yale University Press, 1945.

17. Jiménez 2010.

18. Alba, Richard. *Ethnic Identity: The Transformation of White America*. New Haven, CT: Yale University Press, 1990; Waters, Mary. *Ethnic Options: Choosing Identities in America*. Berkeley: University of California Press, 1990.

19. McDermott 2006.

20. Park, Robert, and E. W. Burgess. *Introduction to the Science of Sociology*. 1921. Chicago: University of Chicago Press, 1969, 735.

21. Park, Robert. *Race and Culture*. Glencoe, IL: Free Press, 1950.

22. Haney-Lopez, Ian. *White by Law: The Legal Construction of Race*. New York: New York University Press, 1996; Wilson, Steven. "Brown over 'Other White': Mexican Americans' Legal Litigation Strategy in School Desegregation Lawsuits." *Law and History Review* 21.1 (2003): 145–94.

23. Ngai, Mae M. *Impossible Subjects: Illegal Aliens and the Making of Modern America*. Princeton, NJ: Princeton University Press, 2004.

24. Baldoz, Rick. *The Third Asiatic Invasion: Migration and Empire in Filipino America, 1898–1946*. New York: New York University Press, 2011; Ngai 2004.

25. Baldoz 2011. Restrictive immigration laws mainly applied to Asians and Southern and Eastern Europeans; however, immigration from other parts of Europe and the Western Hemisphere was still permitted. The Hart-Celler Act eliminated the restrictions targeted against the former. It should be noted that while the 1924 Immigration Act did not technically restrict immigrants from Mexico and Latin America, there were numerous other measures aimed at keeping them out, such as literacy tests.

26. Hondagneu-Sotelo, Pierrette. *Doméstica: Immigrant Workers Cleaning and Caring in the Shadows of Affluence*. Berkeley: University of California Press, 2007; Portes, Alejandro, and Min Zhou. "The New Second Generation: Segmented Assimilation and its Variants." *Annals of the American Academy of Political and Social Science* 530 (1993): 74–96; Waldinger and Lichter 2002.

27. Ochoa 2004; Portes and Rumbaut 2001; Tuan, Mia. *Forever Foreigners or Honorary Whites? The Asian Ethnic Experience Today*. New Brunswick, NJ: Rutgers University Press, 1998.

28. Jiménez 2010; Tuan 1998.

29. Bonilla-Silva, Eduardo. *White Supremacy and Racism in the Post-Civil Rights Era*. Boulder, CO: Lynne Rienner Publishers, 2001; McDermott 2006.

30. Covert, Bryce. "Only White, Male CEOs Make the Big Bucks." *Think Progress*, http://thinkprogress.org/economy/2013/10/22/2816041/white-men-ceos/; Jha, Rega. "Race and Gender Diversity on Television vs. in the United States." *BuzzFeed*, http://www.buzzfeed.com/regajha/race-and-gender-diversity-on-television-vs-in-the-united-sta#2p11587; Murse, Tom. "113th Congress: Information and Details About the 2013–14 Session." *U.S. Politics*, http://uspolitics.about.com/od/thecongress/a/113th-Congress.htm.

31. Zhou, Min. *Chinatown: The Socioeconomic Potential of an Urban Enclave*. Philadelphia: Temple University Press, 1998; Portes and Rumbaut 2006.

32. Zhou, Min. "How Neighborhoods Matter for Immigrant Children: The Formation of Educational Resources in Chinatown, Koreatown, and Pico Union, Los Angeles." *Journal of Ethnic and Migration Studies* 35.7 (2009): 1153–79.

33. Espiritu 1992.

34. Espiritu 1992; Mora, G. Cristina. *Making Hispanics: How Activists, Bureaucrats, and Media Constructed a New American*. Chicago: University of Chicago Press, 2014.

35. Portes and Rumbaut 2001; Portes and Zhou 1993.

36. Espiritu 1992.

37. Said, Edward. *Orientalism*. New York: Vintage, 1978; Tuan 1998.

38. Espiritu 1992.

39. Ibid., 107.

40. Chiang, Mark. *The Cultural Capital of Asian American Studies: Autonomy and Representation in the University*. New York: New York University Press, 2009.

41. Ibid., 172.

42. Mora 2014.

43. Mabalon, Dawn. *Little Manila Is in the Heart: The Making of the Filipina/o American Community in Stockton, California*. Durham, NC: Duke University Press, 2013; Scharlin, Craig, and Lilia Villanueva. *Phillip Vera Cruz: A Personal History of Filipino Immigrants and the Farmworkers Movement*. Seattle: University of Washington Press, 2000.

44. "LULAC Ranks Grow, Yet Gains Superficial." *Houston Chronicle*, http://www.freerepublic.com/focus/f-news/704840/posts.

45. Guevarra, Rudy. *Becoming Mexipino: Multiethnic Identities and Communities in San Diego*. Rutgers, NJ: Rutgers University Press, 2012.

46. Ocampo 2014.

47. Omi, Michael, and Howard Winant. *Racial Formation in the United States: From the 1960s to the 1990s*. New York, NY: Routledge, 1994.

48. Waters, Mary. *Black Identities: West Immigrant Dreams and American Realities*. Cambridge, MA: Harvard University Press, 1999.

49. Itzigsohn, John. *Encountering American Faultlines: Race, Class, and Dominican Experience in Providence*. New York: Russell Sage Foundation, 2009.

50. Warikoo 2011.

51. Roth, Wendy D. *Race Migrations: Latinos and the Cultural Transformation of Race*. Stanford, CA: Stanford University Press, 2012.

52. To maintain the confidentiality of my respondents, I opted to use pseudonyms in lieu of their real names. To further ensure their confidentiality, I also used pseudonyms for their elementary and high schools, places of worship, and organizations that might have helped to reveal their identity.

53. Matilla, Dexter. "Pulitzer Prize–Winning Novelist Junot Diaz." *Philippine Inquirer*, December 26, 2011, http://lifestyle.inquirer.net/28907/pulitzer-prize-winning-novelist-junot-diaz; Matilla, Dexter. "Ronreads Interview: Junot Diaz." Personal blog, November 23, 2011, http://ronreads.com/author-interview/ronreads-interview-junot-diaz/.

54. From what I could gather, it was a Filipino beef steak dish that Alicia thought was *carne asada*, and it was *lechón* (roasted pig) that she thought was *pastor*.

Chapter 2

1. Lowe, Lisa. *Immigrant Acts*. Durham, NC: Duke University Press, 1996.

2. Baldoz 2011; Many Filipinos managed to still migrate during this period of restriction by joining the US military and supporting American forces during World War II.

3. Guevarra 2012.

4. Agoncillo, Teodoro. *History of the Filipino People*. Makati City, Philippines: GP Press, 1990.

5. Portes and Rumbaut 2006.

6. Rodriguez, Evelyn. "Primerang Bituin: Philippines-Mexico Relations at the Dawn of the Pacific Rim Century." *Asia Pacific Perspectives* 6.1 (2006): 4–12.

7. Clavería, Narciso. *Catalogo Alfabetico de Apallidos*. Manila: Philippine National Archives, 1849; Guevarra 2012; Kramer, Paul. *The Blood of Government: Race, Empire, the United States, and the Philippines*. Chapel Hill: University of North Carolina Press, 2006. Originally, the Spanish anointed Filipinos with Spanish surnames as part of a strategy to both Christianize them and preempt their resistance movements.

8. Guevarra 2012, 20.

9. Kramer 2006. Even after the US military was able to quell the Filipino resistance in certain regions of the Philippines, the Moros in the southern islands continued to fight the Americans well into the first few years of the colonial period.

10. Francisco, Luzviminda. "The Philippine American War," in *The Philippines Reader: A History of Colonialism, Neocolonialism, Dictatorship, and Resistance*, ed. D. Schirmer and S. Shalom, 8–20. Brooklyn, NY: South End Press, 1987; Zinn, Howard. *A People's History of the United States: 1492–Present*. New York: Harper Collins, 2003; Go, Julian. *American Empire and the Politics of Meaning: Elite Political Cultures in the Philippines and Puerto Rico During U.S. Colonialism*. Durham, NC: Duke University Press, 2008; Rodriguez, Dylan. "A Million Deaths? Genocide and the 'Filipino American' Condition of Possibility," in *Positively No Filipinos Allowed: Building Communities and Discourse*, ed. A. Tiongson, E. Gutierrez, and R. Gutierrez, 145–61. Philadelphia: Temple University Press, 2003.

11. Anderson, Warwick. *Colonial Pathologies: American Tropical Medicine, Race, and Hygiene in the Philippines*. Durham, NC: Duke University Press, 2006; Wolff, Leon. *Little Brown Brother: How the United States Purchased and Pacified the Philippine Islands at the Century's Turn*. Garden City, NY: Doubleday, 1961.

12. Rusling, James F. "Interview with President McKinley." *Christian Advocate*, January 1903.

13. The name *Thomasites* was derived from the name of the vessel, the USS *Thomas*, that transported these teachers from the United States to the Philippines.

14. Tuason, Julie. "The Ideology of Empire in *National Geographic* Magazine's Coverage of the Philippines, 1898–1908." *Geographical Review* 89.1 (1999): 34–53, 49.

15. Posadas, Barbara M. *The Filipino Americans*. Westport, CT: Greenwood Press, 1999.

16. Baldoz 2011; Coloma, Roland Sintos. "Empire and Education: Filipino Schooling Under United States Rule, 1900–1910" (PhD diss., Ohio State University, 2004); Kramer 2006. Baldoz has noted that a significant number of *pensionados* opted not to return to the Philippines in lieu of building a new life in the United States.

17. Ignacio, Abe, et al. *The Forbidden Book: The Philippine American War in Political Cartoons*. San Francisco, CA: T'Boli Press, 2004; Tuason 1999.

18. Ignacio et al. 2004, 56.

19. Mabalon, Dawn. *Little Manila Is in the Heart: The Making of the Filipina/o American Community in Stockton, California*. Durham, NC: Duke University Press, 2013.

20. Bello, Walden, Herbert Decena, Marissa de Guzman, and Mary Lou Malig. *The Anti-Development State: The Political Economy of Permanent Crisis in the Philippines*. London: Zed Books, 2005; Rodriguez, Robyn. *Migrants for Export: How the Philippine State Brokers Labor to the World*. Minneapolis: University of Minnesota Press, 2010.

21. Takaki 1998; Yang, Dean. "Migrant Remittances." *Journal of Economic Perspectives* 25.3 (2011): 129–51.

22. Takaki 1998.

23. Yang 2011.

24. Baldoz, Rick. "Valorizing Racial Boundaries: Hegemony and Conflict in the Racialization of Filipino Migrant Labour in the United States." *Ethnic and Racial Studies* 27.6 (2004): 969–86.

25. Mabalon 2013.

26. Ibid.

27. Baldoz 2011.

28. Ngai 2004.

29. Ignacio et al. 2004; Tuason 1999.

30. Cabranes, Jose. *Citizenship and the American Empire*. New Haven, CT: Yale University Press, 1979.

31. Cabranes 1979; Poblete, Joanna. *Islanders in the Empire: Filipino and Puerto Rican Laborers in Hawai'i*. Urbana: University of Illinois Press, 2014.

32. Baldoz 2011.

33. Cordova 1983; Guevarra 2012; Melendy, H. Brett. *Asians in America: Filipinos, Koreans, and East Indians*. New York: Hippocrene Books, 1982. A

significant proportion of Filipinos who came to California for work in the early twentieth century were migrating from Hawai'i to escape the severe labor exploitation and harsh working conditions on the islands.

34. Cordova, Fred. *Filipinos: Forgotten Asian Americans*. Dubuque, IA: Kendall/Hunt Publishing, 1983, 37.

35. Takaki 1998.

36. Cordova 1983, 43.

37. Baldoz 2004.

38. Cabranes 1979.

39. Cordova 1983; Takaki 1998.

40. Guevarra 2011; Mabalon 2013.

41. Mabalon 2013, 93.

42. Ibid.

43. Ngai 2004.

44. Mabalon 2013; Ngai 2004.

45. Baldoz 2011.

46. Mabalon 2013.

47. Cordova 1983; Mabalon 2014; Takaki 1998. Historian Dawn Mabalon documents how the migration of war brides during World War II played a major role in sustaining the Filipino community in the United States. They, along with Filipino interethnic couples, were able to build coethnic ties during the 1940s and 1950s, which was especially important because Filipinos were no longer able to freely migrate to the United States.

48. Choy, Catherine. *Empire of Care: Nursing and Migration in Filipino American History*. Durham, NC: Duke University Press, 2003; Espiritu, Yen Le. *Home Bound: Filipino American Lives Across Cultures, Communities, and Countries*. Berkeley: University of California Press, 2003.

49. Espiritu, Yen Le. "Filipino Navy Stewards and Filipina Health Care Professionals: Immigration, Work and Family Relations." *Asian and Pacific Migration Journal* 11.1 (2002): 47–66.

50. Reza, H. G. "Navy to Stop Recruiting Filipino Nationals: Defense: The End of the Military Base Agreement with the Philippines Will Terminate the Nearly Century-Old Program." *Los Angeles Times*, February 27, 1992, http://articles.latimes.com/1992-02-27/local/me-3911_1_filipino-sailors.

51. Schirmer, Daniel B., and Stephen Shalom. *The Philippines Reader: A History of Colonialism, Neocolonialism, Dictatorship, and Resistance*. Cambridge, MA: South End Press, 1987.

52. Mydans, Seth. "Hunt for Marcos's Billions Yields More Dead Ends than Hard Cash." *New York Times*, March 31, 1991, http://www.nytimes.com/1991/03/31/world/hunt-for-marcos-s-billions-yields-more-dead-ends-than-hard-cash.html?src=pm&pagewanted=1&pagewanted=all.

53. Boyce, James K. *The Philippines: The Political Economy of Growth and Impoverishment in the Marcos Era.* Honolulu: University of Hawai'i Press, 1993.

54. Rodriguez 2010.

55. Guevarra, Anna. *Marketing Dreams, Manufacturing Heroes: The Transnational Labor Brokering of Filipino Workers.* New Brunswick, NJ: Rutgers University Press, 2010.

56. Rodriguez 2010.

57. Blanc, Cristina Szanton. "Balikbayan: A Filipino Extension of the National Imaginary and of State Boundaries." *Philippine Sociological Review* 44 (1996): 178–93.

58. Hernández-León, Rubén. *Metropolitan Migrants: The Migration of Urban Mexicans to the United States.* Berkeley: University of California Press, 2008.

59. Hernández-León, Rubén. "The Migration Industry in the Mexico-U.S. Migratory System." California Center for Population Research, Los Angeles, 2005.

60. Rodriguez 2010.

61. During the colonial period, the Americans had first established nursing schools and health facilities to help "sanitize" the Filipino people, whom they viewed as uncivilized and unhygienic (Anderson 2006). Even after the Americans' official departure, these nursing schools remained in place. Eventually, nursing evolved to become a primary career strategy for Filipinos who could not manage to find work in the Philippines (Choy 2003).

62. Quoted by Espiritu 2003, 71; De Quiros, Carlos, "Bracing for Balikbayan," in *Flowers from the Rubble.* Pasig City, Philippines: Anvil Publishing, 1990.

63. Golash Boza 2014.

64. Filipinos use the acronym *TNT*, which stands for *tago nang tago*, or "always hiding," in reference to immigrants who overstay their visas. Romero, Sophia. *Always Hiding.* New York: William Morrow and Company, 1998.

65. Espiritu 2003; Liu, John, Paul Ong, and Carolyn Rosenstein. "Dual Chain Migration: Post-1965 Filipino Immigration to the United States."

International Migration Review 25.3 (1991): 487–513; Ong, Paul, and Tania Azores. "The Migration and Incorporation of Filipino Nurses," in *The New Asian Immigration in Los Angeles and Global Restructuring*, ed. Paul Ong, Edna Bonacich, and Lucie Cheng, 164–95. Philadelphia: Temple University Press, 1994.

66. Portes and Rumbaut 2006; Storey, Sierra, and Jeanne Batalova, "Filipino Immigrants in the United States." Migration Policy Institute, June 5, 2013, http://www.migrationpolicy.org/article/filipino-immigrants -united-states. The gender breakdown of Filipino migrants balanced out significantly in the post-1965 period. Today, about 60 percent of Filipino immigrants living in the United States are women, largely because of the influx of Filipino migrant nurses. Although more Filipino women migrate to the United States than men, the gender distribution of the second generation is about even.

67. Sassen, Saskia. *Globalization and Its Discontents: Essays on the New Mobility of People and Money*. New York: New Press, 1998.

68. Portes and Zhou 1993.

69. Choy 2003; Espiritu 2003.

70. Espiritu 2003.

71. Liu, Ong, and Rosenstein 1991.

72. Feliciano, Cynthia. 2005. "Does Selective Migration Matter? Explaining Ethnic Disparities in Educational Attainment Among Immigrants' Children." *International Migration Review* 39.4 (2005): 841–71.

73. Espiritu 2003. Espiritu notes that immigrants who came through family reunification visas tended to have less educational and occupational capital than those coming through employment visas. Unlike the family member who was in the United States through a professional work visa, these relatives who were petitioned sometimes had to find work within the low-wage service sector.

74. Parreñas, Rhacel. *Servants of Globalization: Women, Migration, and Domestic Work*. Stanford, CA: Stanford University Press, 2001.

75. Warner and Srole 1945.

76. Portes and Rumbaut 2006.

77. Asian Pacific American Legal Center and Asian American Justice Center. *A Community of Contrasts: Asian Americans in the United States, 2011*, http://www.advancingjustice-la.org/system/files/ENTERED _Community_of_Contrasts_2011.pdf.

78. Parreñas 2001.

79. Portes and Rumbaut 2001.

80. Bonus, Rick. *Locating Filipino Americans: Ethnicity and the Cultural Politics of Space*. Philadelphia: Temple University Press, 2000; Espiritu 2003.

81. Portes and Rumbaut 2006.

82. Zhou and Xiong 2005.

83. Portes and Rumbaut 2006.

84. Bonus 2000; Espiritu 2003; Waldinger and Lichter 2002.

85. Espiritu 2003.

86. Lowe 1996.

87. Rodriguez 2010.

88. Cornelius, W. A., and T. J. Espenshade. "The International Migration of the Highly Skilled: 'High-Tech Braceros' in the Global Labor Market," in *The International Migration of the Highly Skilled: Supply, Demand, and Development Consequences in Sending and Receiving Countries*, ed. W. A. Cornelius, Thomas J. Espenshade, and Idean Salehyan, 3–19. La Jolla, CA: Center for Comparative Immigration Studies, University of California, San Diego, 2001.

89. Espiritu 2003.

Chapter 3

1. Gans, Herbert J. *Urban Villagers*. New York: Simon and Schuster, 1962; Ignatiev 1997.

2. Roediger 2005.

3. Takaki 1998.

4. Zhou, Min. *Contemporary Chinese America*. Philadelphia: Temple University Press, 2009; Zhou, Min, and Carl L. Bankston III. *Growing Up American: How Vietnamese Children Adapt to Life in the United States*. New York: Russell Sage Foundation, 1998.

5. Hernández-León 2008; Zhou, Min. *Chinatown: The Socioeconomic Potential of an Ethnic Enclave*. Philadelphia: Temple University Press, 1995.

6. Zhou 2009.

7. Cornelius and Espenshade 2001; Portes and Rumbaut 2006.

8. Dhingra, Pawan. *Managing Multicultural Lives: Asian American Professionals and the Challenge of Multiple Identities*. Stanford, CA: Stanford University Press, 2008; Portes and Rumbaut 2001.

9. Espiritu 2003.

10. Zhou 2009.

11. Fong, Timothy. *The First Suburban Chinatown: The Remaking of Monterey Park, California*. Philadelphia: Temple University Press, 1994.

12. Shyong, Frank. "Monterey Park Sign Ordinance Debate Recalls '80s Ethnic Controversy." *Los Angeles Times*, August 4, 2013, http://articles.latimes.com/2013/aug/03/ local/la-me-english-signs-20130804.

13. Saito, Leland T. *Race and Politics: Asian Americans, Latinos, and Whites in a Los Angeles Suburb*. Champaign: University of Illinois Press, 1998; Saito, Leland T. *The Politics of Exclusion: The Failure of Race-Neutral Policies in Urban America*. Stanford, CA: Stanford University Press, 2009; Vuong, Zen. "Monterey Park Postpones Decision on 'Modern Latin' Sign Ordinance." *San Gabriel Valley Tribune*, October 4, 2013, http://www.sgvtribune.com/government-and-politics/20131004/monterey-park-postpones-decision-on-modern-latin-sign-ordinance.

14. Saito 1998, 2009.

15. Portes and Rumbaut 2006.

16. Vergara, Benito, Jr. *Pinoy Capital: The Filipino Nation in Daly City*. Philadelphia: Temple University Press, 2008.

17. Zhou 1995.

18. Sanchez, Gabriel, and Paul Ong. "Affordable Housing Challenges in Historic Filipinotown." Working paper. UCLA Asian American Studies Center, Los Angeles, 2013.

19. Kang, K. Connie. "Filipinos Happy with Life in U.S., but Lack United Voice." *Los Angeles Times*, January 1996.

20. Ibid.

21. Ibid.

22. Gordon, Larry. "Eagle Rock to Celebrate Its Close-Knit Identity." *Los Angeles Times*, September 19, 1985, http://articles.latimes.com/1985-09-19/news/gl-2131_1_eagle-rock-s-incorporation.

23. Hamilton, Denise. "Filipinos Bring a New, Exotic Touch to Eagle Rock." *Los Angeles Times*, May 1, 1986.

24. Ibid.

25. Ochoa 2004; Saito 1998.

26. Peterson, Jonathan. "Southland Rifts: Filipinos—A Search for Community." *Los Angeles Times*, May 1989.

27. Hamilton 1986.

28. Ibid.

29. Gorman, Anna. "Mall Anchors Thriving Filipino Community." *Los Angeles Times*, August 22, 2007.

30. Ramos, George. "City Approves Sign Honoring Filipino Center." *Los Angeles Times*, December 19, 2002.

31. Gorman 2007.

32. Cordova 1983; Takaki 1998; Ibañez, Florante P., and Roselyn Estepa Ibañez. *Filipinos in Carson and the South Bay*. Mount Pleasant, SC: Arcadia Publishing, 2009.

33. Baldoz 2011; Mabalon 2013.

34. Ibañez and Ibañez 2009.

35. Guevarra 2012.

36. Texeira, Erin. "Carson, a Model of Multiracial Politics, Hit by Discord." *Los Angeles Times*, November 27, 2000.

37. Toward the end of his second term, charges of corruption and bribery emerged and eventually damaged his political reputation beyond repair.

38. "Officials Want to Rename Street: Jose Rizal Who?" *NBC 4: Southern California*, January 7, 2010, http://www.nbclosangeles.com/news/local/Officials-Want-to-Rename-Street-Jose-Rizal-Who.html.

39. Portes and Rumbaut 2001; Zhou 2009.

40. Cornell, Stephen, and Douglas Hartmann. *Ethnicity and Race: Making Identities in a Changing World*. Thousand Oaks, CA: Pine Forge Press, 1998; Ochoa 2004.

41. Espiritu 2003.

42. Portes and Rumbaut 2001; Zhou and Bankston 1998.

43. Cheng, Wendy. *The Changs Next Door to the Diazes: Remapping Race in Suburban California*. Minneapolis: University of Minnesota Press; Ochoa 2013.

Chapter 4

1. Some of the findings from this chapter were published in my 2014 article "Are Second Generation Filipinos 'Becoming' Asian American or Latino? Historical Colonialism, Culture, and Panethnicity." Copyright © 2014 Taylor & Francis. The chapter is derived in part from an article published in *Ethnic and Racial Studies* 37.4: 425–45. http://dx.doi.org/10.1080/014198 70.2013.765022.

2. Omi and Winant 1994.

3. Parreñas 2001; Rodriguez 2010.

4. My analysis of the Immigrant and Intergenerational Mobility in Metropolitan Los Angeles data (IIMMLA) revealed that 45 percent of Filipinos identified as Pacific Islander, a mere 2 percent shy of the percentage that had identified as Asian American. Ocampo 2014.

5. Cornell and Hartmann 1998; Omi and Winant 1994.

6. Statistics of the language patterns of immigrant and second-generation Asians in Los Angeles can be found in Chapter 2.

7. Portes and Rumbaut 2001; Zhou and Xiong 2005.

8. Espiritu 2003; Portes and Rumbaut 2001.

9. Min, Pyong Gap. *Preserving Ethnicity Through Religion in America: Korean Protestants and Indian Hindus Across Generation.* New York: New York University Press, 2002; Portes and Rumbaut 2006.

10. Portes and Rumbaut 2006.

11. Portes and Rumbaut 2006; Rodriguez, Evelyn I. *Celebrating Debutantes and Quinceañeras: Coming of Age in American Ethnic Communities.* Philadelphia: Temple University Press, 2013.

Chapter 5

1. Some of the findings from Chapters 5 and 6 were previously published in my 2013 article "Am I Really Asian? Educational Experiences and Panethnic Identity Among Second Generation Filipinos." Copyright © 2013 The Johns Hopkins University Press. The article first appeared in *Journal of Asian American Studies* 16.3 (October 2013): 295–321.

2. Carter 2005. The negative looks and stares that Lupe received constitute a method symbolic "boundary work" that helps reinforce not only the social organization of the school but also the parameters for behaviors that are deemed acceptable by her coethnics.

3. Oakes, Jeannie. *Keeping Track: How Schools Structure Inequality.* New Haven, CT: Yale University Press, 1985.

4. Ochoa 2013.

5. Although the South Bay alumni whom I interviewed had graduated in different years (from 2000 to 2008), they were remarkably consistent in their descriptions of the different tracks.

6. Ochoa 2013, 79.

7. Ibid.

8. Carter 2005. Rios, Victor M. *Punished: Policing the Lives of Black and Latino Boys.* New York: New York University Press, 2011.

9. Alsaybar, Bangele D. "Youth Groups and Youth Savers: Gangs, Crews, and the Rise of Filipino American Youth Culture in Los Angeles." PhD diss., Department of Anthropology, UCLA, 2007; Teranishi, Robert T. "Asian Pacific Americans and Critical Race Theory: An Examination of School Racial Climate. *Equity & Excellence in Education* 35.2 (2002): 144–54.

10. Losen, Daniel J. *Discipline Policies, Successful Schools, and Racial Justice.* Boulder, CO: National Education Policy Center, 2011, http://nepc .colorado.edu/publication/discipline-policies; Losen, Daniel J., and Jonathan Gillespie. "Opportunities Suspended: The Disparate Impact of Disciplinary Exclusion from School." Civil Rights Project, Los Angeles, August 2012; Rios 2011.

11. Kasinitz et al. 2008; Ocampo, Anthony C. "Am I Really Asian? Educational Experiences and Panethnic Identification Among Second Generation Filipino Americans." *Journal of Asian American Studies* 16.3 (2013): 295–324.

12. A *courtesy stigma* is a term coined by sociologist Victor Rios (2011) that describes the way different authorities would automatically label friends and family of gang members as gang affiliated.

13. Ochoa 2013.

14. Rios 2011.

15. The name of the gang is a pseudonym.

16. Alba, Richard, and Victor Nee. *Remaking the American Mainstream: Assimilation and Contemporary Immigration.* Cambridge, MA: Harvard University Press, 2003; Portes and Rumbaut 2001, 2006.

Chapter 6

1. Filipinos lost their official designation as "underrepresented minorities" a few years before the passage of Proposition 209.

2. Smith, Sandra S., and Mignon Moore. "Intraracial Diversity and Relations Among African Americans: Feelings of Closeness Among Black Students at a Predominantly White University." *American Journal of Sociology* 106.1 (2000): 1–39.

3. Ibid.

4. McIntosh, Peggy. "White Privilege: Unpacking the Invisible Knapsack." *Peace and Freedom* (1989): 31–36.

5. Agius Vallejo, Jody. *From Barrios to Burbs: The Making of the Mexican American Middle Class*. Stanford, CA: Stanford University Press, 2012.

6. Fuligni, Andrew J. "Family Obligation and the Academic Motivation of Adolescents from Asian, Latin American, and European Backgrounds." *New Directions for Child and Adolescent Development* 94 (2001): 61–76; Sue, Stanley, and Sumie Okazaki. "Asian American Educational Achievements: In Search of an Explanation." *American Psychologist* 45.8 (1990): 913–20; Zhou and Bankston 1998.

7. Fuligni 2001.

8. McDermott 2006.

9. Lacy, Karyn. *Blue-Chip Black: Race, Class, and Status in the New Black Middle Class*. Berkeley: University of California Press, 2008; Neckerman, Kathryn, Prudence Carter, and Jennifer Lee. "Segmented Assimilation and Minority Cultures of Mobility." *Ethnic and Racial Studies* 22 (1999): 945–65; Pattillo, Mary. *Black Picket Fences*. Chicago: University of Chicago Press, 2013.

10. Zhou, Min. "Are Asian Americans Becoming White?" *Contexts* 3.1 (2004): 29–37.

11. Nickerson, Kim J., Janet E. Helms, and Francis Terrell. "Cultural Mistrust, Opinions About Mental Illness, and Black Students' Attitudes Toward Seeking Psychological Help from White Counselors." *Journal of Counseling Psychology* 41.3 (1994): 378–85; Whaley, Arthur L. "Cultural Mistrust: An Important Psychological Construct for Diagnosis and Treatment of African Americans." *Professional Psychology: Research and Practice* 32.6 (2001): 555–62.

12. Portes and Rumbaut 2001; Portes and Zhou 1993; Neckerman, Carter, and Lee 1999.

13. Agius Vallejo 2012; Lacy 2008; Neckerman, Carter, and Lee 1999; Pattillo 2013.

14. University of California. *Statistical Summary of Students and Staff: Fall 2012*, http://legacy-its.ucop.edu/uwnews/stat/statsum/fall2012/statsumm 2012.pdf.

15. "New Freshman Enrollment by Ethnicity." *UC Berkeley Fall Enrollment Data*, http://opa.berkeley.edu/uc-berkeley-fall-enrollment-data.

16. Okamura, Jonathan. "Filipino American Access to Public Higher Education in California and Hawai'i," in *The Other Students: Filipino Americans, Education, and Power*, ed. Dina C. Maramba and Rick Bonus, 213–36. Scottsdale, AZ: Information Age Publishing, 2013.

17. Dobruck, Jeremiah. "FBI Ranks Irvine as Safest Big City in U.S. for 10th Year in a Row." *Los Angeles Times*, November 11, 2014, http://www.latimes.com/local/lanow/la-me-ln-fbi-ranks-irvine-safest-big-us-city-10th-year-20141111-story.html.

18. Teranishi, Robert, Miguel Ceja, Anthony Lising Antonio, Walter Allen, and Patricia McDonough. "The College-Choice Process for Asian Americans: Ethnicity and Social Class in Context." *Review of Higher Education* 27 (2004): 527–51.

19. Louie, Vivian S. *Compelled to Excel: Immigration, Education, and Opportunity Among Chinese Americans*. Stanford, CA: Stanford University Press, 2004.

20. Bourdieu, Pierre. *Homo academicus*. Stanford, CA: Stanford University Press, 1990.

21. Goffman, Erving. *Presentation of Self in Everyday Life*. New York: Anchor Books, 1959.

22. West, Candace, and Don H. Zimmerman. "Doing Gender." *Gender & Society* 1.2 (1988): 125–51.

23. Omi and Winant 1994.

24. Cornell and Hartmann 1998.

25. Sue, Derald, Christina Capodilupo, Gina Torino, Jennifer Bucceri, Aisha Holder, Kevin Nadal, and Marta Esquilin. "Racial Microaggressions in Everyday Life: Implications for Clinical Practice." *American Psychologist* 62.4 (2007): 271–86.

26. Blow, Charles M. "The Curious Case of Trayvon Martin." *New York Times*, March 16, 2012; Cooper, Michael. "Officers in Bronx Fire 41 Shots, and an Unarmed Man Is Killed." *New York Times*, February 5, 1999, http://www.nytimes.com/1999/02/05/nyregion/officers-in-bronx-fire-41-shots-and-an-unarmed-man-is-killed.html.

27. Morales, Erica. "Black Boundary Lines: Race, Class, and Gender among Black Undergraduate Students." PhD diss., Department of Sociology, UCLA, 2012; Smith and Moore 2000.

28. *MEChA* stands for Movimiento Estudiantil Chican@ de Aztlán. Chicano students in high schools and colleges throughout the country

have established chapters of MEChA as a way to empower their community through promoting historical knowledge and political activism.

29. Carter 2005; Ocampo, Anthony C. "Making Masculinity: Negotiations of Gender Presentation Among Latino Gay Men." *Latino Studies* 10.4 (2012): 448–72; Rios 2011.

30. Cornell and Hartmann 1998.

31. Roth 2012.

Chapter 7

1. Pattillo 2013.

2. "Final Enrollment Figures for Fall 2000 Undergraduate and Graduate Students at the University of California, Berkeley." *UC Berkeley Campus News*, November 30, 2000, http://www.berkeley.edu/news/media/releases/2000/11/30_enrol.html.

3. Lapidario, Millie. "UC Berkeley May Create Spot for Filipino American Studies Professor." *Daily Californian*, February 11, 2002, http://archive.dailycal.org/article.php?id=7648.

4. Espiritu 1992; Portes and Rumbaut 2006.

5. Espiritu 1992; Chiang 2009.

6. Smith-Barrow, Delece. "10 Medical Schools with the Lowest Acceptance Rates." *US News and World Report*, March 27, 2014, http://www.usnews.com/education/best-graduate-schools/the-short-list-grad-school/articles/2014/03/27/10-medical-schools-with-the-lowest-acceptance-rates.

7. Over the past decade, the percentage of African American and Latino medical school matriculants sits at around 7 percent and 8 percent, respectively. Association of American Medical Colleges. "Race and Ethnicity (One Race Response) of Applicants to U.S. Medical Schools, 2003–2012," https://www.aamc.org/download/321488/data/2012factstable15.pdf.

8. Ignacio, Laurie, and Nelly Gonzalez. "Closing Data Gaps: Shifting the Perspective on AA/NHPI University of California Medical Student Representation." Report prepared for Greenlining Institute, Berkeley, CA, http://greenlining.org/wp-content/uploads/2013/02/ClosingDataGapsAANHPIUCMedicalSchoolDiversity.pdf.

9. Association of American Medical Colleges. "Total Enrollment by U.S. Medical School and Race and Ethnicity," https://www.aamc.org/download/321540/data/2012factstable31.pdf.

Chapter 8

1. Vargas, Jose Antonio. "My Life as an Undocumented Immigrant." *New York Times Magazine*, June 22, 2011, http://www.nytimes.com/2011/06/26/magazine/my-life-as-an-undocumented-immigrant.html?pagewanted=all.

2. Ibid.

3. Ibid.

4. Ibid.

5. Ibid.

6. Ibid.

7. Vargas, Jose Antonio. Facebook post. July 7, 2014, https://www.facebook.com/jav/posts/827057037304578.

8. Hsieh, Steven. "Living Undocumented: A Conversation with Jose Antonio Vargas." May 1, 2014. *Nation*, http://www.thenation.com/blog/179633/living-undocumented-conversation-jose-antonio-vargas#.

9. Vargas, Facebook post, July 7, 2014.

10. Vargas, Jose Antonio. Facebook post. August 24, 2012, https://www.facebook.com/joseiswriting/posts/10152031055650062.

11. Lauderdale and Kestenbaum 2002; Perez-Stable et al. 1995.

12. Asian American Donor Program, http://www.aadp.org.

13. Volpp, Leti. "American Mestizo: Filipinos and Antimiscegenation Laws in California." *UC Davis Law Review* 33 (2000): 795–835.

14. Root, Maria P. P. *Love's Revolution: Interracial Marriage*. Philadelphia: Temple University Press, 2001.

15. Morales, Erica. "Parental Messages Concerning Latino/Black Interracial Dating: An Exploratory Study Among Latina/o Young Adults." *Latino Studies* 10 (2012): 314–33.

16. Osuji, Chinyere. "Racial Boundary-Policing: Perceptions of Black-White Interracial Couples in Los Angeles and Rio de Janeiro." *DuBois Review: Social Science on Race* 10.1 (2013): 179–203.

17. Vasquez, Jessica. "The Whitening Hypothesis Challenged: Biculturalism in Latino and Non-Hispanic White Intermarriage." *Sociological Forum* 29.2 (2014): 386–407.

18. Waters and Jiménez 2005, 110; Rosenfeld, Michael. "The Salience of Pan-national Hispanic and Asian Identities in U.S. Marriage Markets." *Demography* 38 (2001): 161–75.

19. Waters and Jiménez 2005.

20. Jiménez, Tomás. "Affiliative Ethnic Identity: A More Elastic Link Between Ethnic Ancestry and Culture." *Ethnic and Racial Studies* 33.10 (2010): 1756–75.

21. Steele, Claude. *Whistling Vivaldi: How Stereotypes Affect Us and What We Can Do.* New York: W. W. Norton, 2010.

22. Gonzales, Patricia, Hart Blanton, and Kevin Williams. "The Effects of Stereotype Threat and Double-Minority Status on the Test Performance of Latino Women." *Personality and Social Psychology Bulletin* 28.5 (2002): 659–70; Lee, J. "Asian American Exceptionalism and Stereotype Promise." *Society Pages*, May 4, 2012, http://thesocietypages.org/papers/asian-ameri can-exceptionalism-and-stereotype-promise/; Shih, Margaret, Nalina Ambady, Jennifer Richeson, Kentaro Fujita, and Heather Gray. "Stereotype Performance Boosts: The Impact of Self-Relevance and the Manner of Stereotype Activation." *Journal of Personality and Social Psychology* 83 (2002): 638–47; Shih, M., T. L. Pittinsky, and A. Trahan. "Domain-Specific Effects of Stereotypes on Performance." *Self and Identity* 5 (2006): 1–14; Steele 2010.

23. Ochoa 2013, 115.

24. Teranishi 2002.

25. Ocampo, Anthony C. "Becoming Asian or Latino: Historical Colonialisms, Changing Racial Contexts, and the Divergent Incorporation Outcomes of Second Generation Filipino Americans." PhD diss., Department of Sociology, UCLA, 2011.

26. Bertrand and Mullainathan 2004; Luo, Michael. "Whitening the Resume," *New York Times*, December 6, 2009.

27. Matthews, Cate. "He Dropped One Letter from His Name, and the Responses Rolled In." *BuzzFeed*, September 2, 2014, http://www.huffington post.com/2014/09/02/jose-joe-job-discrimination_n_5753880.html.

28. Bertrand and Mullainathan 2004; Milkman, Katherine L., Modupe Akinola, and Dolly Chugh. 2015, April 13. "What Happens Before? A Field Experiment Exploring How Pay and Representation Differentially Shape Bias on the Pathway into Organizations." *Journal of Applied Psychology.* Advanced online publication. http://dx.doi.org/10.1037/apl0000022.

Appendix

1. Portes and Rumbaut 2001; Portes and Zhou 1993.

2. Agius Vallejo 2012; Lacy 2008.

3. Cornell and Hartmann 1998.

4. Roth 2012. The US Census considers "Hispanic/Latino" an ethnicity and not a race (at this particular moment), but many sociologists have made the case that "Latino" is a racial category.

5. Lacy 2008.

6. Espiritu 1992; Mora 2013.

7. Carter 2005; Ocampo 2014.

8. Cheng 2013.

9. Guevarra 2012; Ocampo 2014.

10. Pisares, Elizabeth. "Daly City Is My Nation: Race, Imperialism, and the Claiming of Pinay/Pinoy Identities in Filipino American Culture." PhD diss., University of California, Berkeley, 1999.

11. Portes and Rumbaut 2001; Waters 1999.

12. Massey et al. 1993.

Index

Page numbers followed by "f" or "t" indicate material in figures or tables. Names in **bold** refer to interviewees and associates.

Made in the USA
Middletown, DE
22 June 2020